1

CONTENTS

Chapter 1. From Cain And Abel To The Destruction Of Babel's Tower

AND Adam knew Eve his wife, and she conceived and bore him two sons and three daughters.

The first-born she called "Cain," saying, "I have gotten a man from the Lord."

Her second son she called "Abel," saying, "With nothing we come into the world, and with nothing will we be taken from it"

When the lads grew up, their father gave to each of them a possession in the land. Cain became a tiller of the soil, and Abel a shepherd.

And after a time it came to pass that the lads each brought an offering to the Lord. Cain brought from the fruit of the ground, and Abel brought from the firstlings of his flock. But while Abel selected the finest and best-conditioned animals, Cain offered fruit of an inferior quality, the poorest which the earth offered. Therefore Cain's offering was unheeded, while the fire of acceptance fell from heaven, consuming the gracious gift which his brother had presented to his Maker. Thus a feeling of jealousy found birth in Cain's heart, and he resolved, when a good opportunity should offer, to slay his brother.

This time came upon an occasion when Cain was ploughing his fields. Abel, leading his flocks to pasture, crossed the ground which his brother was tilling.

In a wrathful spirit, Cain approached Abel, saying, "Wherefore comest thou with thy flocks to dwell in and to feed upon the land which belongs to me?"

And Abel answered:

"Wherefore eatest thou of the flesh of my sheep? Wherefore clothe thyself in garments fashioned from their wool? Pay me for the flesh which thou hast eaten, for the garments in which thou art clothed, for they are mine, even as this ground is thine; then will I go out of it, aye, and fly through the air, so that I may not touch it."

Then said Cain to his brother:

"Behold, thou art in my power. If I should see fit to slay thee now, to-day, who would avenge thy death?"

"God, who has placed us upon this earth," replied Abel. "He is the judge who rewardeth the pious man according to his deeds, and the wicked according to his wickedness. Thou canst not slay me and hide from Him the action. He will surely punish thee, aye, even for the evil words which thou hast spoken to me but now."

This answer increased Cain's wrathful feelings, and, raising the implement of his labour which he was holding in his hand, he struck his brother suddenly therewith, and killed him.

Thus was the blood of Abel spilled by Cain his brother, and the blood ran along the ground, even to the place where Abel's flocks were staying.

And it came to pass, after this rash action, that Cain grieved and wept bitterly. Then, arising, he dug a hole in the ground, and buried therein his brother's body from the light of day.

And after this, the Lord appeared to Cain, and said to him:

"Where is Abel, thy brother, who was With thee?"

And Cain replied unto the Lord:

"I know not! Am I my brother's keeper?"

Then said the Lord:

"What hast thou done! Thy brother's blood cries to me from the ground. Thou thinkest I know not of thy action, of the crime which thou hast committed, which thou wouldst now deny. Cursed be thou from the ground which oped to swallow up thy brother's blood. No longer shall it give its strength to thee and answer to thy efforts; no longer shall it give thee aught but thorns. A fugitive and wanderer shalt thou henceforth be upon the earth."

And Cain went forth a wanderer from the presence of his Maker, forth to the land on the east of Eden.

Now, after this time, when God began to give Cain rest, his wife conceived and bore a son. And Cain called his son "Enoch," because God had at last given him rest upon the earth. And he began to build a city, and this, too, he called "Enoch," for the same reason, because he was no longer a fugitive and a wanderer as before.

Now, when Adam was one hundred and thirty years old, he begat another son, whom he called "Seth."

And Seth lived one hundred and five years, and begat "Enosh."

Then the people increased and grew many upon the face of the earth. And they polluted their souls by sin and rebellion against the Lord. Their wickedness and their transgressions increased day by day. They forgot the Eternal who had formed them and given them the earth as a possession. They made images of copper and iron, of wood and of stone, to which they prostrated themselves in worship.

During the entire lifetime of Enosh the people continued thus unrighteous.

Therefore God's wrath was kindled against them, and he caused the river Gichon to overflow, and destroy and consume them. But though one-third of the earth was thus destroyed, the remaining people did not repent; they continued in their evil ways, displeasing in the eyes of the Lord.

During this time there was neither sowing nor reaping. There was a grievous famine in the land, for when the people became corrupt, the land was also corrupted, and, instead of fruit for man's sustenance, it brought forth thorns and thistles.

And Enosh lived ninety years, and begat "Kenan."

Kenan was a wise man who understood all things, and when he grew to be forty years of age, he ruled over the whole human race. Being an intelligent man, he instructed the people, and imparted to them his wisdom and understanding. He foresaw that the people would be punished for their continued wickedness, and he prophesied concerning the future and the flood which God would bring upon the earth, and he wrote down his prophecies on stone tablets, and deposited them in the Treasury.

When Kenan was seventy years old he begat children, three sons and two daughters. These two daughters became the wives of Lemech, the son of Methushael, the fifth of the generations of Cain. Ada, his first wife, bore him a son, whom she called "Jabal," and another son, whom she called "Jubal;" but Zillah, her sister, was barren for many years.

But it came to pass, even in her old age, that Zillah became the mother of a son, whom she called "Tubal-Cain," saying, "After I have grown old, Almighty God has granted me a son." Then Zillah conceived again, and bore a daughter, whom she called "Naäma," which signifies joy and pleasure in old age.

Now as Lemech grew old, his eyes grew very dim, and finally all sight was taken from them, and Tubal-Cain, his son, led him by the hand when he walked abroad.

And it came to pass, when Tubal-Cain was still quite young, that he led his father into the fields to hunt, and he said to his father:

"Lo, yonder is a beast of prey, shoot thy arrow in that direction."

Lemech did as his son had spoken, and the arrow struck Cain, who was walking afar off, and killed him. Thus was Cain's blood shed even as he had shed the blood of Abel his brother.

Now when Lemech and his son drew near and saw that instead of a beast of prey they had killed their progenitor Cain, Lemech trembled exceedingly and clapped his hands heavily together in surprise, grief, and fright. Being blind, he saw not his son, and struck the lad's head between his hands, killing him instantly. When his wives discovered what their husband had done they upbraided and despised him. And he spoke to them, saying:

"Ada and Zillah, listen to my voice! Oh, wives of Lemech, give ear unto my speech! I have slain a man to my hurt, a child to my wounding, but not in cruelty or with design. Ye know that I am old and hoary, that my eyes are sightless; accidentally I did this thing to my own wounding and my own hurt."

Then his wives became reconciled to their husband, according to the advice of Adam, their father, but they bore no more children.

"Mehalalel begat Jared, and Jared begat Enoch, and Enoch begat Methusaleh."

And Enoch served the Lord and walked with him, despising the wicked ones about him, and cleaving with knowledge and understanding to the ways of the Most High.

Enoch did not mix with the people, but lived alone as a hermit for many years.

And it came to pass as he was praying in his apartment an angel of the Lord called to him from heaven, saying, "Enoch, Enoch," and he answered, "Here am I."

Then said the angel:

"Arise, go forth from thy solitude and walk among the people of the land. Teach to them the way they should go, and instruct them in the actions they should perform." And Enoch did as the Lord commanded him.

He walked among the people and taught them the ways of the Creator, assembling them together and addressing them in earnestness and truth. And he charged his followers to proclaim in all places where men dwelt

"Who is he that desires to know the ways of the Lord and to do righteously? Let him seek Enoch." And Enoch reigned over the human race and the people obeyed him, and while Enoch was among them they served God. And princes and rulers came to listen to his words of wisdom and to make obeisance before him. And he made peace through all the land.

And Enoch reigned over the human race for three hundred and fifty-three years. In justice and righteousness he ruled, and peace blessed the land during all this period.

Methusaleh was the son of Enoch, and Lemech was the son of Methusaleh. Adam died, nine hundred and thirty years old, when Lemech was sixty-five years of age. He was buried with great honours by Seth, Enoch, and Methusaleh, His body was placed in a cave, which according to some authorities was the cave of Machpelah. From this time, the time of Adam's burial, it has been the custom to perform funeral obsequies over the dead.

Adam died because he had eaten of the fruit of the tree of knowledge, and through his sin must all his descendants likewise die, even as the Lord has spoken.

The year in which Adam died was the two hundred and fifty-third year of the reign of Enoch.

And it came to pass about this time that Enoch again felt a longing for solitude take possession of him, and he again withdrew from frequent communion with his people. He did not separate himself from them altogether; for three days he remained alone, and on the fourth he appeared to exhort and instruct them. But when a few years had passed he increased the periods of his withdrawal from the world, and separating himself from the people for six days, he preached to them upon the seventh. And after this he appeared before the people but one time in a year, and though they were desirous of seeing him and hearkening to his voice, save at this one time, they were unable to behold him.

And Enoch became so holy that the people feared him and dared not approach when he appeared before them, for the glory of heaven rested on his face. Yet when he spoke they assembled and listened to his words, and learning from his knowledge, they bowed before him, and cried aloud, "Long live the King!"

And it came to pass when the inhabitants of the world had learned from Enoch the ways of the Lord, an angel called to him from heaven, saying:

"Ascend, Enoch, ascend to heaven, and reign over the children of God in heaven as thou hast reigned over the children of men on earth."

Then Enoch assembled the people and said to them, "I have been summoned to heaven, but I know not the day I shall ascend. Therefore let me teach you ere I go, reiterating the lessons which you have heard from my lips."

And Enoch made peace and harmony among the people, and pointed out to them the path to everlasting life. And his followers proclaimed aloud wherever men dwelt, "Who is he that wishes to live and to know the ways of the Lord? Let him seek Enoch and learn, ere he is taken from us and earth."

So Enoch taught the people and united them in peace and harmony.

Then Enoch mounted his horse and rode away, and a multitude of people followed him a day's journey.

And it came to pass on the second day that Enoch spoke to those who followed him, saying:

"Return to your tents! Wherefore follow me? Return, lest death overtake ye."

A number of the followers returned at these words, but others continued to journey with him; and every day he spoke to them, saying:

"Return, lest death overtake ye."

And on the sixth day there were still some who followed after him, and they said, "Where thou goest will we go; as the Lord liveth naught but death shall separate us;" so when Enoch saw that they were thus determined he spoke to them no more.

Those who went back on the sixth day knew how many they had left following, but of those whom they left on the sixth day not one returned.

And on the seventh day Enoch ascended to heaven in a whirlwind, with chariot and horses of fire.

And it came to pass after Enoch had gone up to heaven that the people started out to search for those men who had followed after him. And on the spot where they had left them they found deep snow and ice. They cut through the ice and they found there the dead bodies of the men for whom they were searching, but Enoch they did not find. Therefore is this the meaning of the words of Scripture, "And Enoch walked with God; and he was not" (he was not where search was made), "for God had taken him" (Gen. 5: 24).

And Enoch ascended to heaven when Lemech the son of Methusaleh was one hundred and thirteen years old.

And it came to pass after Enoch had ascended to heaven that the people appointed Methusaleh, his son, king over them. And Methusaleh lived in the way of righteousness which his father had taught him, and he continued to instruct the people in morality and goodness even as Enoch had done before him. But in the latter part of his reign the people grew regardless of his teachings. They disregarded the personal rights of one another, and rebelled against the commands of God.

And the wrath of the Lord was again kindled against them, and the earth brought forth thorns and thistles instead of its fruit for sustenance, yet they repented not, nor turned from their evil deeds. Therefore did God resolve to destroy them entirely from the face of the earth.

Now when Lemech, the son of Methusaleh, was one hundred and eighty-six years old, Seth, the son of Adam, died and was buried.

And about this time Lemech took to himself Ashmua, the daughter of Elishua, the son of Enoch, for a wife, and he begat a son and called him Noah.

Noah grew up in righteousness and followed zealously in the ways of truth which Methusaleh taught him; but the others of the people practised wickedness towards God and deceit towards one another.

Then said God:

"The whole earth is corrupt. I will destroy this man whom I have created, the fowls of the heaven and the beasts of the earth, for the wickedness of man proves him undeserving of life, and I repent that I have made him."

But the Lord stayed his wrath until every man who walked in His ways was dead, before He brought to pass the evil which He had spoken, so that his faithful servants might not see the punishment of their fellow-man.

But Noah found grace in the eyes of the Lord; and God selected Noah and his family from all the people of the earth, to keep them alive through the destruction which He designed.

And it came to pass in the eighty-fourth year of Noah's life that Enosh, the son of Seth, died at the age of nine hundred and five years. And when Noah was one hundred and seventy, Kenan died nine hundred and ten years old. And Mehalel died at the age of eight hundred and ninety-five years, when Noah was two hundred and thirty years of age; and when Noah was three hundred and sixty, Jared died at the age of nine hundred and sixty-two years. And also those people who fulfilled the words of the Lord died in those days before He showed them the evil which He had decreed.

And it came to pass in the four hundred and eightieth year of the life of Noah, that the only righteous ones left in that generation were Methusaleh, and Noah with his family.

Then the word of the Lord came to Methusaleh and Noah, saying:

"Go forth, proclaim to all mankind, 'Thus saith the Lord: Turn from your evil inclinations, abandon your unrighteous ways, then may God forgive and spare you on the face of the earth. For thus saith the Eternal, one hundred and twenty years will I give ye to repent; if ye forsake your evil ways, then will I forsake my intentions of destruction.'"

And Noah and Methusaleh went forth and spoke these words of the Lord to the people. Every day, from morning until night, they addressed the people, but the people heeded not their words.

Noah was a righteous man in his generation, and the Lord chose Noah's seed to be spread over the whole earth. Then said God to Noah:

"Take thyself a wife, and beget children, for I have seen thee to be a righteous man before me; only thyself, thy wife, and thy sons, shall live on earth of all this generation."

And Noah did as God commanded him, and took to wife Naamah, the daughter of Enoch; and Noah was four hundred and ninety-eight years old when he married Naamah. And Naamah conceived and bore a son, whom she called "Japhet," saying, "God has enlarged us through the land." And she bore a second son, and called him "Ham." And she bore a third son, and called him "Shem," saying, "God has given me a great *name* on earth." And Noah was five hundred and two years old when she bore to him his third son, Shem.

And the lads grew up and walked in the way of God, as they were taught by Noah and by Methusaleh. And in these days died Lemech, the father of Noah. He was not as righteous either as his father or his son. He was seven hundred and seventy-seven years old when he died.

And again the Lord spoke to Methusaleh and Noah, saying:

"Once more call mankind to repentance; call once again, ere my punishment falls upon the people."

But the people listened not, and the words of warning were unheeded.

Then the Lord said unto Noah:

"The end of all flesh cometh before me, because of its evil ways; behold, I will destroy the people with the earth. But thou, take for thyself gopher wood, and build for thee an ark. In this manner build it: Three hundred cubits in length, fifty cubits in breadth, and thirty cubits in height; make a door in its side, and to a cubit finish it above."

In the five hundred and ninety-fifth year of his age Noah commenced building this ark, and he completed it in his six hundredth year, and during the time of its building his three sons married the three daughters of Methusaleh.

And it came to pass, also, during this time, that Methusaleh, the son of Enoch, died at the age of nine hundred and sixty-nine years.

After his death the Lord spoke to Noah, saying:

"Go thou with all thy household into the ark, and, behold, I will gather to thee all the beasts and fowls, and they will surround the ark.

"Then place thyself in the doorway of the ark, and the beasts and fowls will place themselves opposite to thee. Those that lie down before thee let thy sons lead into the ark, and those that remain standing thou shalt abandon."

As the Lord had spoken so happened it. The animals assembled in a great multitude opposite the ark. Those which lay down were led into the ark, and the others were abandoned.

And at the end of seven days the thunder and lightnings of the heavens frighted all the earth. The glory of the sun was darkened, the heavy rain fell, and the fury of the storm exceeded all that man had heard of or imagined.

And the people came to the ark and clung to it, and cried to Noah for help, but he answered them:

"For a hundred and twenty years I entreated ye to follow my words; alas, 'tis now too late."

For forty days and forty nights the rain fell, and with such violence that even those in the ark were in trouble and agony of mind, for they feared their vessel would not be able to withstand its might.

Each animal in the ark, according to its nature, uttered its cry of fear, of rage, of helplessness, and the noise was loud and terrible.

Then Noah addressed the Eternal in prayer:

"O Lord, I beseech Thee, save us now! Without strength to face this great calamity, we come to Thee. The rivers of water terrify us, and death plays in waves about us. Lift up Thy countenance upon us, O Lord! Be gracious to us. Redeem us, our God; deliver us, and save us!"

And God heard the voice of Noah, and remembered him.

"And God caused a wind to pass over the earth, and the waters were assuaged, ... and the ark rested in the seventh month .... upon the mountain of Ararat."

And Noah opened the window of the ark, and again called to God, saying

"O Lord, God of heaven and of earth, release our souls from confinement, bring us out from the prison in which we live; verily our hearts are weary with sighing."

And God answered Noah, saying:

"At the close of the year thou and thy family may go forth out of the ark."

And it came to pass in the second month, on the seven-and-twentieth day of the month, the earth was perfectly dry. Yet Noah and his family still tarried in the ark, and they did not leave it until God called to them and said, "Go out of the ark."

All the people and living things then departed from the vessel in which their lives had been preserved.

Noah and his children served the Lord all the days of their lives, and God blessed them. And the human race increased rapidly after the flood, and the names of the generations are written in the Bible.

Cush, the son of Ham and grandson of Noah, married in his old age a young wife, and begat a son whom he called "Nimrod," because in those days the people were beginning to rebel again against the Lord's command, and Nimrod signifies rebellion.

Now Nimrod grew up, and his father loved him exceedingly, because he was the child of his old age. And there was a certain coat of skins which God had made for Adam. When Adam died this coat became the possession of Enoch; from him it descended to Methusaleh, his son; Methusaleh gave it to Noah, who took it with him into the ark. And when the people left the ark Ham stole this coat, and hid it from his brothers, giving it secretly thereafter to Cush, his son. Cush kept it hidden for many years, until out of his great love he gave it to Nimrod, the child of his old age. When Nimrod was twenty years of age he put on this coat, and it gave him strength and might; might as a hunter in the fields, and might as a warrior in the subjection of his enemies and opponents. And his wars and undertakings prospered until he became king over all the earth.

Behold, to this day his power is a proverb among men, and he who instructs the youthful arm in the wielding of weapons, and the youthful mind in the secrets of the chase, wishes his pupils "even as Nimrod, who was a mighty hunter in the land, and prosperous in his wars."

When Nimrod was forty years old his brethren, the sons of Ham, quarrelled with the sons of Japhet. And Nimrod assembled the tribe of Cush, and went forth to battle with the sons of Japhet. And he addressed his army, saying:

"Be not dismayed, and banish fear from your hearts. Our enemies shall surely be your booty, and ye shall do with them as ye please."

Nimrod was victorious, and the opposing armies became his subjects. And when he and his soldiers returned home rejoicing the people gathered around and made him king, and placed a crown upon his head. And he appointed counsellors, judges, chiefs, generals, and captains. He established a national government, and he made Therach, the son of Nahor, his chief officer.

When Nimrod had thus established his power he decided to build a city, a walled town, which should be the capital of his country. And he selected a certain plain and built a large city thereon, and called it Shinar. And Nimrod dwelt in Shinar in safety, and gradually became ruler over all the world; and at that time all the people of the earth were of one language and of one speech.

Nimrod in his prosperity did not regard the Lord. He made gods of wood and stone, and the people copied after his doings. His son Mordon served idols also, from which we have, even to this day, the proverb, "From the wicked, wickedness comes forth."

And it came to pass about this time that the officers of Nimrod and the descendants of Phut, Mitzrayim, Cush, and Canaan took counsel together, and they said to one another:

"Let us build a city and also in its midst a tall tower for a stronghold, a tower the top of which shall reach even to the heavens. Then shall we truly make for ourselves a great and mighty name, before which all our enemies shall tremble. None will then be able to harm us, and no wars may disperse our ranks."

And they spoke these words to the king, and he approved of their design.

Therefore these families gathered together and selected a suitable spot for their city and its tower on a plain towards the east, in the land of Shinar.

And while they were building rebellion budded in their hearts, rebellion against God, and they imagined that they could scale the heavens and war with him.

They divided into three parties; the first party said:

"We will ascend to heaven and place there our gods, and worship them."

The second party said:

"We will pour into the heavens of the Lord and match our strength with His."

And the third party said:

"Yea, we will smite Him with arrow and with spear."

And God watched their evil enterprise, and knew their thoughts, yet they builded on. If one of the stones which they had raised to its height fell, they were sad at heart, and even wept; yet when any of their brethren fell from the building and were killed, none took account of the life thus lost. Thus they continued for a space of years, till God said, "We will confuse their language." Then the people forgot their language, and they spoke to one another in a strange tongue.

And they quarrelled and fought on account of the many misunderstandings occasioned by this confusion of language, and many were destroyed in these quarrels, till at last they were compelled to cease building. According to their deserts did God punish the three rebellious parties. Those who had said, "We will place our gods in the heavens," were changed in appearance, and became like apes; those who had said, "We will smite Him with arrows," killed one another through misunderstandings; and those who had said, "Let us try our strength with His," were scattered over the face of the earth.

The tower was exceedingly tall. The third part of it sunk down into the ground, a second third was burned down, but the remaining third was standing until the time of the destruction of Babylon.

Thus were the people dispersed over the globe, and divided into nations.

Chapter 2. From The Birth Of Abram To The Destruction Of Sodom And Gomorrah

THERACH, the son of Nahor, was the chief officer of King Nimrod, and a great favourite with his royal master; and when his wife Amtheta, the daughter of Karnebo, bore him a son, she called the child *Ab-ram*, meaning "Great father;" and Therach was seventy years old when his son Abram was born.

Now it came to pass on the night of Abram's birth that Therach entertained a number of his friends, including the wise men and magicians of Nimrod the king. They passed the night in revelry and merriment, and when they went forth from the house of their host morn was dawning. Lifting their eyes heavenward, they beheld a large and brilliant star rise before them in the east, and swallow up or consume four stars from the four corners of the heavens. The magicians wondered much at this occurrence, and they said one to the other:

"Verily, this is an omen connected with the newly-born child of Therach. When he grows up he will be fruitful and increase' greatly in power and excellence, and his descendants will destroy this kingdom and possess its lands."

And they went home and pondered over the matter, and when they met in the house of assembly, they said:

"Behold, we had better inform the king of the wonderful occurrence which greeted our sight. Should it come to his knowledge indirectly, he will be wroth with us for keeping it from him; he may even slay us for our neglect. Let us go to him at once that we may be free from blame in the matter."

Entering into the presence of the king, his wise men saluted him, saying, "O king, live for ever!"

And the chief of the wise men then related to the king the phenomenon which they had witnessed, and the interpretation or meaning which they assigned to it. Concluding the relation, he added:

"And now, if it be pleasing to the king, we would advise him to pay the value of this child unto his father and destroy him while in his infancy, lest in the days to come, through him and his descendants, we and our children be utterly destroyed."

The king listened attentively to the words of his servants and approved of their advice. He sent a messenger for Therach, and when the latter appeared before him he told him all that the wise men had related, and said:

"Now, therefore, give up the child, that we may slay him before misfortune falls upon us, and in payment we will fill thy coffers with silver and with gold!"

Then answered Therach:

"I have listened to the words of my lord, and all that he wishes I will do; yet first I beg, let me tell the king of a request made to me but yesterday, and ask his advice thereon."

"It is well," replied Nimrod; "speak."

"Yesterday," said Therach, "Ayon, the son of Morad, came to my house desiring to purchase from me the beautiful steed, which thou, oh king, didst graciously present to me. 'Sell me the horse,' said Ayon, 'and I will pay thee his full value and likewise fill thy stables with straw and provender.' And I answered him that I did not feel at liberty to so dispose of the king's gift without the king's approval; and now, oh king! I ask thee for advice." Angrily the king answered:

"And thou wouldst think of selling my gift, of parting with that noble steed for gold and silver, straw and provender! Art thou in such need of these things that thou wouldst barter for them the horse which I have given thee, a steed unequalled in the land?"

Then Therach bowed before the king, and said, "And if such is thy feeling in regard to this horse, how canst thou ask me to give up my child? Gold and silver cannot pay me for the gift of my king, neither can gold or silver replace for me my child?"

This application of his advice was exceedingly disagreeable to the king, and his feeling was so plainly pictured on his countenance that Therach quickly added:

"All my possessions are my king's, even my child, without money and without price."

"No," said the king, "for money will I buy him."

"Pardon, my lord," returned Therach, "give me three days for consideration, and I will speak of this matter with the mother of the boy."

Nimrod granted this request, and Therach departed from his presence.

At the end of the three days the king sent a message to Therach, commanding him to send the child or be himself destroyed with all his family.

When Therach received this message, realising that the king was determined in his purpose, he took the child of one of his slaves, a child born on the day of Abram's birth, and sent it to King Nimrod, receiving the money for it and declaring it to be his child.

The king himself slew the child, and Therach hid his wife, Abram, and the child's nurse in a lonely cave, sending them food secretly every week. And Abram remained in this cave until he was ten years old.

At the end of ten years Nimrod and his officers had forgotten all about Abram and the episode of his birth, and Abram came forth from the cave and was sent to live with Noah and his son Shem to learn from them the ways of the Lord; and he lived there thirty-nine years.

During these years Charan, the son of Therach, the elder brother of Abram, married, and his wife bore him a son whom he called "Lot;" she bore him also two daughters, one of whom he called Milcah and the other Sarai. At the time of Sarai's birth, Abram was about forty-two years of age.

From his earliest childhood Abram was a lover of the Lord. God had granted him a wise heart ready to comprehend and understand the majesty of the Eternal, and able to despise the vanity of idolatry.

When quite a child, beholding the brilliant splendour of the noonday sun and the reflected glory which it cast upon all objects around, he said, "Surely this brilliant light must be a god, to him will I render worship." And he worshipped the sun and prayed to it. But as the day lengthened the sun's brightness faded, the radiance which it last upon the earth was lost in the lowering clouds of night, and as the twilight deepened the youth ceased his supplications, saying, "No, this cannot be a god. Where then can I find the Creator, He who made the heavens and the earth?" He looked towards the west, the south, the north, and to the east. The sun disappeared from his view, nature became enveloped in the pall of a past day. Then the moon rose, and when Abram saw it shining in the heavens surrounded by its myriads of stars, he said, "Perhaps these are the gods who have created all things," and he uttered prayers to them. But when the morning dawned and the stars paled, and the moon faded into silvery whiteness and was lost in the returning glory of the sun, Abram knew God, and said, "There is a higher power, a Supreme Being, and these luminaries are but His servants, the work of His hands." From that day, even until the day of his death, Abram knew the Lord and walked in all His ways.

While Abram, the son of Therach, added daily to his wisdom and knowledge in the house of Noah, none knowing aught of his whereabouts, the subjects of King Nimrod, who then reigned in Babel, continued in their evil ways, despite of the warnings which they had received of the destruction of the wicked. And the servants of Nimrod called him Amraphel. Merdon, the son of Nimrod, was more unrighteous than his father, and even Therach, who still remained chief officer to the king, became a worshipper of idols. In his house he had twelve large images of wood and stone, a separate god for each month in the year, and to these he prayed and made obeisance.

When Abram was fifty years of age he left the house of his instructor, Noah, and returned to Therach, his father. He beheld the twelve idols occupying the places of honour in his father's house, and his soul waxed full with wrath, and he uttered a vow, saying:

"By the life of the Lord, if these images remain here three days longer, may the God who created me make me even such as they."

And Abram sought his father when he was surrounded by his officers, and he spoke to him, saying:

"Father, tell me, I pray, where I may find the God who created the heavens and the earth, thee, me, and all the people in the world."

And Therach answered:

"My son, the creator of all things is here with us in the house."

Then said Abram:

"Show him to me, my father."

And Therach led Abram into an inner apartment, and pointing to the twelve large idols and the many smaller ones around, he said:

"These are the gods who created the heavens and the earth, thee, me, and all the people of the world."

Abram then sought his mother, saying:

"My mother, behold, my father has shown to me the gods who have created the earth and all that it contains, therefore, prepare for me, I pray thee, a kid for a sacrifice, that the gods of my father may partake of the same and receive it favourably."

Abram's mother did as her son had requested her, and Abram placed the food which she prepared before the idols, but none stretched forth a hand to eat.

Then Abram jested, and said, "Perchance ‘tis not exactly to their taste, or mayhap the quantity appears stinted. I will prepare a larger offering, and strive to make it still more savoury."

Next day Abram requested his mother to prepare two kids and with her greatest skill, and placing them before the idols he watched with the same result as on the previous day.

Then Abram exclaimed:

"Woe to my father and to this evil generation; woe to those who incline their hearts to vanity and worship senseless images without the power to smell or eat, to see or hear. Mouths they have, but sounds they cannot utter; eyes they have, but lack all power to see; they have ears that cannot hear, hands that cannot move, and feet that cannot walk. Senseless as they are the men who wrought them, senseless all who trust in them and bow before them."

And seizing an iron implement, he destroyed and broke with it all the images save one, into the hands of which he placed the iron which he had used.

The noise of this proceeding reached the ears of Therach, who hurried to the apartment, where he found the broken idols and the food which Abram had placed before them. In wrath and indignation he cried out unto his son, saying:

"What is this that thou hast done unto my gods?" And Abram answered:

"I brought them savoury food, and behold they all grasped for it with eagerness at the same time, all save the largest one, who, annoyed and displeased with their greed, seized that iron which he holds and destroyed them."

"False are thy words," answered Therach in anger. "Had these images the breath of life, that they could move and act as thou hast spoken? Did I not fashion them with my own hands? How, then, could the larger destroy the smaller ones?"

"Then why serve senseless, powerless gods?" replied Abram, "gods who can neither help thee in thy need nor hear thy supplications? Evil is it of thee and those who unite with thee to serve images of stone and wood, forgetting the Lord God who made the heaven and the earth and all that is therein. Ye bring guilt upon your souls, the same guilt for which your ancestors were punished by the waters of the flood. Cease, oh, my father, to serve such gods, lest evil fall upon thy soul and the souls of all thy family."

And seizing the iron from the hands of the remaining idol, he destroyed that also, before his father's eyes.

When Therach witnessed this deed of his son, he hastened before King Nimrod and denounced Abram, saying, "A son born to me fifty years ago has acted so and so,--let him be brought before thee, I pray, for judgment."

When Abram was summoned before the king, Nimrod said to him:

"What is this that thou hast done unto thy father's gods?"

And Abram answered the king in the same words that he had spoken to his father. And when Nimrod replied:

"The large god had no strength nor power to do this thing," Abram continued, saying:

"Then wherefore serve him? Why cause thy subjects to follow in thy vain ways? Rather serve the great Lord of the world who has power to do all things; who has the power to kill, the power to keep alive. Woe to thee, thou man of foolish heart. Turn from thy evil ways, serve Him in whose hands is thy life and the lives of all thy people, or die in reproach, thou and all who follow thee."

The king commanded his officers to seize Abram and lead him to confinement, and he remained in prison ten days. During this time Nimrod convened his council, and thus addressed his princes and his officers:

"Ye have heard of the deeds of Abram, the son of Therach. He has treated me with disrespect and shown no dread of my power. Behold, he is in prison; therefore speak and tell me what punishment should be inflicted on this man, who has acted so audaciously before me."

And the counsellors replied:

"He who acts disrespectfully to the king should meet death upon the gallows; this man has done more; he is guilty of sacrilege, he has insulted our gods; therefore he should be burned to death. If it be pleasing to the king let a furnace be heated, day and night, and then let this Abram be cast therein."

This advice pleased the king, and he commanded such measures to be taken forthwith.

And when the furnace was heated to a great and consuming heat, all the officers assembled, and the people, both great and small, to witness the carrying out of the king's orders. The women, carrying their children with them, ascended to the roofs of their houses, and the men gathered in great numbers; but all stood afar off, for none dared approach the great heat to look into the furnace.

And it came to pass, when Abram was brought out from prison and the wise men and magicians beheld him, that they cried aloud unto Nimrod:

"Oh, king, we know this man! This is none other than the child, at whose birth, fifty years ago, one large star consumed four other stars. His father has mocked thee and played thee false in sending another child in his stead, to be slain according to thy will."

When the king heard these words he grew fiercely angry, and ordered Therach to be immediately brought before him. And he said to Therach:

"Thou hast heard what these magicians have asserted. Tell me, now, have they spoken truly?"

And Therach, observing the great anger of the king, answered truly:

"It is as these wise men have spoken. I had compassion upon my child, and sent thee in his stead the child of one of my slaves."

"Who advised thee to this? Speak truly, and thou shalt live?" demanded Nimrod.

The king's manner terrified Therach, and he answered quickly, not knowing what he said, and altogether without foundation:

"Charan, my other son, advised me to the thing."

Now Charan was a man without strength of mind in faith, and undecided as to whether the idols of his father or the God of Abram deserved his worship. When Abram was cast in prison, Charan said in his heart, "Now will I see what God is powerful. If Abram prevails I will profess his faith, and if he perishes I will follow the leading of the king."

When Therach thus accused his son, Nimrod answered:

"Then Charan must suffer with Abram, and both thy sons be cast into the furnace."

And both Abram and Charan were brought before the king, and in the presence of all the inhabitants their robes were removed from them, their hands and feet were bound, and they were cast into the flaming furnace.

Now the heat of the fire was so great that the twelve men who cast them therein were consumed by it, yet God had compassion upon his servant Abram, and though the ropes which bound him were burned from off his limbs, he walked upright through the fire, unharmed. But Charan, his brother, whose heart was not the Lord's, met instantaneous death in the flames. And the servants of the king called out to their master:

"Behold, Abram walks unhurt through the flames, the ropes with which we bound him are consumed, yet he is uninjured."

The king refused to believe so wonderful a thing, and sent trusted officers to look into the furnace, and when they corroborated the words of their inferiors the king was lost in amazement, and commanded his officers to take Abram out of the fire. They were not able, however, to execute his order, for the forks of flame blazed in their faces and they fled from the great heat.

And the king reproached them, saying ironically:

"Haste ye,--take Abram out, else he may die!"

But their second attempt was fruitless as the first, and in it eight men were burned to death.

Then the king called to Abram, saying:

"Servant of the God of Heaven, come forth from the fire and stand before me."

And Abram walked out of the fire and the furnace and stood before the king. And when the king saw that not even a hair of Abram's head was singed by the flame, he expressed wonder and amazement.

"The God of Heaven, in whom I trust," said Abram, "and in whose hand are all things, hath delivered me from the flames."

And the princes of the king bowed before Abram, but he said to them:

"Bow not to me, but to the great God of the Universe, who hath created you. Serve Him and walk in His ways; He is powerful to deliver and to save from death."

The king, too, looked on Abram with awe, and made him many valuable presents, and parted from him in peace.

And it came to pass after this that Nahor and Abram took to themselves wives; the name of Nahor's wife was Milcah, and the name of Abram's wife Sarai, or Yiska. They were both the daughters of Charan, the brother of their husbands.

About two years after Abram's deliverance from death by fire, King Nimrod dreamed. And behold, in this dream, he was standing with his army in a valley, opposite to a great furnace, in which a fire blazed; and a man, resembling Abram, came forth from the furnace and stood before the king, holding in his hand a drawn sword. And the man approached Nimrod with this sword uplifted, and Nimrod turned and fled. Then, as the king fled, the man threw after him an egg, and a huge river of water flowed forth from this egg, engulfing the king and all his army, and all were drowned save the king with three men. As they fled, the king turned to look at the companions who had been saved with him, and behold they were men of tall stature and commanding appearance, and attired in royal apparel. And the river disappeared and only an egg remained. And further in his dream, King Nimrod beheld a bird issue forth from this egg, and the bird flew upon his head and pecked out his eyes. Then the king awoke in great terror, and lo, his heart was beating rapidly and his blood was feverish.

In the morning the king sent for his wise men, and relating to them his dream, he demanded its interpretation. And one of the wise men, whose name was Anuki, answered, saying:

"Behold, this dream foreshadows the evil which Abram and his descendants will cause the king in time to come. It foretells the day when they will rise and smite our lord the king with all his hosts, and there will none be saved except the king, with three other kings who will battle on his side. And the river and the bird, these that came forth from the egg, lo, they but typify the descendants of this man, who will work much evil to our nation and our people in after days.

"This is the interpretation of the dream, its only meaning. And well thou knowest, oh, any lord the king, that many years ago thy wise men beheld this very thing, and yet to thy own misfortune thou hast still allowed this man to live. While he walks on earth thy kingdom remains imperilled."

The words of Anuki made a deep impression on the king, and he sent secret emissaries to take Abram's life. The king's design, however, was frustrated by Eleazer, a slave of Abram's, whom Nimrod had presented to him. He learned of the king's intention, and warned his master, saying:

"Arise, get thee quickly hence, that thou mayest escape destruction."

And he told Abram of the king's dream, and the interpretation which the wise men had given to it.

So Abram hastened to the house of Noah, and remained there hiding while the servants of the king searched his own home and the surrounding country in vain, and he remained a longer time, even until the people had forgotten him.

And it came to pass during this period of concealment that Therach, who was still a favourite with the king, came in secret to visit his son. And Abram spoke to him, saying:

"Come, let us all journey to another land; let us go to Canaan. Thou knowest that the king seeks my life, and even though he honours and exalts thee, yet wealth and power amount to naught in the hour of death and trouble. Journey with me, oh, my father; abandon the vanity which thou pursuest; let us live in safety, worshipping the great God who created us in happiness and peace."

And Noah and his son Shem added their entreaties to those of Abram, till Therach consented to do as they wished. And Therach with Abram his son, and Lot his son's son, and Sarai his daughter-in-law, and all his family, went forth from *Ur Chaldee*, from the city of Babel to the land of Charan, and there they tarried.

And the country around them was pleasant and fertile, and there was ample space for the men and the cattle they had with them. And the people of Charan respected and honoured them, and God blessed them and looked with favour on their household.

And it came to pass after Abram had dwelt in Charan about three years, that the Lord appeared to him, and said:

"I am the Lord who brought thee safely through the fire of the Chaldeans, and delivered thee from the strength of thy enemies. If thou wilt hearken earnestly to my words and follow diligently my commands, I will make thy seed even as the stars of the heaven, and those who hate shall likewise fear thee. My blessing shall rest upon thee and my favour on thy doings. Now, arise, take Sarai thy wife, and those who belong to thee, and all thy possessions, and journey to Canaan and dwell there, and I will be thy God and bless thee."

And Abram journeyed with his family to Canaan in obedience to the Lord's command. And he was fifty-five years old when he left Charan.

When Abram had pitched his tent in Canaan, among the inhabitants of the land, God again appeared to him, and said:

"This is the land which I have given as a permanent possession to thee and thy descendants. For the generations to spring from thee shall be numerous as the stars in heaven, and the countries which I have shown thee shall be their heritage on earth."

Then Abram built an altar to God, and called it by the name of the Lord. And he continued to dwell in Canaan, and when he had lived there about three years Noah died at the age of nine hundred and fifty years.

After this Abram returned to Charan to visit his father and mother, and he remained with them in Charan for five years. During this time he endeavoured to spread a knowledge of the Eternal, and he succeeded in gaining among the Charanites many followers of the one God.

And the Lord appeared to him in Charan, saying:

"Arise and return to the land of Canaan, thou and thy wife and all born in thy house, and all the souls which thou hast made in Charan. To thee have I given the land from the river of Egypt even unto the great river, the river Euphrates."

And Abram did as the Lord commanded, and Lot, the son of his brother, went with him out of Charan to the land of Canaan.

Now Lot possessed large herds of cattle, for God had prospered him in his undertakings. And it happened that the herdsmen of Lot and the herdsmen of Abram quarrelled and disputed in regard to rights of pasturage and water, and they strove one with the other. Therefore Abram said to Lot:

"Thou hast done wrong, and through thy herdsmen thou wilt cause me to be hated by our neighbours. Thy shepherds have pastured their flocks on lands which belong to others, and I must bear the reproach therefor. Thou knowest that I am but a stranger and sojourner in this land, and thou shouldst bid thy servants to be heedful."

Despite the frequent rebukes of Abram, however, the herdsmen of Lot continued to quarrel with Abram's men, and to trespass upon the pastures of their neighbours. At last Abram spoke earnestly, saying:

"Let there be no strife between us, for we are near relations, yet we must separate. Go thou whither thou pleasest, choose thy dwelling-place where thou wilt, thou and thy cattle and all thy possessions, but bide no longer with me. If thou art in danger I will haste to aid thee, and in all things will I be with thee, but separate thyself from me I pray."

And Lot lifted up his eyes and looked upon the land opposite the river Jordan. He saw rich plains and fertile fields, a country pleasant for man, and with wide pastures for flocks, rich in water and gratifying to the sight. And Lot was much pleased with the country, and journeyed thither even to Sodom, departing in peace from Abram with his flocks and all his possessions. And Abram remained and dwelt in the groves of Mamre, near to Hebron.

"The men of Sodom were wicked, and sinners before the Lord exceedingly."

Now, in these days Sodom and four other cities were inhabited by men of evil actions, who provoked the anger and indignation of the Most High. They planted in the valley a beautiful garden many miles in extent, a place adorned with fruits and flowers, and objects pleasing to the sight and intoxicating to the senses. Thither the people flocked four times a year with music and with dancing, indulging in all sorts of excesses and acts of idolatrous worship, with none to utter a word of warning or rebuke.

In their daily life they were both cruel and treacherous, oppressing the stranger and taking advantage of all persons thrown in contact with them. If a trader entered their city they would seize his goods either with violence or through trickery, and if he remonstrated they but mocked him and drove him from the place.

It happened once that a man from Elam, journeying to a place beyond Sodom, reached this latter city even as the sun was setting. He had with him an ass bearing a valuable saddle to which some rare and precious merchandise was attached. Unable to find a lodging for himself and stabling for the animal, he resolved to pass the night in the streets of Sodom, and journey on in the morning. A certain citizen of Sodom, named Hidud, chanced to observe this stranger, and being cunning and treacherous, he accosted him, saying:

"Whence comest thou, and whither art thou travelling?"

"I am journeying from Hebron," replied the stranger; "my destination is beyond this place; but lo, the sun has set; I can obtain no lodging, and so I remain here in the streets. I have bread and water for myself and straw and provender for my beast, so I need not be under obligation to anybody."

"Nay, this is wrong," returned Hidud, "come pass the night with me, thy lodging shall cost thee naught, and I will attend also to the wants of thy animal."

Hidud led the stranger to his house. He removed the valuable saddle from the ass, and the merchandise which was attached to it he also removed, placing them in the closet in his house, then he gave the ass provender and set meat and drink before the stranger, who partook of the meal, and lodged that night with him.

In the morning the stranger rose up early intending to pursue his journey, but Hidud said to him, "Take first thy morning meal, then go thy way."

After the man had eaten he rose to go on his way, but Hidud stopped him, saying, "It is late in the day, remain I pray thee, bide with me yet this day and then depart."

The stranger remained in Hidud's house until the following morning, and then, declining another pressing invitation to remain one day more, he prepared for his departure.

Then said Hidud's wife:

"This man has lived with us two days and paid us naught."

But Hidud answered:

"Keep thy peace."

He then brought forth the stranger's ass, and bade him "fare thee well."

"Hold," said the stranger, "my saddle, the spread of many colours, and the strings attached to it, together with my merchandise, where are they?"

"What!" exclaimed Hidud.

"I gave thee," returned the stranger, "a beautiful spread with strings attached to it; thou hast hidden it in thy house."

"Ah!" said Hidud pleasantly, "I will interpret thy dream. That thou hast dreamed of strings, signifies that thy days will be prolonged even as strings may be stretched from end to end; that thou hast dreamed of a spread of many colours signifieth that thou wilt one day possess a garden rich in flowers and luscious fruits."

The stranger answered:

"No, my lord, I dreamed not; I gave to thee a spread of many colours with strings attached, and thou hast hidden it in thy house."

And Hidud said:

"And I have interpreted thy dream; I have told thee its meaning, 'tis useless to repeat it. For the interpretation of a dream people generally pay me four pieces of silver, but as for thee, behold I will ask of thee only three."

The stranger was very angry at this outrageous conduct, and he accused Hidud in the court of Sodom of stealing his goods. Then when each man told his story, the judge said:

"Hidud speaks the truth; he is an interpreter of dreams; he is well known as such."

And Hidud said to the stranger:

"And as thou art such a liar, thou must even pay me the full price, four pieces of silver, as well as for the four meals eaten in my house."

"Willingly will I pay thee for thy meals," replied the other, "if thou wilt but return my saddle and my goods."

Then the two men wrangled with angry words, and they were driven forth from the court-house, and the men in the streets joined on Hidud's side, and they fought the stranger and thrust him forth from the city, robbed of all his possessions.

When a poor man entered the city of Sodom the people would give him money in order to save a reputation for charity, but they made an agreement among themselves that no one should either give or sell him food, or allow him to depart from the city. The man would consequently die of starvation, and the people would then regain the money they had given him. They would even rob the body of the rags which covered it, and bury it naked in the wilderness.

Upon one occasion Sarai sent her servant Eleazer to Sodom to inquire concerning the welfare of Lot and his family. As he entered the city, Eleazer observed a Sodomite fighting with a stranger whom he had defrauded, and who, running to Eleazer, implored him for assistance.

"What art thou doing to this poor man?" said Eleazer to the Sodomite; "shame upon thee to act in this manner towards a stranger in your midst!"

And the Sodomite replied:

"Is he thy brother? What is our quarrel to thee?" and picking up a stone, he struck Eleazer with it on the forehead, causing his blood to flow freely in the street. When the Sodomite saw the blood, he caught hold of Eleazer, crying

"Pay me my fee as a leech; see, I have freed thee of this impure blood; pay me quickly, for such is our law."

"What!" exclaimed Eleazer, "thou hast wounded me and I am to pay thee for it!"

This Eleazer refused to do, and the Sodomite had him brought into the court, and there before the judge reiterated his demand for a fee.

"Thou must pay the man his fee," said the judge, addressing Eleazer; "he has let thy blood, and such is our law."

Eleazer paid the money, and then lifting up the stone he struck the judge heavily with it, and the blood spurted out in a strong stream.

"There!" exclaimed Eleazer, "follow thy law and pay my fee to this man; I want not the money," and he left the court-house.

At another time a certain poor man entered Sodom, and as everybody refused to give him food, he was very nearly starved to death when Lot's daughter chanced to meet him. For many days she supported him, carrying him bread whenever she went to draw water for her father. The people of the city, seeing the poor man still living, wondered greatly as to how he managed to support life without food, and three men constituted themselves a committee to watch his goings and his doings. They saw Lot's daughter giving aim bread, and seizing her they carried her before the fudges, who condemned her to death by burning, and this punishment was inflicted on her.

Another maiden, who assisted a poor stranger, was smeared with honey, and left to be stung to death by bees.

For such acts were Sodom and her sister cities destroyed by fire from Heaven, and only Lot and his family spared through God's love for his servant Abram.

Chapter 3. From The Birth Of Isaac To The Wars Of Shechem

"AND the Lord visited Sarah and she bore a son unto Abraham in his old age."

When Isaac was born Abraham prepared a great feast in his honour, and invited thereto all the chiefs and men of birth and position who were his neighbours, such as Abimelech and the captains of his armies. Therach, Abraham's father, and Nahor, his brother, journeyed also from Charan to join in the festivities, and Shem with Eber, his son, were likewise of the party. They were all hearty in their congratulations, and Abraham's heart was full with gladness.

Ishmael, the son of Hagar and Abraham, was very fond of hunting and field sports. He carried his bow with him at all times, and upon one occasion, when Isaac was about five years of age, Ishmael aimed his arrow at the child, crying, "Now I am going to shoot thee." Sarah witnessed this action, and fearing for the life of her son, and disliking the child of her handmaid, she made many complaints to Abraham of the boy's doings, and urged him to dismiss both Hagar and Ishmael froth his tent, and send them to live at some other place.

For some time Ishmael lived with his mother in the wilderness of Paran, always indulging in his great passion for hunting; then they journeyed to Egypt, where Ishmael married, and where four sons and a daughter were born to him. But soon he returned to his favourite home in the wilderness, building there tents for himself, his people and his family, for God had blessed him, and he was the master of large flocks and herds.

And it came to pass after many years that Abraham, yielding to a longing which had always possessed him, determined to visit his son, and informing Sarah of his intention he started off alone upon a camel.

He reached Ishmael's dwelling-place about noontime, and found that his son was away from home, hunting. He was rudely treated by Ishmael's wife, who did not know him, and who refused him the bread and water which he asked for. Therefore he said to her, "When thy husband returns say thus to him, describing my appearance, An old man from the land of the Philistines came to our door during thy absence, and he said to me, when thy husband returns, tell him to remove the nail which he has driven in his tent and to replace it with one more worthy," with which words Abraham rode away.

When Ishmael returned home his wife related to him the occurrence, describing the man and repeating his words, and Ishmael knew that his father had visited him and been treated with disrespect. For which cause Ishmael divorced his wife, and married a maiden from the land of Canaan.

Some three years after this Abraham again visited his son's tent, and again his son was away from home; but his wife was pleasant and hospitable, and begged the stranger, whom she did not know, to alight from his camel, and she set before him bread and meat. Therefore he said to her, "When thy husband returns, describe to him my appearance, and say, 'This old man came to thee from the land of the Philistines, and this message he left for thee: the nail which thou hast driven in thy tent is good and worthy, see that it is properly esteemed;" and blessing Ishmael and his family, Abraham returned to his home.

When Ishmael returned he was much pleased to hear his father's message, and he thanked God for a good and worthy wife, and after a time he and his family visited Abraham, and remained with him in the land of the Philistines for many days.

When Abraham had dwelt here for six-and-twenty years, he removed with all his family and possessions to *Bear Sheba*, near Hebron. Here he planted a grove and built large houses, which he kept always open for the poor and needy. Those who were hungry entered freely and partook of food according to their desire, and those who were needy were liberally supplied with the necessaries of life. When any of the grateful ones would seek to Abraham to thank him for his benevolence he replied to them:

"Address thy thanks to God. To the Eternal, who created all things, all that we receive belongs; through His bounty we are fed and clothed."

To feed the hungry, to clothe the naked, to speak kindly to the unfortunate, to act justly towards all mankind, and to be ever grateful to the Eternal, formed the articles of the creed according to which Abraham fashioned his life.

And the word of the Lord came unto Abraham, saying, "Take now thy son whom thou lovest, and offer him for a burnt-offering upon one of the mountains which I will tell thee of."

When this command was delivered to Abraham, chief among the many griefs and anxieties which oppressed his mind, was the necessity of separating Isaac from his mother. He could not tell her of his intention, and yet the lad was always with her. Finally he proceeded to Sarah's tent, and seating himself beside her, he said:

"Thy son is growing to manhood, and he has not yet learned the service of heaven. To-morrow I will take him with me to learn the ways of the Lord, with Shem and Eber."

And Sarah replied:

"Go, my lord, and do as thou hast spoken; but do not take the lad too great a distance, and keep him not a long time from my presence."

And Abraham said:

"Pray to God for the happiness of thy son, for my happiness, and for thy own."

During that night Sarah was much troubled on account of the approaching separation from Isaac; she was unable to sleep, and when her husband and the lads who accompanied him appeared early in the morning, ready to start upon their journey, she pressed Isaac to her bosom, and weeping bitterly she sobbed:

"Oh, my son, my son! how can I allow thee to wander from me; my only child, my pride, my hope." Then turning to Abraham she said:

"Watch carefully the lad, for he is young and tender; let him not travel in the heat, nor journey so as to weary his frame."

She clothed Isaac in his richest garments, and she and her maidens accompanied him on his way till Abraham bid them depart and return unto their homes.

Abraham and Isaac journeyed on with the two lads, who were Ishmael, Abraham's son, and Eleazer, the steward of his house.

As they journeyed Ishmael spoke to Eleazer, saying:

"My father intends to sacrifice his son Isaac for a burnt offering; therefore, I will be his heir, for am I not his first-born son?"

"Nay," answered Eleazer, "thy father drove thee forth that thou shouldst not inherit his possessions; to me, his faithful servant, will all his wealth descend."

As they proceeded on their way Isaac addressed his father, saying:

"Behold, my father, here is the fire and the wood, but where is the lamb for the sacrifice?"

And Abraham answered:

"Our God hath chosen thee, my son; thee, a creature without blemish, as an acceptable burnt-offering to His glory in place of the lamb."

And then said Isaac:

"To the will of the living God in thankfulness I bow."

"My son," said Abraham, "is there any secret evil in thy heart, or any wrong upon thy mind; if so, dell me freely, my son, keep naught from me in this great hour."

And Isaac answered:

"By the life of God, my father, I know no evil, I am conscious of no regret. Blessed be the Lord who has desired me this day."

This answer of his son was very gratifying to the father's heart, and they continued on in silence, until they reached the spot which God had selected.

Then Abraham built an altar to the Lord, and his son handed him the stones and assisted him in the work.

They who trust in God are ever strengthened, and though their eyes were wet with tears their hearts were firm, confiding in their God.

When the altar was built Abraham laid the wood upon it in order, and then he bound his son Isaac upon the wood.

And Isaac spoke to his father, saying:

"My father, bind me well, in order that I may not, by struggling, profane the sacrifice; be firm, my father, and sharpen well the knife. Tell my mother that her joy is gone; the son she bore at ninety years surrendered to the flame. When I am consumed, take with thee of the ashes left, and say to Sarah, This is thy Isaac, who to God was offered."

When Abraham heard these words he wept bitterly, but Isaac continued with a firm voice:

"Now quickly, father, do the will of God." And he stretched his neck to meet the knife which rested in his father's hand.

"And Abraham went and took the ram, and offered him up for a burnt-offering in the stead of his son."

Abraham sprinkled the ram's blood upon the altar, saying:

"May this blood be considered even as the blood of my son, offered as a sacrifice before the Lord."

And so through the entire sacrificial service Abraham prayed:

"May this be received even as the blood of my son, offered as a burnt-offering before the Lord."

While Abraham and Isaac were away upon this mission an old man approached Sarah, near her tent, and said to her:

"Knowest thou that Abraham has offered up thy Isaac as a sacrifice before the Lord. Aye, despite his struggles and his cries, thy son has been made a victim to the knife."

Then Sarah uttered a heart-rending cry, and throwing herself upon the ground she sobbed bitterly:

"My son, my son, would that I had perished this day for thee. Thee, whom I have raised and nourished, my life and all my love was thine. Now is my pride and gladness turned to mourning, for the fire has consumed my joy. Take comfort, oh, my heart! the lives of all God carries in the hollow of his hand. Blessed are they who follow Thy commands, for Thou art righteous, and Thy words are truth; therefore, oh Lord, though mine eyes weep bitter tears, my heart is glad."

Then Sarah rose and journeyed from *Bear Sheba* to Hebron, and she inquired upon the road concerning her husband and her son, but she was unable to ascertain their whereabouts.

Returning to her tents she was met by the same old man who had before addressed her, and thus he spoke:

"Verily I did inform thee falsely, for Isaac, thy son, lives."

Sarah's heart was stronger for grief than joy. These tidings and the revulsion in her feelings killed her; she died and was gathered to her people.

And when Abraham and Isaac returned and found the dead body of Sarah, they lifted up their voices in bitter lamentation, and all their servants joined with Abraham and Isaac in grief for the departed.

Now Isaac was fifty-nine years of age, and his wife Rebecca was barren, and Isaac prayed unto the Lord to visit his wife even as he had visited Sarah, his mother, saying:

"Oh Lord, God of heaven and of earth, thou fittest both with thy goodness and mercy. From the house of his father, and from his kindred's home, thou didst bring my father to this place, promising to increase his seed, even as the stars of the heavens, and to give to them this land as a heritage and possession. Fulfil, oh God, these words which thou hast spoken. To thee, oh God, we look in hope and pray for children, for those whom thou hast promised us. Oh, my God, to thee I look, in hope."

And God hearkened to the prayer of Isaac, and his wife bore him two sons, twins. The one, the first, she called "Esau," and the other "Jacob."

And Esau was fond of outdoor life, while Jacob stayed at home learning from Abraham, his grandfather, the ways and teachings of the Lord.

When the lads were about fifteen years old, Abraham died at the age of one hundred and seventy-one years. And when the inhabitants of Canaan learned of his decease they, with all its kings and princes, hastened to do honour to his remains, and all his relatives, who lived in Charan, and the sons of his concubines, came also to the funeral. And Isaac and Ishmael buried him in the cave of Machpelah, and all who knew him mourned for him a year.

Very few men like Abraham has the sun looked upon. From his youth he served his Maker and walked upright before Him, and from his birth even unto the moment of his death his God was with him. He spoke of God's goodness to all with whom he came in contact; he built a grove for travellers and opened his doors in wide and generous hospitality to the needy, the weary, and all who passed his way. For Abraham's sake the Lord looked kindly on the people of the earth, and after his death God blessed Isaac, his son, and prospered him greatly.

And the sons of Isaac grew in strength and years. Esau was a man of evil thoughts, of quick passions, and a lover of outdoor life, Jacob was a shepherd, an intelligent and domestic man, following in the path which Abraham had pointed out to him.

And it came to pass that Esau went hunting in the field upon a certain day, when Nimrod, too, was engaged in the same pursuit. Both being mighty hunters a rivalry existed between the two, a deadly jealousy. Esau happened to see Nimrod when all his attendants, save two men, had left him. Esau concealed himself, and when Nimrod passed the place where he was hiding pointed his arrow, pulled the cord, and shot Nimrod through the heart. Then rushing from his concealment, Esau engaged in a deadly struggle with Nimrod's two attendants, and overcame and killed them both. Then stripping from Nimrod's shoulders the wonderful coat, before mentioned, which God had made for Adam, Esau hastened home, reaching his father's tent weary, hungry, tired, and faint. Then Esau said to Jacob, his brother:

"Give me of yonder red pottage,--let me eat of it, I pray, for I am faint."

And Jacob said:

"Sell me this day thy right of first born."

And Esau thought in his heart, "They will surely avenge upon me the death of Nimrod," and he answered:

"Behold, I am going to die. What can the right of first born profit me?"

So Jacob bought from Esau his right of first born, and also a burial plot for himself in the cave of Machpelah.

Then Jacob gave Esau bread and pottage of lentils, and Esau eat and drank and went his way.

For money did Jacob purchase these rights, and after the bargain was concluded, he gave his brother the food he had asked for.

The body of Nimrod was found and brought to Babel and buried there, And Nimrod lived two hundred and fifteen years, and was killed by a descendant of Abraham, even as he had foreseen in his dream.

When Jacob received the blessing which was intended for Esau, Isaac was very old, and Esau said:

"My father will soon die, and then I will take vengeance on Jacob for this wrong which he has done me." This threat was repeated to Rebecca, who called Jacob and bade him flee to Charan, to her brother Laban, to tarry there until his brother's fury had abated.

Then Isaac sent messengers after Jacob, with a repetition of his blessing and this charge: "Take not a wife from the daughters of Canaan, for thus has said my father Abraham, in the word of the Lord, the word which has promised this land to our seed if we obey the Lord and observe faithfully his commands. Arise, go to Charan, to the house of Bethuel, thy mother's father, and take heed that thou forgettest not the Lord thy God and all His ways. Turn neither to the right nor to the left after the vanities of the people among whom thou goest. The Almighty will give thee grace in the eyes of the men of the land, and thou shalt take a wife there according to thy desire, that God may grant thee the blessing of Abraham, and make thee fruitful and multiply thee until thou becomest an assembly in the land. That He may bring thee back to this land with children, gladness, and prosperity."

Jacob obeyed his father and journeyed on towards Mesopotamia. He was seventy-seven years of age when he started forth from *Bear Sheba*.

When Jacob had departed from his father's house, Esau called to him his son Eliphas, and said to him in secrecy, "Go follow after Jacob with thy bow in thy hand, lie in wait for him, slay him upon the mountains, take for thy own what treasure he has with him, and then return to me."

Eliphas was then but thirteen years of age, yet he was remarkably swift of foot and understood well the handling of the bow. He obeyed his father, and taking some men with him, followed after Jacob and overtook him on the borders of Canaan.

When Jacob saw Eliphas coming after him he halted and awaited his approach, thinking that his nephew carried some message from home. When Eliphas came near he drew his sword. Jacob inquired the reason of his pursuit, and the lad answered, "Thus and thus has my father commanded me, and I dare not disobey his orders."

When Jacob learned Esau's intention, and saw that the lad seemed determined to do as he had been bidden, he turned to him and the men with him, and said:

"Take all that I have, all that my father and my mother gave into my hands, but spare my life. Your kindness will be accounted to you as righteousness."

The Lord gave Jacob favour in their eyes, and they allowed him to proceed unharmed on his journey. His gold and silver, however, everything of value that he had taken with him from his father's house, Eliphas and his comrades seized and carried to Esau. Esau was strongly displeased because they had listened to Jacob's pleadings, and the treasure which they had seized he added to his own store.

Jacob proceeded on his journey towards Charan. When he reached the Mount of Moriah he tarried there and slept that night. And the Lord appeared to him and said, "I am the Lord, the God of Abraham and Isaac, thy father The ground whereon thou liest will I give to thy children and behold I will be with thee, therefore fear not. I will guard thee wheresoever thou goest, and I will increase thy seed as the stars of the heaven. I will disperse thy enemies before thee; they will fight against thee, but they will not prevail. With gladness and great wealth will I bring thee back to thy father's land."

Jacob awoke from his sleep enchanted with the remembrance of the beautiful and encouraging vision which had blessed his slumbers. He called the place *Beth El.*

When Jacob arrived in Charan he told his uncle Laban how Eliphas, the son of Esau, had despoiled him, and bursting into tears, proclaimed himself a beggar.

"Then," said Laban, "surely thou art my bone and my flesh. I will take care of thee even though thou art penniless."

After Laban's fruitless pursuit after Jacob when he left with his wives, children, and chattels, and God had said to the son of Bethuel, "Take heed to thee, speak with Jacob neither good nor evil," he sent, after parting with his son-in-law, messengers to Esau, charged to deliver these words:

"We come from Laban, thy relative, thy mother's brother, and in his words we say, 'Knowest thou what Jacob, thy brother, has done to me? Faint and needy he came to me, and I received him into my house with honours and affection. I gave him my daughters for wives, and the handmaids of my daughters did I also give him. God blessed him for my sake, and he accumulated much wealth. He begat children and acquired men-servants and maid-servants, sheep, oxen, and cattle of all kinds, a great multitude, and likewise silver and gold. With all this he left me, fled secretly with all his possessions towards the land of Canaan, his father's home. He denied me even the privilege of kissing my daughters; as captives he led them with him, and worse than all, my gods he stole. By the brook of Jabak I left him with all his substance, and if thou desirest to pursue him, there will he be found. Go, then, and do with him what is pleasing to thy heart.'"

When Esau heard these words of the messengers of Laban, all the wrong which Jacob had done him freshened in his memory, and his anger and hate against his brother burned once more fiercely in his heart. He gathered together his sons and servants, and all the family of Seer, a company of four hundred men, and at their head he set out to meet Jacob and to smite him.

After the messengers of Laban left Esau, they journeyed to Canaan, and there informed Rebecca of her son Esau's preparations and his intention to waylay and punish Jacob. Rebecca immediately sent seventy-two of Isaac's men to assist her favourite child. They met him at the brook Jabak, and when he saw them he said, "Surely here is help from heaven," and he called the place *Machanayim*.

Jacob recognised his father's servitors, and asked after the wellbeing of his parents, to which the messengers responded, "They live in peace, and farther we bring this message from thy mother. 'I have heard, my son, that Esau, thy brother, intends to meet thee on the road with the men of Seer. Therefore, I pray thee, heed my words. When thou shalt see him, be not rash nor headstrong, but greet him humbly and with a gracious present from the abundance with which God hath blessed thee. When he addresses thee, answer meekly, kindly, and thus will his wrath be turned from thee. Remember, he is thy elder brother, and to him is thy respect and honour due.'"

Jacob wept at these words of his mother, but he obeyed her request. He sent messengers to meet Esau on the road, and to offer him such words as his mother had directed. These messengers met Esau and his company, and spoke as Jacob had commanded them, but Esau answered with pride:

"Nay, nay, the truth I have heard. I know how Jacob treated Laban; how he repaid the kindness of the relative who gave him wives and substance; how he fled, taking the children of Laban with him, as though they had been captives of the sword. Not Laban only has he wronged; twice he supplanted me. Therefore I come to meet him, and the vengeance for which I have waited twenty years shall now be mine."

When these words were carried to Jacob he was sorely distressed. Earthly help seemed unavailable; with a full heart he cast himself before the Lord and prayed earnestly for deliverance from the trouble which threatened him and all his people.

Then he divided his people and his flocks into two companies. One detachment he placed under the command of Eleazer of Damascus, the servant of Abraham, with his sons, and the other under Elinus, the son of Eleazer, and his sons. And thus he commanded them:

"Travel apart, so that if one company shall perchance be smitten, the other may escape."

Then, when he met Esau, he bowed to the ground before him seven times, and God gave him grace in his brother's eyes. Esau's hate died away, and natural affection gaining the mastery, he raised Jacob from the ground and embraced and kissed him.

Jacob encamped with all his family before the city of Shechem, and purchased a lot of land for a dwelling from the sons of Chamor for the sum of fifty shekels.

Here he made his home, and lived in peace and safety for about eighteen months.

Then the inhabitants of Shechem made a great feast, an occasion of joyousness, dancing, singing, and merriment of all kinds, and all the daughters of the land joined in the general revelry. And it came to pass that

Rachel and Leah, the wives of Jacob, and Dinah, his daughter, felt a great desire to witness this scene of enjoyment, and together they repaired to the place where the festivities were held. All the nobles of the city were present, and Shechem, the son of the king, was also one of the participants.

He happened to see Dinah, and was immediately attracted by her great beauty and modest appearance. He inquired as to who she was, and learned that she was the daughter of Jacob the Hebrew, who had lately settled in his father's land. His passion grew very strong, and taking advantage of an opportunity he carried the frightened girl forcibly to his house.

Rachel and Leah hurried home and informed Jacob of the occurrence. He immediately sent twelve servants to the house of Shechem to demand the girl, but they were insolently met by the prince's retainers and driven back to Jacob. He said nothing, but waited quietly until his sons should return to their home.

Shechem, in the meantime, sent a messenger to his father, requesting him to visit Jacob and demand Dinah as a wife for him. The king was much displeased with the affair, and seeking his son, he said, "Canst thou not find a wife among the daughters of our land? Why shouldst thou desire this Hebrew damsel, a stranger among thy race?"

Shechem replied to his father, "She is pleasing in my eyes," and he impressed his father so completely with his love for the maiden that the king at length consented to seek the patriarch, Jacob, and gain his consent to the marriage.

Now when the sons of Jacob returned home, and learned of the occurrence and the violence with which their only sister had been treated, their hearts burned with indignation.

"The penalty for this crime is death," they exclaimed; our sister has been sinned against with the sin which God warned Noah and his children to shun if they desired life. Death shall be the punishment of this violator of our home, death at our hands, to him, his family, and the whole city."

While the sons of Jacob were thus speaking, Chamor, the father of Shechem, entered into their presence, and addressed Jacob:

"My son Shechem desires thy daughter for a wife; give her to him, I pray thee, and thy people may intermarry with the daughters of our land. Our country is large, and it is all before thee to trade therein, or do soever as thou pleasest, if thou wilt but consent to the wishes of my son."

As Chamor concluded, his son, Shechem, entered, and continued his father's propositions:

"Let me find grace in your eyes," he said to the men before him. "Give me the damsel for a wife, and whatever dowry you may demand shall be cheerfully given."

Simeon and Levi, desiring time to perfect a plan for inflicting punishment for the wrong done their sister, replied to Shechem and his father with a cunning tongue:

"What thou hast said to us we will consider. Our sister is in thy hands. Give us time, however, to consult with our grandfather, Isaac; he is wise, and knows well what should be done in a case like this; according to his welds we will act."

Shechem acquiesced in this arrangement, and withdrew, with his father, from Jacob's house.

When they had departed the sons of Jacob reiterated their determination to put the man of violence to death, and with him the men of the city who had encouraged him in the act.

"Listen," said Simeon, "to my advice. We will say to these men, 'Our God hath enjoined upon us the act of circumcision, and we cannot give our daughters and sisters to those who have not entered into this covenant. Become like us, and then we may freely intermarry; if not, we will take our sister and go from among you;' then when they are weak and suffering we will fall upon them, and all their males shall die by the sword."

This advice was pleasing to his brethren, and when Shechem and Chamor came again to them for their decision, they proclaimed this as the counsel of Isaac, saying that their grandfather had decided that for them to give their sister to an uncircumcised man would be a reproach to them for ever.

Shechem and his father then gathered the people at the gates of the city, and made known to them the proposition of the Israelites, counselling them to accept the same.

All the citizens seemed willing to do the pleasure of their king save Hadkam, the son of Pered, the father of Chamor, and his six brothers. They scorned Jacob and his sons, and defended the mothers of their city who refused to allow their children to undergo the operation.

"Shame to you that you should consider such a thing," said they. "Are not the daughters of the Canaanites good enough for wives, that you wish to wed the daughters of this Hebrew, this stranger among you? Beware of this rash act, which your fathers never enjoined upon you; the undertaking cannot be prosperous. What answer can you make to your brethren, the Canaanites, when they demand your reason for this folly? And how will you appear in the eyes of your brethren, the children of Ham, when 'tis said, 'For a Hebrew woman did Shechem, his father, and all the inhabitants of his city, commit an abomination?' Whither will ye flee? Where will ye be able to hide your shame? We will not bend beneath this yoke, which you take so willingly upon you; we will gather our brethren, and we will smite you, aye to death."

Chamor and Shechem began to regret their impulsive proceeding, but they answered:

"Think not that we did this because we love the Hebrews; no, merely to blind their eyes, and obtain their daughter. Wait but till we have recovered from the operation, and they and all that is theirs shall be ours, to use according to our pleasure."

Dinah overheard the discussion, and she sent a hand-maiden to her father's house to inform him and her brethren of the designs of Shechem.

"By the life of the Lord, the God of the universe," swore Simeon and Levi, "to-morrow will we fall upon this people, and not a remnant shall escape our just anger."

They carried out their intention, and coming suddenly upon the people next day, while they were suffering from the effects of their doing, the sons of

Jacob slew Chamor, Shechem, and all the inhabitants of the city, and carried their sister Dinah to her home.

When Jacob realised the result of their rashness he was grieved, angered, and alarmed.

"What is this that you have done to me!" he exclaimed. "In this country I thought I had found rest, and now when the relatives of these people learn what you have done they will fall upon me and destroy me and my house."

But his sons answered:

"All this lies at the door of Shechem. Wouldst thou have us hold our peace and suffer quietly this immoral conduct and cruel wrong!"

The number of men killed by the Hebrews was forty-seven. The women they took for slaves.

And it came to pass when Simeon and Levi left the city of Shechem that two men, who had been in hiding, hastened to the city of Thapnah and told to its king and its inhabitants all that the sons of Jacob had wrought in Shechem. The king refused to believe that ten men could thus overcome a city, and he sent messengers to ascertain whether the report was true. "Even in the time of Nimrod, when men were mighty," said he, "such a thing would have been impossible." When his messengers returned, however, and reported that in all Shechem they found but weeping women, he gathered his men together, and said:

"Prepare yourselves to go and fight these Hebrews. We will do to them even as they have done to our brethren of Shechem."

But his princes answered his words, and said:

"With our people alone we cannot prevail over these Hebrews. Ten men destroyed a city, and not one man was able to stand up against them. Let us send to the kings around us for help, and then perchance we may be able to cope with them."

This advice seemed reasonable to the king, and he sent to the kings of the Emorites who dwelt around him, informing them of the action of Jacob's sons, and begging their assistance in dealing out punishment for the same.

The Emorites answered his appeal, and gathered together about ten thousand men, who started out to fight the children of Jacob.

Jacob was greatly terrified at this, and again upbraided his sons for their rashness.

Then Judah spoke to his father, and said:

"Did we act without cause, Simeon, Levi, and the rest of us? Cruelly they wronged our sister, violating the chastity of our house, and transgressing the command of our God. For this reason did the Lord deliver the city into our hands Wherefore fear? Why grieve, and find displeasure in thy heart against thy sons? The same God who gave the men of Shechem into our hands will deliver to us also these Emorites who come against us. Keep thy peace, oh our father! fear not, but pray to the Lord our God that he may protect us and deliver our enemies into our power."

Then Judah summoned his servants and bade them go and discover what men, and how many, were marching against them. Then he addressed Simeon and Levi, and said to them:

"Prepare yourselves, and act like heroes. The Lord our God is with us. Gird on each man his sword and his bow; trusting in heaven, we will fight these Emorites and find deliverance."

The sons of Jacob and their servants and the servants of Isaac, who lived in Hebron, then prepared themselves for battle; and Isaac, the head of their house, prayed to God for their success in these words:

"Oh Lord God, thou didst speak unto my father and make a promise to him, saying, 'I will increase thy seed as the stars in heaven.' To me hast Thou reiterated this promise; and now, behold, the strength of Canaan comes to wrestle with my son. Oh Lord God of the universe, turn the purpose of these kings; let the dread of my children fall upon them and humble their pride. Even that they withdraw and return to their homes without shedding blood.

Deliver my children and their servants from the strength of these kings, for in Thy hand is the might, the power, and the strength."

Jacob also uttered a solemn prayer to the same effect.

When the Emorites drew near to Jacob's sons and their hosts, the kings and princes met to consult before beginning the attack, for their hearts were not thoroughly rid of the fear which the prowess of the Hebrews had cast upon them. The Lord answered the prayers of Isaac and Jacob, and this dread and fear augmented, and at last found vent in these words from one of their number, words which the others echoed in their hearts:

"We are acting foolishly in attempting to fight these Hebrews; we are marching to our deaths. Ten men overcame the inhabitants of Shechem, and now these same ten men with all their servants stand before us. Their God delights in them, and they live under His especial protection. None of the gods of other nations are able to perform such wonders as their God has wrought in behalf of this, his favourite people. Did not Nimrod endeavour to destroy their progenitor Abraham, and did not their God deliver him even from a furnace of fire? Did not this same Abraham defeat four kings who had carried off his relative Lot, who lived in Sodom? Their God is powerful, He delights in them, and He will give them the victory over us. This same Jacob He delivered from Esau and four hundred men. Could ten men have destroyed a city without assistance from heaven? Were we a hundred times greater in number than we are we should meet but with defeat, for we do not fight against them, but against their God. Let us turn back and attack them not."

One by one the kings of the Emorites withdrew and journeyed homeward without disturbing Jacob. The Hebrews remained in position awaiting the attack until evening, but when the Emorites came not they returned unto their homes. Then the Lord appeared to Jacob, saying, "Arise, go up to *Beth El*, and dwell there, and raise there an altar to the God who hath delivered thee and thy children from trouble." And Jacob and his sons journeyed to *Beth El* according to the commands of God.

Jacob was then ninety-and-nine years of age. He had lived at *Beth El* formerly called *Luz*, for about six months when the nurse of Rebecca, Deborah, died, and Jacob buried her under an oak tree at*Beth El*. Rebecca, the daughter of Bethuel, his mother, died also about this time, and was buried in the cave of Machpelah. When Jacob was one hundred years old the Lord appeared to him and called him "Israel." He then journeyed with his family to Hebron, to live with Isaac, his father. While on this journey his wife, Rachel, died, at the age of forty-five years. And Jacob and his family lived with Isaac in the land of Canaan, as the Lord had commanded Abraham, their father.

Chapter 4. From Joseph's Youth To His Elevation Over Egypt

JOSEPH, the son of Jacob and Rachel, did not take part in the war of Shechem: he was but a lad, too young to associate with his brothers. Yet he experienced a desire to emulate their greatness, and he felt that his fame would yet be superior to theirs. His father loved him tenderly as the son of his old age, and as a token of this love he made him a handsome coat, a garment of many colours. This especial mark of distinction increased Joseph's natural feeling of superiority, and as he found fault with his brothers' doings and carried tales to his father he soon gained their enmity; they could not even speak to him in a peaceable manner.

When Joseph was seventeen years of age he dreamed his well-known dream, and related it to his brethren.

"What!" they exclaimed, "do you presume to tell us that you shall reign over us?"

Joseph then related the dream to his father, who listened attentively, and in his great love kissed and blessed the lad. And when the other sons of Jacob learned of this action of their father they hated Joseph still more. But when the second dream was told them, and Joseph stated that the sun, the moon, and eleven stars bowed down to him, their anger reached a climax, and even Jacob felt himself called upon to rebuke the ambitious dreamer.

And it came to pass, on a certain day, the sons of Jacob started out to feed their father's flocks, and remained away so long a time that Jacob became troubled, for their welfare. He thought that perhaps the men of Shechem had received aid and wrought vengeance on his sons for the warfare they had brought upon that city.

So Jacob called Joseph to him; and said:

"Thy brothers started out to feed the flocks in Shechem, and they have not yet returned. Go, I pray, and seek them, and bring me back word of their well-doing."

Joseph wandered around some time in the neighbourhood of Shechem without seeing aught of his brethren, and he did not know which way to turn to seek them, when a man espied him straying aimlessly about, and asked, "Whom seekest thou?" Joseph answered, "I am looking for my brethren; knowest thou which way they have travelled?" "I do," replied the man; "I saw thy brethren, and I heard them say, 'Let us go to Dothan.'"

When Joseph's brethren saw the lad approaching them they conspired against him, and resolved to kill him.

"Behold," said Simeon, "the great master of dreams comes this way. Now let us destroy him; we can cast his body into one of the pits in the wilderness, and when our father inquires concerning him we can say that a wild beast has devoured him."

But when Reuben heard these words he said:

"No, we must not do this thing. Our father could never pardon us for such a crime. Rather cast him in one of the pits and let him perish there, but shed not his blood."

This proposition was made by Reuben with the purpose of rescuing the lad later, and returning him safely to his father.

When Joseph was cast into the pit, in accordance with this suggestion, he cried loudly to his brethren:

"What are ye doing? wherefore are ye treating me thus? What have I done,--what is my sin? Have ye no fear of the Lord that ye do this thing, for am I not of your flesh and blood, the son of Jacob? Reuben, Judah, Levi, Simeon," he cried, "lift me up out of this pit,--oh, sons of Jacob, have mercy upon me! If I have sinned against you, remember the precepts of your father, of Abraham, Isaac, and Jacob, to have mercy on the fatherless, to give food to the hungry, drink to those who thirst, clothing to the naked; and will ye deny mercy to your own flesh and blood? If I have sinned against you, oh pardon me for the sake of our father, Jacob."

His brothers, however, moved away from the pit, that they might not hear his cries, and they sat down to partake of their usual meal. While eating they consulted as to the final disposition of their brother; they were undecided whether to leave him as he was, to kill him, or to restore him to his father.

While considering the matter they saw a party of Ishmaelites approaching, on their way down to Egypt, and Judah said to his brethren, "What would it profit us to kill our brother? Let us sell him to this party of Ishmaelites, let them carry him whither they will; perchance he may be destroyed among the people of the earth; but our hands will not have shed his blood."

The brothers agreed to this proposition, and resolved to sell Joseph to the Ishmaelites.

But it happened that while they were discussing the question, a party of Midianites on a journey were seeking for a well of water. They lighted by chance upon the pit in which Joseph was concealed, and looking in, they were astonished to meet the gaze of a bright and handsome lad. They drew Joseph up from the pit and carried him along with them. As they passed by, the sons of Jacob saw Joseph with them, and called aloud:

"Hold! Wherefore have ye done this, to steal our slave whom we cast into the pit for disobedience? Come, give him up."

"And is he your slave?" answered the Midianites; "does he serve you? Likely it is the reverse, for he is handsomer and nobler than any among ye. We found the lad in the pit, and we shall take him with us."

"Give us our slave," repeated the sons of Jacob, or peradventure we shall kill you."

The Midianites drew their weapons, and were ready to enter upon a bloody fray at once.

"Beware," said Simeon, "do ye not know that we killed a whole city? Beware, if ye give us not our slave we may treat you as we treated the city of Shechem."

Upon hearing these words the Midianites lowered their tone, and assumed a more amicable attitude.

"What do you want," they asked, "with a disobedient slave? Sell him to us; we will pay you whatever you may ask."

A bargain was at once concluded, and the sons of Jacob sold their brother Joseph to the Midianites for twenty pieces of silver, for Reuben was absent, unable to speak a word to change their purpose.

The Midianites, taking Joseph with them, journeyed on towards Gilead. As they journeyed, however, they regretted the purchase which they had made, and they said one to the other, "See, this is a lad of noble appearance; doubtless the men from whom we bought him stole him from the land of the Hebrews, and if search is made for him he may be found in our hands; this will surely be death to us."

While they were speaking in this strain, the body of Ishmaelites which the sons of Jacob had seen, approached the Midianites, and the latter hailing them, sold Joseph for the same amount they had paid for him, glad to be rid of the fear which had seized them.

The Ishmaelites placed Joseph upon one of their camels and carried him with them into Egypt. Joseph wept bitterly during this journey at the thought that each step took him farther away from his father's house, and shut the gates of hope more securely behind him. The Ishmaelites were provoked at his sighs and weeping, and treated him quite cruelly.

On their way they passed the spot where Rachel, Joseph's mother, lay buried. Joseph knew the spot, and throwing himself upon his mother's grave, he gave free vent to the anguish of his soul.

"My mother, oh my mother," he cried, "rise from thy grave and look upon thy son! He is sold for a slave, and there is no eye to pity him. Arise and look upon thy son, weep with him for his trouble and his distress! Answer me, oh my mother! Awake from thy sleep, and take up arms against my brethren for thy son! My coat they have torn from me, and they have consigned me into bondage; twice have I been sold, separated from my father, from every compassionate heart, from every pitying eye. Arise, my mother, call upon thy God! See, my mother, whom the Eternal will justify, and whom He will condemn! Wake from thy sleep, my mother, seek my father, stricken down in grief, whisper to him words of comfort and glad tidings, that his heart may live again. Arise, my mother, and look upon thy son!"

The Ishmaelites drove Joseph from his mother's grave with blows and threats. Then Joseph spoke to them: "Let me find grace in your eyes," said he; "take me home, I pray you, to my father's house, and he will make all of you rich."

But they laughed, and answered him:

"Art thou not a slave? Who is thy father? Lo, thou hast been twice sold; thou art a slave, and a disobedient slave; hadst thou been worthy thou wouldst not have been twice sold."

Joseph wept, and pined, and grew sick; and his masters said:

"Behold, the boy will die upon our hands, and the money which we have paid for him will be lost to us. He wishes to go home to his father's house; let us carry him thither, and 'tis likely we shall receive the money that we paid for him."

But others answered, "No, the distance is too great; should we turn back now, we shall be kept but so much longer from our own homes. Let us take the lad to Egypt; we will be able to sell him there, and for a large price."

This advice met with the approval of the majority of the party, and they carried Joseph into Egypt.

Now when the sons of Jacob had sold their brother their consciences smote them, and they wished to repurchase him; but on account of the second sale they were unable to find him. While they were seeking for him Reuben returned to the pit in which Joseph had been placed, designing to release him. He stood at the edge of the pit, but he heard no sound. Then he called aloud, "Joseph, Joseph!" but still there came no answer--all was still. Reuben became greatly terrified; he thought that Joseph had died of fright, and he descended into the pit, hoping that the body might not be beyond resuscitation. When he found the pit empty he rent his garments and cried aloud, "How can I return to my father! How look upon his face and Joseph dead!"

He then hurried after his brethren, and found them consulting as to the manner in which they should inform their father of Joseph's loss. Reuben upbraided his brethren, and said to them, "Evil has been your behaviour; our father's old age you bring in sorrow to the grave."

The brothers agreed to keep the fact of Joseph's fate a secret, and acting upon the advice of Issachar, they took Joseph's coat, tore it in several places, and killing a kid dipped the garment in its blood, and then trampled it in the dust. Then they sent the coat to their father by the hands of Naphtali, and these words they charged him to deliver with the coat:

"Behold, we gathered our herds together and proceeded upon the read to Sheehan, and this coat we found by the way, in the wilderness, torn, smeared with blood, and trampled in the dust. Examine it, we pray thee, and see whether or not it be the coat of thy son."

Jacob immediately recognised Joseph's coat, and fell with his face to the ground. He remained motionless for a long time, and then he arose and wept aloud, crying, "It is my son's coat."

Towards evening he sent for his sons, and the messenger found them with their clothing rent and dust upon their heads.

When they reached home the bitter lamentation of their father touched their hearts, and it was with self-accusing consciences that they denied having seen Joseph and repeated their story of the finding of the coat.

Jacob gave himself up to the abandonment of grief, and lay with his face to the ground. Judah raised his father's head and wiped the tears from his father's eyes, but Jacob refused to be comforted. "Some wild beast has devoured Joseph," he said, "I shall never see him more;" and he mourned for Joseph many years.

The Ishmaelites carried Joseph down to Egypt, and when they came near to the place they met four men, the descendants of Medan, the son of Abraham and Ketura, and they said to them:

"Do you not wish to purchase this slave from us?"

The men saw that Joseph was a handsome and likely lad, and they bought him from the Ishmaelites for nine shekels, and carried him into Egypt.

Then these Medanites said, "Behold, Potiphar, the officer of Pharaoh, captain of the guard, desires to buy a slave, a trusty, active youth, to superintend his household. Let us see whether we can sell this lad to him."

The Medanites carried Joseph before Potiphar, and the latter was very favourably impressed with his bearing and appearance.

"What is his price?" he inquired.

"Four pieces of silver," replied the Medanites.

"I will buy him," said Potiphar, "provided you bring before me the man from whom you purchased him. He does not look like a slave, and I fear he has been stolen from his country and his home."

The Medanites then hutted up the Ishmaelites from whom they had bought Joseph, and Potiphar, satisfied with their account of the manner in which they had obtained possession of the lad, paid the four pieces of silver, and purchased Joseph for his slave.

Joseph found grace in the eyes of Potiphar, and was placed over the house of the latter, and over all his possessions. And the Lord was with Joseph, and for his sake blessed Potiphar and all his household.

At this time Joseph was about eighteen years of age, and a lad of such beautiful appearance that his equal could not be found in the land of Egypt. Being obliged, in the pursuance of his duties, to enter freely all parts of his master's house, he attracted the attention of Zelicha, Potiphar's wife. She was fascinated by his manners and handsome form and face, and declared to him day by day her passion, praying for a return upon his part of the favour with which she regarded him. Joseph refused to listen to her, and endeavoured to rid himself of her attentions. When she praised his beauty, and said, "Thou art fairer than all the rest of the world," he replied, "The same One who created me created also all mankind." When she admired his fine eyes, he replied, "What can they avail me; they will not move or sparkle in the grave."

When Zelicha found that Joseph could not be induced by fair words to desecrate his master's house, she tried threats of death and loss of freedom in case of further obstinacy; but Joseph replied to them, "The God who hath created man, looseneth the fetters of those who are bound, and He will deliver me from thy chastisement."

Her female friends who called to see her also admired Joseph, and lauded his beauty. On one occasion when fruit was set before the visitors, one of them, paring the same, cut her fingers, and knew nothing of the accident till her attention was called to the blood upon her garments, for her eyes were fixed on Joseph, and her mind was filled with thoughts of his appearance.

Thus time passed on, and though Zelicha still entreated, Joseph remained cold to her allurements.

And it came to pass at the time of the overflowing of the Nile, that all the inhabitants of Egypt left their houses, the king, the princes, and all the people, to see the overflow and make a holiday in its honour. And with the rest of the people the family of Potiphar went also, all save Joseph, who remained to protect his master's goods, and Zelicha, who remained to be alone with Joseph.

She attired herself in her richest garments, and was more ardent than ever in her appeals to Joseph, so that to escape them he turned and fled abruptly from her presence. As he did so she caught his garment to stay him, but it sundered, and a portion remained in her hand. As she looked upon it, and became conscious of how she had been shamed, a deep feeling of hate entered her heart, and she was also terrified lest the affair might now become known to her husband. She quickly replaced her elegant clothing with her ordinary wear, and calling a lad she sent him to summon home the men of the house. When they arrived she met them with loud wailing, and related to them a story of Joseph's presumption, crediting him with the entreaties and protestations which she had herself made, and adding to them a charge of violence. "I caught hold of his garment," she said, "and cried with a loud voice; he became frightened and fled, leaving this portion of his cloth in my hand."

The men repeated these charges to Potiphar, who returned to his house in a great rage against Joseph, and commanded at once that the lad should be whipped severely. During the infliction of this punishment Joseph cried aloud, raising his hands to Heaven, "Thou knowest, oh God," said he, "that I am innocent of all these things; wherefore, shall I die through falsehood!"

Potiphar carried Joseph before the judges, and made an accusation against him, saying, "Thus and thus has the slave done." The judges then addressed Joseph, and he gave his version of the story, saying, "Not so; but thus and thus did it occur." The judges then ordered that the rent garment should be brought to them, and upon an examination of the same they pronounced Joseph "not guilty." But still they sent him to prison, that the character of the wife of one as high in the state as Potiphar might not suffer.

For twelve long years Joseph was confined in prison, and during this time Zelicha visited him, offering to restore him to honour and liberty if he would but do her will. Yet steadfastly he refused, till finally she abandoned the attempt. And while Joseph was thus in custody, deprived of his freedom, his father Jacob, in Canaan, mourned for him as a father mourns for a beloved child torn from him by death.

It came to pass about this time that Pharaoh gave a feast to his officers and princes, and the chief butler and the chief baker waited upon the guests. The princes found stone grits in the bread, and one of them discovered a fly in his wine. Pharaoh was very angry at this, and condemned the two officials to prison, where they remained a whole year.

Then a son, his first child, was born to Pharaoh, and there was great rejoicing in the land. When the infant was three days old Pharaoh ordered a grand banquet, and released the chief butler that he might attend to the same. But the butler forgot his promise to Joseph to remember him in the return to prosperity which he had predicted, and for two years longer the prison was his home.

At this time Isaac, the son of Abraham, was still living in the land of Canaan; he was one hundred and eight years old. Esau, his son, was living then in Edom. When Esau learned that his father had grown very feeble, and that his last days on earth were approaching, he and his entire family journeyed to Canaan, to his father's house. Jacob and his sons, from Hebron, also journeyed thither, Jacob still mourning for the lost Joseph.

And Isaac said to Jacob, "Bring near to me thy children, in order that I may bless them," and Jacob placed his eleven sons and one daughter by his father's side.

Isaac laid his hands upon the heads of Jacob's children and embraced them each in turn, and he said to them:

"The God of your fathers will bless you, and will increase your seed as the stars of the heaven."

Isaac also blessed the children of Esau, saying:

"The dread of you shall be upon your enemies; your God will fill their hearts with fear."

Then Isaac called them all together, children and grandchildren, and thus addressed them, speaking especially to Jacob:

"The Lord, the God of the Universe, spoke unto me saying: 'Unto thy seed will I give this land to possess it, it thy children will keep my statutes and my ways; and I will establish the oath which I have sworn unto thy father Abraham.' And now, my son, teach thy children, and thy children's children, to fear the Lord and traverse the path which is pleasing in his eyes; for if thou wilt diligently follow His statutes, He will keep with you the covenant which He made with Abraham, and He will look with favour on you and your seed for ever."

Then Isaac died, and Jacob and Esau wept together for their father's demise. They carried his body to the cave of Machpelah, which is in Hebron, and all the kings of Canaan followed with the mourners in the funeral train of Isaac. He was buried with great reverence, even as though he had been a king; his children mourned for him twelve months, and the kings of Canaan lamented sorely for thirty days.

Isaac bequeathed his cattle and all his possessions to his two sons.

Esau said then to Jacob, "Behold, this which our father has left us must be divided into two portions, then I will select my share."

Jacob divided all his father's possessions into two portions in the presence of Esau and his sons, and then addressing his brother, said:

"Take unto thyself both these portions which thou seest before thee. Behold, the God of Heaven and Earth spoke unto our ancestors, Abraham and Isaac, saying, 'Unto thy seed will I give this land as an everlasting possession.' Now, all that our father left is before thee; if thou desirest the promised possession, the land of Canaan, take it, and this other wealth shall be mine; or if thou desirest these two portions, be it as it is pleasing in thy eyes, and the land of Canaan shall be the share for me and mine."

Before Esau replied and made his choice, he sought Nebaioth, the son of Ishmael, who was in that country, and asked his advice as to the selection.

Nebaioth answered:

"Behold the Canaanites are now living in the land in peace and safety; at present it is theirs; let Jacob believe that he may inherit it some day; take thou the substance, the personal wealth of thy father."

Esau followed this advice, and taking the personal substance, he gave Jacob for his portion the land of Canaan from the river of Egypt unto the great river, the river Euphrates, also the cave of Machpelah, in Hebron, which Abraham purchased from Ephron for a burying-place. Jacob took it as a burying-place for himself and his seed forever. Jacob drew up a deed and recorded all the particulars of the contract, which was duly witnessed and sealed. The following is the expression of the same:

"The land of Canaan and all the cities which it contains,--the Hittites, the Hivites, the Jebusites, the Amorites, the Perizites, and all the seven nations, from the river of Egypt to the river Euphrates; the city of Hebron, which is *Kiriath arbah*, and the cave which is in it. All this hath Jacob bought with money from his brother Esau, as a possession to him and an inheritance to his sons and their descendants forever."

Jacob put this deed in an earthen vessel, that it might be kept safely, and gave the same as a charge to his children.

Esau took what his father had left and parted from his brother Jacob, as it is written:

"And Esau took his wives, and his sons, and his daughters, and all the persons of his house, and his cattle and his beasts, and all his substance which he had got in the land of Canaan, and went into another country from the face of his brother Jacob" (Gen. 37: 6). He went with all his possessions to the land of Sëir, and never returned to Canaan, which became an inheritance unto Israel for everlasting.

Then Pharaoh, the king, issued a proclamation throughout the whole land of Egypt to the wise men thereof. And he called upon all the wise men to seek his presence and listen to the dreams which troubled him.

"He who can properly interpret to me the meaning of these visions, shall have his dearest wishes granted as they issue from his lips; but he who is able to read dreams and neglects my bidding, shall surely be put to death.'

Then the wise men, and the soothsayers, and the magicians of the land of Egypt, came and stood before the king.

And the king related to them his dream, and though many interpreted no two agreed as to its meaning. They contradicted one another, and they served but to confuse the king. Many were the interpretations. "The seven fat cows," said one, "are seven kings who will arise over Egypt from royal families, and the seven lean cows are seven princes who will arise from them, and in the end of days destroy the seven kings. The seven rank ears are seven great princes of this land who shall in a coming time of war fall into the power of seven princes, now weak and in no wise to be feared."

"The seven fat cows," said another, "are seven queens whom thou shalt marry in the coming days, and the seven lean cows declare that these queens shall die during thy life, oh king! The seven rank ears and the seven lean ears are fourteen children whom thou shalt beget, and they will fight among themselves, and the seven weaker ones shall conquer their stronger brethren."

But the king was not satisfied with these interpretations. His mind was still unquiet, for the Lord had ordained that Joseph was to be released from his prison and elevated to a princely position therefore did Pharaoh remain unsatisfied with the words of his wise men.

And the king was wroth, and he dismissed the wise men from his presence; and all the wise men and the soothsayers and magicians of Egypt went out from the presence of their king in shame and confusion. And the king commanded in his wrath that all these men should be put to death.

When the chief butler heard this he sought the presence of the king, and in deep obeisance before him spoke as follows:

"Oh king, live forever! May thy greatness, oh king, increase forever through the land. Lo, thou wast wroth with thy servant, and thou didst place him in confinement. For a year was I imprisoned, I and the chief baker. And with us in our dungeon was a Hebrew servant who belonged to the captain of the guard. His name was Joseph, and his master growing wroth with him, had placed him in prison, where he served the captain of the guard, and he served us also.

"And it came to pass when we had been in the prison for a year we dreamed, each, a dream, and the Hebrew slave interpreted for each of us his dream. And lo, as he interpreted our dreams so was the reality. As he spoke so did it come to pass.

"Therefore, my lord king, I pray thee, do not kill the wise men of Egypt for naught. Behold, this slave is still in the prison. If it be pleasing in the eyes of the king let him be sent for. Let him listen to the dreams which trouble the mind of the king, and he will be able to solve them correctly."

The king listened to the words of the chief butler, and he ordered that Joseph should be brought before him. But he commanded his officers to be careful not to frighten the lad, lest through fear he should be unable to interpret correctly.

And the servants of the king brought Joseph forth from his dungeon, and shaved him and clothed him in new garments, and carried him before the king. The king was seated upon his throne, and the glare and glitter of the jewels which ornamented the throne dazzled and astonished the eyes of Joseph.

Now the throne of the king was reached by seven steps and it was the custom of Egypt for a prince or noble who held audience with the king, to ascend to the sixth step; but when an inferior or a private citizen of the land was called into his presence, the king descended to the third step and from there spoke with him. So when Joseph came into the presence of the king he bowed to the ground at the foot of the throne, and the king descended to the third step and spoke to him.

And he said:

"Behold, I have dreamed a dream, and among all the wise men and magicians of the land there is not one able to read for me its meaning. I have heard that thou art far-sighted and blest with the gift of divination, and I have sent for thee to solve my dream."

And Joseph answered:

"Oh king, the power is not with me; but God will answer and give Pharaoh peace."

And Joseph found favour in the eyes of the king, and he told to him his dream. And the spirit of God was upon Joseph, and the king inclined his ears and heart to the words of Joseph.

And Joseph said to Pharaoh:

"Let not the king think that his dreams are two and distinct; they have but a single portent, and what the Lord intends doing upon the earth He has shown to Pharaoh in a vision. Let me advise thee, oh king, how thou mayest preserve thy life and the lives of all the inhabitants of thy land from the grievous evils of the famine which is soon to drain and dry up its fruitfulness and its plenty. Let the king appoint a man wise and discreet, a man well versed in the laws of the country, and let him appoint other officers under him to go out through all the length and breadth of the land to gather food during the years of plenty and store it carefully away for future use, that the land may not die in the years of famine which will follow. And let the king command the people of the land, that they shall each and every one gather and store up in the years of plenty of the produce of the fields, to provide for their wants when the ground shall be barren and the fields unproductive."

And the king answered, "How knowest thou that thou hast read the dream aright?"

And Joseph said, "Lo, this shall be a sign that my words are true. A son shall be born to the king, and upon the day of his birth, thy first-born son, who is now two years old, shall die."

And when Joseph finished speaking these words, he bowed low before the king and departed from his presence.

The occurrence which Joseph predicted came to pass. The queen bore a son, and upon the day when it was told to the king he rejoiced greatly. But as the messenger of glad tidings retired, the servants of the king found his first-born son dead, and there was a great crying and wailing in the palace of the king.

And when Pharaoh inquired as to the cause of this great cry he was informed of his loss, and remembering the words of Joseph he acknowledged them as true.

After these things the king sent and gathered together all his princes, officers, and men of rank, and when they came before him, he said, "You have seen and heard all the words of this Hebrew, and you know that as he spoke so has the thing occurred; therefore must we believe that his solution of my dream was the correct one, and that his words of advice were of good weight and consideration. We must take measures of protection against the famine which is surely to come upon us. Therefore search, I pray you, over all Egypt for a man with wisdom and knowledge in his heart, that we may appoint him governor over the land."

And they answered the king, "The advice of this Hebrew was very good; behold, the country is in the hands of the king to do with it what is pleasing in his eyes; but the Hebrew has proved himself wise and skilful, why should our lord the king not select and appoint him as governor over the land."

"Yea, surely," said the king, "if God has made these things known to the Hebrew, then there is none among us as wise and discreet as he is, What you have suggested is in accordance with my own thoughts; we will appoint the Hebrew our governor, and through his wisdom shall our country be saved the pangs of want."

And Pharaoh sent for Joseph and said to him, "Thou didst advise me to appoint a wise and discreet man to deliver the land from the anguish of famine. Surely, there can be none more discreet than thyself to whom God has made known all these things. Thy name shall no more be Joseph, but '*Zaphenath-Päaneeth*' (Revealer of hidden things) shalt thou hereafter be called among men.

"Thou shalt be second to me only, and according to thy words shall the land of Egypt be ruled; only upon the throne shall I be greater than thyself."

Then the king removed his ring from his finger and placed it upon the hand of Joseph. And he dressed Joseph in royal apparel, and placed a crown upon his head and a chain of gold about his neck. And Pharaoh commanded that Joseph should ride in his second chariot throughout the land of Egypt. And the people followed him with music, and a large concourse accompanied him upon his journey.

Five thousand soldiers with drawn swords in their hands, swords glittering in the sunlight, preceded him, and twenty thousand soldiers followed. And the people of the land, men, women, and children gazed upon the pageant from windows and from house-tops, and the beauty of Joseph pleased all eyes.

And flowers were strewn in his path when he walked, and the air was made sweet with perfume, and the savoury odour of balms and spices, And proclamations were placed in prominent places declaring the authority of

Joseph, and threatening death to those who failed to pay him homage; for he was considered as dishonouring his king who failed to honour the man made second in the kingdom. The people bowed down and shouted, "Long live the king and his viceroy!" And Joseph, seated in his chariot, lifted his eyes to Heaven, and exclaimed in the fulness of his heart:

"He raiseth the poor from the dust; from the dunghill He lifteth up the needy. Oh Lord of Hosts, happy is the man who trusteth in thee!

Chapter 5. Joseph's Greatness And Jacob's Entry Into Egypt

AND it came to pass after this, that Joseph saw Osnath, the daughter of Potipharah, a pearl among the beauties of the land, and he loved her and she became his wife. And Joseph was but thirty years old when he was elevated to his honourable and trustworthy position. He built for himself a palace, elegant and complete in its details and surroundings, so elaborate that three years' time was required for its completion. And the Lord was with Joseph, and increased his wisdom and understanding, and blessed him with manners so affable and deserving that he quickly won the love and favour of all the inhabitants of the country.

And during seven years, as Joseph had foretold, the Lord increased the produce of Egypt sevenfold. And Joseph appointed officers to gather up the plenty. They built huge storehouses and heaped up corn during the seven years of plenty, till the amount stored grew so great that no man could number it. And Joseph and his officers were watchful and diligent that their stores of grain should not suffer from moth or mould. The people of the land, too, stored up their surplus crop, but they were not as careful and watchful as was Joseph and his assistants.

And the wife of Joseph bore him two sons, Manassah and Ephraim, and their father taught them diligently the way of truth; they listened to his words and departed not from the paths of pleasantness either to the right hand or to the left. They grew up bright and intelligent lads, and, were honoured among the people as were the children of the king.

But the seven years of plenty drew to an end, and the fields became barren and the trees gave forth no fruit, and the famine which Joseph had predicted threw its gloomy shadow and threatening presence over the once fruitful land.

And when the people opened their storehouses, they found to their sorrow that the moth and mould had taken advantage of their neglect. And they cried aloud to Pharaoh, "Give us food;--let us not die of hunger before thee, we and our children; give to us, we pray thee, from the plenty of thy storehouses."

And Pharaoh answered, "Why cry ye unto me, oh careless people? did Joseph not tell ye of the famine which has come upon us? Why did ye not hearken to his voice, and obey his commands to be frugal and painstaking?"

"By thy life, our lord," replied the people, "as Joseph spoke, so did we, and gathered in our corn during the years of plenty, but lo, when the pangs of hunger and the barrenness of the land bid us open our granaries, the moth had destroyed the provisions which we had garnered."

The king became alarmed lest all their precaution should prove unavailing against the famine's blight, and he bade the people to go to Joseph. "Obey his commands and rebel not against his words."

And the people repeated to Joseph the cry for food they had addressed to Pharaoh.

When Joseph heard the words of the people and learned the result of their want of care, he opened the storehouses of the king and sold food unto the hungry people.

And the famine grew sore in the land of Egypt and spread through Canaan and the land of the Philistines, and to the other side of the Jordan. And when the inhabitants of these countries heard that corn could be obtained in Egypt, they came all of them into that country to buy, so that Joseph was obliged to appoint many officers to sell corn to the large multitude of people.

And Joseph's thoughts reverted to his father's home, and he knew that his brothers would be obliged to come to Egypt to purchase food, for the famine was very grievous in their neighbourhood. Therefore he gave orders that no man desiring corn should send his servant to purchase it, but the head of each family should personally appear as a purchaser; either the father of a family or his sons. He proclaimed also as the order of the king and his viceroy, that no man should be allowed to purchase corn in Egypt to sell it again in other countries, but only such as he required for the support of his immediate family; neither should any purchaser be allowed to buy more corn than one animal could carry.

And he put guards at all the gates of Egypt, and every man who passed through the gates was obliged to record his name and the name of his father in a book, which was brought by the guards every night for Joseph's inspection.

Thus did Joseph design to ascertain when his brothers came to buy food; and all the commands which he had given were faithfully executed.

Now, when the patriarch Jacob learned that food could be purchased in Egypt, he bade his sons proceed thither and obtain a stock of provisions, for the famine was growing very severe, and he feared that his family would suffer from its pangs. Jacob instructed his sons to enter the city by different gates, so that no objection should be made to the amount of their purchases, and as he commanded so they did.

Thus did the sons of Jacob go down to Egypt, and while upon the way they thought of their brother Joseph, and their hearts chid them for their cruelty towards him, and they said one to the other:

"Behold, we know that Joseph was carried down to Egypt; now when we come to the city let us seek for him, perchance we may discover his whereabouts, and then we will redeem him from his master."

And so did Jacob's ten sons travel to Egypt. Benjamin was not with them, for his father feared that mischief might befall him as it did the other son of Rachel, and he kept him at home by his side.

By ten different gates did the ten sons of the patriarch enter into the land of Egypt, and the guards at the gates took down their names, which were sent with the other names to Joseph at the close of the day. When Joseph read the names he commanded that all the storehouses save one should be closed, and he ordered further, that every purchaser at this storehouse should be required to give his name; and mentioning the names of his brethren, he said, "If these men come before ye, see that ye seize them, every one."

When the sons of Jacob had entered the city they met together, and before buying their corn they resolved to make a thorough search for their brother. They visited all places of public resort, and the houses of divination, but though they continued their search for three days, it proved unavailing.

Now when three days had passed, and his brothers had not put in an appearance at the storehouse, Joseph wondered at their delay, and he sent sixteen of his servants to search for them quietly through the city. They were found among the Egyptian players, and brought straightway before the viceroy.

Joseph was seated upon his throne dressed in his royal apparel, with his officers around him, when his brothers bowed to the ground before him. They wondered exceedingly at the magnificence, the handsome appearance and the majestic presence of the powerful man before them, but they did not recognise in him their brother.

And Joseph spoke to them, saying, "Whence came ye?"

"From the land of Canaan," they answered, "and to buy food, for to! the famine is sore in the land; and thy servants learning that corn might be purchased in Egypt, have journeyed hither to provide for their support and the support of their families."

But Joseph said, "Nay, ye are spies, else why did ye enter the city by ten different gates?"

They answered, "We are true men; thy servants have never been spies. Thy servants are brothers, the sons of one father, and by his command did we enter the city separately, for coming together he feared our appearance might attract unfavourable attention."

But Joseph repeated, "Ye are spies; to spy out the nakedness of our land have ye come. Behold, every man who comer to buy corn, makes his purchase and departs; but ye, lo, three days have ye been in the city, in public places and among the players; it is as I have spoken, ye are spies."

"God forbid!" they exclaimed; "our lord misjudges us. We are altogether twelve brothers, the sons of Jacob, in the land of Canaan; Jacob, the son of

Isaac, and grandson of Abraham the Hebrew. Behold, our youngest brother is with his father, we ten are here, and the other brother, alas, he is not with us, we know not where he is. We thought perchance he might be in your land, therefore have we searched all public places these three days."

"And what should the son of Jacob be doing in the public places?" asked Joseph.

"We heard," they answered, "that the Ishmaelites had sold him in Egypt, and being of very handsome appearance we thought it likely he might have been sold in one of the play-houses, therefore we went there hoping to find and to redeem him."

"Suppose you had found him," said Joseph, "and his master had asked for him an enormous amount of money; were you prepared to comply with extraordinary demands?"

The brothers answered in the affirmative, and Joseph continued:

"Suppose again that you should find him and his master should refuse to sell or deliver him to you under any circumstances, what would you do in such a case?"

"In such a case," they answered, "if neither prayers nor money should prove of avail, we would rescue our brother by violence: aye, even the death of his master, and flee with him to our father's house."

"It is as I have said," retorted Joseph; "ye are spies; lo, with evil designs upon the inhabitants of our city ye have come. We have heard and know indeed how ye killed all the males of Shechem in the land of Canaan on your sister's account, and now ye would treat the men of Egypt in the same way for the sake of a brother. But yet we will give ye an opportunity to prove yourselves true men. Send one of your number to your father's house to bring hither the youngest brother of whom you have spoken. If ye will do this, I shall know that you have spoken truly. Take three days to consider."

And in obedience to Joseph's commands his brothers were held in ward for three days.

After this time the brothers concluded to leave one of their number as a hostage, while the others returned to Canaan to bring Benjamin down to Egypt. So Menasseh, the son of Joseph, chose Simeon as the hostage, and he was kept in ward.

Ere his brothers departed, Joseph spoke to them once more.

"Take heed," said he, "that ye forget not my commands. If ye bring this brother to me, I shall consider ye true men, and ye shall be free to traffic in the land; neither will I do harm to your brother; he shall be at liberty to return with ye to your father's house, in peace."

And they bowed down to the ground and departed from Egypt. As they proceeded upon their homeward journey, they stopped at an inn to feed their asses, and Levi opened his sack to provide the corn for the meal. And lo, when he opened the sack, his money which he had paid for the corn was lying on the top. And he was exceedingly afraid, and he told the thing to his brethren, and they, too, were filled with alarm. And when every man found his money returned they cried aloud:

"What is this that God has done to us? Has the Lord withdrawn from us the mercy which He showed to our ancestors, to Abraham, to Isaac, and to Jacob, that He has given us into the hands of Egypt's prince to mock us and make merry with us?"

But Judah said, "It is just! Are we not guilty and sinful before the Lord? We sold our brother, our flesh. Why should we now complain that the favour God has lavished on our ancestors is denied to us?"

"Did I not warn ye, 'sin not against the child?'" said Reuben, "and ye would not hearken to my words. His blood is upon us,--why do ye say, therefore, 'Where is the kindness which the Lord promised unto our fathers?' Verily we have forfeited His protection."

When Jacob's sons approached their home, and the patriarch came forth to meet them, he quickly missed the face of Simeon, and he asked, "Where is Simeon, your brother?"

Then the brothers told their father all that had happened to them in Egypt, and Jacob said to them:

"What is this that ye have done to me? Your brother Joseph I sent to ye to inquire of your welfare, and his face I looked upon no more,--his bloody garments ye brought me, saying, 'Lo, the wild beasts of the forest have destroyed thy son.' Simeon I sent with ye to purchase food, and ye tell me that he is imprisoned in a cruel land; and now Benjamin ye wish to take also,--for Joseph and for Benjamin ye would bring my grey hairs in sorrow to the grave. No, my son shall not go with ye."

And Reuben said, "The lives of my two sons I place in your hands; if we do not bring back Benjamin safely to thee, their lives shall prove the forfeit."

But Jacob said, "Neither shall ye return again to Egypt; stay here, for my son shall not go with ye, to die as did his brother."

And Judah said to his brothers, "Urge him no more at present. Let us wait until these provisions have been consumed, and when cruel want and hunger press us he will consent to what we ask."

And it came to pass when the provisions were gone, that the sons of his children gathered around Jacob and cried to him, "Oh, give us bread."

And the heart of Jacob was torn with anguish at the cry, and summoning his sons, he said to them, "Hear ye not the voices of your children crying for food? 'Give us bread,' they cried to me, and I--I have none to give them. Get ye down to Egypt, I pray ye, and buy us a little food."

Then Judah answered, and said to his father, "If thou wilt send Benjamin with us, we will go,--otherwise we cannot. The king of Egypt is a mighty potentate; we dare not trifle with him. Should we return to Egypt, and our youngest brother be not with us, lo, he would destroy us all. Our father, we cannot disobey this king; greater even is he than Abimelech, the Philistine. Thou hast not seen, as we have, his throne, his palace, his myriads of officers; thou hast not witnessed, as have we, his wisdom, knowledge, and understanding. God has blessed him with unequalled gifts; greater is he than all on earth beside. Our names he told us; what had happened to us in our youth; he inquired of thee, saying, 'Is your father yet alive? Are all things well with him?' Thou hast not heard, as we have, of his power; over his people he is supreme; upon his word they go out, and upon his word they come in; his word governs, and the voice of his master, Pharaoh, is not required. Oh, my father, send the lad,--we cannot go without him if thou refusest, we must see our children die with hunger."

And Jacob said, in his sorrow:

"Why did ye tell the man ye had a brother? Oh, evil, evil is this thing which ye have done!"

"Give the boy into my hands," said Judah, "and let us go down to Egypt and buy the corn. If I do not return him safely to thee, a sinner against my father shall I be considered all my days. Our children weep before thee, and we have naught to stay their cries; have mercy on them, send our brother with us. Hast thou not often told us of the mercy which our God has promised to thee? Lo, He will protect thy son and return him to thee safely. Pray unto the Lord for our sakes, entreat Him to give us grace and favour in the eyes of Egypt's Prince. Lo, had we not tarried thus long, we should have now been back with food; yea, back twice to thee, and with thy son in safety." And Jacob answered:

"The Lord God give you grace in the eyes of the king and officers of Egypt. In Him will I put my trust. Arise, go unto the man, take with ye gifts, the best the land affords; the Lord will be with ye, and ye shall bring back to me your brothers, Benjamin and Simeon."

Then the sons of Jacob went down again to Egypt. And they took Benjamin with them, and they took, also, presents and twofold money.

"Take heed of the lad," were Jacob's parting words; "separate not from him either in Egypt or upon the road;" and when they had gone, he sought the presence of the Almighty in prayer:

"Oh, Lord, God of heaven and of earth, remember, I beseech Thee, the covenant which Thou didst make with our father Abraham; remember, I beseech Thee, the merit of Isaac, my father, and for their sakes show kindness unto my sons. Do not deliver them into the hands of Egypt's king for evil; redeem them, I pray Thee, and bring them back safely with their two brothers."

And the wives of Jacob's sons, and his grandchildren, they, too, lifted their eyes and hearts to Heaven, and cried:

"Deliver, oh Lord, our fathers from the hands of Egypt's king."

Jacob also addressed the following letter, to be delivered by his sons into the hands of Joseph:

"From thy servant, Jacob, the son of Isaac, the son o! Abraham the Hebrew.

"The prince of God unto the mighty and wise kin; Zaphenath-Päaneah, the king of Egypt, peace.

"My lord, the king, knows well that the famine is sore in the land of Canaan; therefore I sent my sons to thee to buy food for our sustenance. I charged them not to enter the city by the same gate, lest coming together they might attract the attention of the inhabitants. And, lo, their obedience to my orders has caused them to he accused by thee as spies. Oh, my lord, could not an intelligent man, such as thou art, read truth upon the faces of my sons? Much have I heard of thy wisdom and the understanding which thou didst display in the interpretation of Pharaoh's dreams, in foretelling this grievous famine,--how, then, was it possible that thou shouldst suspect my sons?

"Behold, I am surrounded with children; I am very old, and my eyes wax dim; tearful have they been for twenty years in lamenting the loss of my son Joseph, and now I have sent to thee his brother Benjamin as thou didst command; I pray thee, oh, my lord, to be good to him, and return him to me with his brothers. The strength of God has ever been with us; He has listened to our prayers, and He has never forsaken us; protect thou my son who is coming unto thee, and God will look favourably upon thee and upon thy kingdom. Send him home again with his brothers, and Simeon also send with them in peace."

This letter was entrusted into Judah's hands.

Thus the sons of Jacob went down again to Egypt with Benjamin and with the presents, and they stood before Joseph. And Joseph released Simeon from prison, and restored him to his brethren. And Simeon told them of the kind treatment which he had received since their departure.

"I was not bound," said he, "or treated as a prisoner, but I was taken to the governor's own house, and received there as a guest."

Then Judah took Benjamin and brought him before Joseph, and they prostrated themselves to the ground.

And the brothers gave Joseph the presents which their father had sent to him. And Joseph asked them whether all went well with their children and with their old father, and they answered, "It is well with all of us."

Then Judah delivered his father's letter to Joseph, and the latter recognised his father's hand, and his feelings grew too strong for him; the recollections of his youth overpowered him, and retiring into a side apartment he wept bitterly.

Returning to the presence of his brother, Joseph's eyes rested upon Benjamin, his mother's son, and he asked, "Is this your youngest brother of whom ye told me?" And when Benjamin drew near, Joseph laid his hand upon his brother's head, and said, "God be gracious unto thee, my son."

Then restraining his feelings, he ordered his officers to prepare the dining-tables.

Then when the meal was ready Joseph took into his hand a cup,--a cup of solid silver, set with precious stones, and holding it in his hand in the presence of his brothers, Joseph said, "I know by this cup that Reuben is the first born of your father, therefore shall he sit first, and Simeon, Levi, Judah, Issachar, and Zebulun shall follow him in this order, according to their ages; the rest shall follow these according to their ages." And he said further, "I know that your youngest brother has no mother, neither have I a mother, therefore will we two sit together."

And the men marvelled much at the words of Joseph, as they ate and drank with Joseph upon that day.

Joseph placed two portions of food before his brother Benjamin, and when his sons, Ephraim and Menasseh, saw this they too gave their portions to Benjamin, and Osnath, Joseph's wife, gave also hers. Thus Benjamin had five portions.

And Joseph brought wine to the board, and bade his brethren drink and be glad, but they refused, saying, "We have not partaken of wine since we lost our brother." Joseph pressed them, however, and forced them to drink and be merry with him. And he said to Benjamin, "Hast thou children?" And Benjamin answered, "Thy servant has ten sons, and I call them by names reminding me of the brother whom I have never seen."

In the morning Joseph dismissed his brethren, and bade them return to their father in peace. But when they had departed he called his servants, and ordered them to pursue after, overtake them, and bring them back.

And when the servants of Joseph overtook them, and said to them:

"Why have ye done this thing to steal our master's cup?" the brothers of Joseph were indignant, and they answered, "If ye find the cup in the possession of any one of us, lo, he shall die, and we, his brethren, shall be your master's slaves;" but when the cup was found where Joseph had ordered it to be put, in Benjamin's sack, they returned, grieving and crestfallen, to the presence of Joseph.

The viceroy was seated upon his throne, and his officers of state were gathered about him when his brethren entered, and speaking roughly to them, he said:

"What evil deed is this which ye have wrought? Why did ye take my silver cup? Is it because you could not find that brother you spoke of in the country that you stole the cup instead? Answer and tell me why have ye done this thing?"

And Judah spoke, saying, "What shall we say unto my lord? What shall we speak, for how shall we justify ourselves? God hath found out the iniquity of thy servants, and sent this calamity upon us."

Then Joseph arose, and grasping hold of Benjamin he led him to another room, and pushing him therein closed the door upon him. He then told the others to return to their homes in peace, saying, "I will keep the one in whose possession the cup was found; return ye in peace."

Then Judah approached Joseph, and said:

"Let not thy anger, I pray thee, burn against thy servant, but let thy servant speak before thee;" and Joseph answered, "Speak."

Then Judah continued:

"From the commencement, from the moment we set foot in Egypt, thou hast mocked us. We have been accused as spies; we have been forced to bring our brother Benjamin hither with us; and now, still at this moment, thou art using us for thy sport. Let the king now hearken to my words, and heed them, and allow our brother to return to his father with us, lest we destroy thee, aye, and all thy officers who are stationed about thee. Thou knowest what two brothers of us did to the city of Shechem for a sister's sake; take heed that they work not the same revenge for their brother Benjamin. Lo, I am stronger and more powerful than both of them; give over thy idle trifling with us, lest I strike thee with thy guard. Knowest thou not the punishment which God ordained upon Pharaoh when he acted wickedly towards Sarai, our great grandmother? Even to this day the people of thy land do tell about it! Beware, therefore, lest He punish thee too for thy wickedness in taking our brother Benjamin from his father. God will not forget the covenant which He made with Abraham, to protect his seed and chastise their enemies; therefore listen, oh, my lord, to the words which I am speaking. Let our brother return to his father, lest I carry my words into effect; beware, you cannot prevail over me."

Then Joseph answered and said:

"Why indulge in this vain self-glorying? Art proud of thy strength? Lo! one word to my officers, and they would destroy thee in a moment with thy brethren."

"By God's life," exclaimed Judah, "if I draw I will commence with thee and end with Pharaoh."

"Thy strength is not equal to thy boast," returned Joseph; "I myself am stronger than thou art; if thou shouldst draw thy sword I would sheathe it in thine own body; aye, with thine own sword would I put thy brothers and thyself to death."

And Judah replied:

"Oh, my lord, God is a witness between us that I seek not to fight; give us our brother and let us go in peace."

"By the life of Pharaoh," answered Joseph, "if all the kings of Canaan should come and second your demand, I would not surrender your brother. Go your way, the rest of ye unto your father, but Benjamin shall be my servant. He stole my cup and his liberty is forfeit to me."

"What profit is the name of king to such as thou?" retorted Judah. "A king's household contains much gold and silver in vessels and utensils, and lo, thou speakest much about a poor silver cup, which thou thyself hast placed in our brother's sack. God forbid that a descendant of Abraham should steal from thee, or from any other king, prince, or whatever he may be. Be silent now about this for thine own sake, lest it become known abroad and people say, 'Lo, for a trifling silver cup the great viceroy of Egypt fought with men and took one of them for a servant;' for thine own sake, say no more."

But Joseph merely repeated what he had said:

"Go ye, and leave your brother with me; the law makes him my servant; get ye gone, and take the cup with ye."

"Never," exclaimed Judah; "we would not forsake our brother for a thousand cups, or for any sum of money which thou couldst name."

Then Joseph replied quickly:

"But you did forsake and abandon your brother; aye, and sold him for twenty silver pieces."

"Give us our brother," reiterated Judah. "God is my witness I desire no quarrel with thee; let us depart without a brawl. What, oh, what can we say to our father if we return without the lad? his grief would kill him; and we, what could we say?"

"Say to him," said Joseph, that the rope followeth the bucket."

"Woe, woe unto the king who speaks a false judgment," cried Judah.

"Say naught of false judgments," replied Joseph, "did ye not speak untruths unto your father, saying, 'A wild beast has devoured Joseph?' Did ye not sell him to the Midianites for twenty pieces? Say naught; be dumb in shame."

"Now does the fire of Shechem burn within me," thundered Judah; "thyself and thy country shall perish in the fierce flame of my wrath."

In the meantime, during this scene, Joseph had despatched Menasseh, his son, to order troops to his palace, and now they came at full speed, armed and equipped at short notice. Five hundred mounted soldiers, two thousand on foot, and four hundred reserve guard of veterans. With cries and shouts they surrounded the sons of Jacob, who were exceedingly terrified and trembled for their lives. Then Joseph said to Judah:

"Tell me, I pray, why thou alone of all thy company didst fight so zealously for the lad?"

And Judah answered:

"Know that I became a surety with our father for the lad's safe return. 'If he comes not back with us,' I said, 'Lo, I shall be considered as sinning before thee all my days.' Oh, my lord, let me find grace in thy eyes; let me but take the lad home to his father, and I will return to take his place as thy servant. See, I am stronger and older than he is, let me be thy servant instead of Benjamin."

"Upon one condition," replied Joseph, "the lad may go with you. Bring before me his brother, his mother's son of whom you have spoken, and I will take him in place of Benjamin. You did not become a surety for him to your father, therefore let me have him, and the brother for whom you did become a surety shall return home with you."

Then Simeon drew near and answered:

"Did we not tell my lord, when first we came before him, that this lost brother we could not find? Wherefore will my lord speak such idle words? We know not, alas, whether this brother be alive or dead."

"Suppose, then," said Joseph, "that I should call him before me, will ye then give him to me in place of Benjamin?" And raising his voice he called aloud, "Joseph! Joseph! Appear Joseph, and sit before thy brethren."

The sons of Jacob wondered much at these words, and their blood grew chill as they looked around in fear and amazement to see from whence their brother was to appear.

And Joseph said to them:

"Why do ye look around? Your brother is before you. I am Joseph whom ye sold to Egypt. But nay, be not alarmed, ye were but instruments, and to save life did God send me hither."

And the men were much frightened, and Judah especially was terrified at the startling words. Benjamin, who was in the inner court, heard them, and hurrying before Joseph, he threw himself upon the latter's breast, and kissing him, they wept together. The other brothers too were much affected, and the people about wondered, and the report of the occurrence reached Pharaoh's palace.

Pharaoh was pleased with the news, and sent a deputation of his officers to welcome Joseph's brethren, and to bid them, in his name, to bring their families and their household goods and make their homes in Egypt.

And Joseph clad his brethren in new and elegant garments, and made them many generous presents, and gave to each of them three hundred pieces of silver; and then he took them before Pharaoh and introduced them to the king.

And when Pharaoh saw what goodly men the sons of Jacob were he was much pleased and very gracious towards them.

And when it became time for them to return to Canaan, Joseph procured eleven of Pharaoh's chariots and added to them his own, for their accommodation. And he sent rich presents to his father, and garments and presents to the children of his brothers and sister, and to his brothers' wives. And he accompanied his brethren upon their journey to the boundaries of Egypt, and parting with them, he said:

"Do not, my brethren, quarrel on the way. This thing was wrought through God's wisdom; ye were but the instruments to save from famine and hunger a vast multitude." He also commanded them to be careful in imparting the great news they carried to their father, lest speaking suddenly it might have a bad effect upon so old a man. And the sons of Jacob returned unto the land of Canaan in gladness with happy hearts.

And it came to pass when they drew near to Canaan that they said one to the other, "How shall we break this news unto our father? We cannot tell him suddenly that Joseph is still alive."

But it chanced when they reached Beer-Shebah that Serach, the daughter of Asher, came to meet her father and her uncles. And Serach was a sweet singer, and she played upon the harp.

So they said unto her, "Take thy harp, and go and sit before our father and play to him, and as thou playest, sing; sing of his son Joseph, and let him know in this manner that Joseph lives."

And the maiden did as she was bid, and sitting before her grandfather, she sang to him a song, wherein she repeated seven times these words:

"Lo, Joseph is not dead; he lives,
My uncle rules o'er Egypt's land."

And Jacob was pleased with her singing and playing; happiness seemed to find birth in his heart at her sweet voice, and he smiled upon the maiden and blessed her. And while he was talking to her his sons arrived with their horses and chariots, and Jacob arose and met them at the door, and they said to him, "We have joyful tidings for our father. Joseph, our brother, is still alive, and he is ruler over all the land of Egypt."

But Jacob remained cool and unaffected, for he did not believe their words, until he saw the presents which Joseph had sent, and all the signs of his greatness; then his eyes brightened and gladness sparkled in their depths, and he said:

"Enough, my son lives; I will go and see him before I die."

And the inhabitants of Beer-Shebah and the surrounding countries heard the news, and came and congratulated Jacob, and he made a great feast for them. And he said, "I will go down to Egypt and see my son, and then will I return to Canaan, as the Lord has spoken to Abraham, giving this land unto his seed."

And the word of the Lord came to Jacob, saying, "Go down to Egypt; be not afraid, for I am with thee, and will make of thee a great nation."

And Jacob commanded his sons and their families to prepare to go down with him to Egypt, as the Lord had spoken, and they arose and started upon the way. And Jacob sent Judah in advance, to announce his coming and to select a place for his residence.

And when Joseph learned that his father was upon the way he gathered together his friends and officers, and soldiers of the realm, and they attired themselves in rich garments and gold and silver ornaments, and the troops were armed with all the implements of war, and they gathered together and formed a great company to meet Jacob upon the way and escort him to Egypt. Music and gladness filled the land, and all the people, the women and the children, assembled upon the house-tops to view the magnificent display.

Joseph was dressed in royal robes, with the crown of state upon his head; and when he came within fifty cubits of his father's company, he descended from his chariot and walked to meet his father. And when the nobles and princes saw this they, too, descended from their steeds and chariots and walked with him.

And when Jacob saw all this great procession he wondered exceedingly, and he was much pleased thereat, and turning to Judah he asked, "Who is the man who marcheth at the head of this great array in royal robes?" and Judah answered, "That is thy son." And when Joseph drew nigh to his father he bowed down before him, and his officers also bowed low to Jacob.

And Jacob ran towards his son and fell upon his neck and kissed him, and they wept. And Joseph greeted his brethren with affection.

And Jacob said to Joseph, "Now let me die. I have seen thy face; my eyes have beheld thee living and in great honour."

And the great company escorted Jacob and his family to Egypt, and there Joseph gave to his relatives the best of the land, even Goshen.

And Joseph lived in the land and governed it wisely. And the two sons of Joseph were great favourites with their grandfather, and were ever in his house. And Jacob taught them the ways of the Lord, and pointed out to them the path of happiness and peace in His service.

And Jacob and his family lived in Goshen, and had possession of the land and multiplied therein exceedingly.

Chapter 6. Death Of Jacob And His Sons--Moses--The Deliverance From Egypt

JACOB lived in the land of Egypt for seventeen years, and all the years of his life were one hundred and forty-seven.

And Jacob grew very sick, and being old and feeble, he sent for his son Joseph, and said to him:

"Behold, I am going to die. Listen, my son. The God of your fathers will surely visit you in the days to come, and carry back His people, as He has sworn, to the land which He has given to you and your descendants. Do not bury me in Egypt, but in the cave of Machpelah, in Hebron, in the land of Canaan, next to my parents."

Jacob made his sons swear to bury him as he had requested, and he said to them:

"Serve the Lord your God, and He will deliver ye from all trouble, even as He delivered your fathers." He bade them call all their children before him, and he blessed them and their fathers also, according to the blessings which are recorded in Holy Writ.

And Jacob said unto Judah:

"Thou, my son, art stronger than all thy brethren, and from thy loins will kings arise. Teach thy children how they may protect themselves from enemies and evil-doers." Then turning to his children, he said:

"Thus shall ye carry me, after my death, to my resting place in the cave of Machpelah. Ye, my sons, and not your children, shall bear me. Judah, Issachar, and Zebulun shall carry the eastward corner of my bier; Reuben, Simeon, and Gad shall carry at the south; Ephraim, Menasseh, and Benjamin at the western end; and Dan, Asher, and Naphtali to the north.

"Levi shall not carry or help to carry my bier, for his descendants will bear the ark of God's covenant through Israel's host; neither shall Joseph assist in carrying, for he is a king; his sons shall take his place, and walk beside his brother Benjamin. As I have spoken do; diminish not from my words.

"And it shall come to pass, if ye do as I have commanded, that God will visit ye with happiness and give peace to your children after ye.

"And now, my sons, honour one another, and live peacefully, family and family, together. Teach your children to love God, and observe His commandments, in order that their days may be prolonged, for God will guard those who do justly and walk in righteousness through all His ways."

And the sons of Jacob responded, "All that you have commanded us, our father, we will do. May God be with us."

And Jacob answered:

"The Lord will be with ye if ye depart not from His ways to the right hand or to the left. Behold. I know that great troubles will come upon ye, upon your children, and your children's children in this land of Egypt in the days to come. But serve God, and He will prove your salvation. He will bring ye out of Egypt, aye, back to the land of your fathers, to inherit it, and dwell therein in safety."

And when Jacob had finished these words he drew his feet into the bed, and was gathered unto his fathers.

And when Joseph saw that his father was dead he fell upon the cold face, and wept bitterly, and cried aloud in anguish, "My father; oh, my father!"

And the family of Jacob, his sons, and their wives and children rent their garments and clothed themselves in sackcloth and ashes, and mourned for the patriarch. And the Egyptians who knew Jacob mourned for him also.

Then Joseph commanded the physicians to embalm his father's body, and he, with all his family and relatives and Egyptian friends, lamented for seventy days.

After these days of mourning Joseph approached Pharaoh the king, and said to him, "Let me go up, I pray thee, to bury my father; I will then return;" and Pharaoh answered, "Go in peace and bury thy father."

And Joseph arose and prepared with his brethren to carry their father's body to Canaan, as he had commanded them.

And Pharaoh issued a proclamation requesting the citizens of Egypt to honour Joseph by participating in Jacob's funeral, and showing the last marks of respect to him. And the citizens, in large numbers, acquiesced in the wishes of the king.

And there went up with Joseph and his brethren all the servants of Pharaoh and the elders of his house, and the elders of the land of Egypt, and the princes and noblemen, and all attached to Joseph's household.

And the sons of Jacob carried the bier on which rested their father's remains, as he had commanded. them, and there rested upon the bier a sceptre and a crown of gold.

And the troops of Egypt followed Jacob's body, infantry and cavalry, and the body-guard of Pharaoh, and Joseph's body-guard also.

And it came to pass, when the funeral train reached the threshing-floor of Atad, beyond the Jordan, they rested there, and mourned with great lamentation.

And when the kings of Canaan heard that the funeral cortege of Jacob was approaching, they started forth to meet the same, to express their grief and love for the departed patriarch.

And Esau, Jacob's brother, came also with his sons and the men of his belonging, and then the funeral proceeded to Hebron, to the cave of Machpelah.

But when they reached the cave, lo, Esau and his sons, and his followers, approached Joseph and his brethren, saying:

"Jacob shall not be buried here; this cave is ours and our father's."

Then Joseph and his brethren were very wroth, and Joseph said to Esau:

"What is this which thou hast spoken? Did not my father, Jacob, buy from thee, after the death of Isaac, all thy possessions in the land of Canaan, aye, five-and-twenty years ago, for a large sum of money, that it might be an inheritance to his children for ever? Why speakest thou in this manner?"

And Esau answered:

"I sold naught to Jacob."

"We have the deeds," returned Joseph, "and thine own signature shall prove that the truth is on our side."

"Bring me the deeds then," said Esau, "and all that I have written will I do."

Then Joseph called to him his brother Naphtali, who was more swift of foot than the roebuck, and so light of step that he could run over the tassel-topped corn and it would bend not beneath his tread.

And Joseph said to Naphtali:

"Get quickly to Egypt and bring to me the deeds for the cave, also the deed whereby Esau sold his birthright to our father; get thee quickly, and return in haste."

And when Esau learned that Naphtali had departed upon this errand he stopped further proceeding in the funeral rites, and Joseph and his brethren guarded their father's body and the burial cave.

With the next day a fight began between the two factions; Esau and his retainers on the one side, and Joseph, the Hebrews, and those who had followed the funeral train from Egypt, on the other.

Now among this latter party was Hushim, the son of Dan. He was dumb, and was placed to keep watch over the coffin containing the remains of his grandfather. Though not in the conflict, he noticed that something unusual was occurring, and asking by signs of those who came near him why the dead was not buried, he learned of Esau's interference, and the stoppage of the rites.

It came to pass, when he fully understood this, that his anger was roused, and hurrying into the midst of the combat, he singled out Esau, and struck his head from his shoulders with one blow. Then the children of Jacob prevailed over their opponents. Of Esau's company forty men were killed, while the other party suffered no loss. So with the death of Esau the fears expressed by Rebecca when Esau intended to kill Jacob, "Why should I be deprived of both of you in one day?" (Gen. 32: 45), seemed to be verified.

Then Jacob was buried in the cave of Machpelah, and the sons of Esau witnessed the interment. For seven days Joseph and his brethren remained in their houses, mourning and attending not to their usual avocations; and after this, though they discharged their daily duties, they mourned for twelve months, and since that time such has been the custom of the Jews on the death of a near relative.

The defeated children of Esau fled with Eliphas, the son of Esau, carrying Esau's body with them. His head was buried in Hebron, where he fell, but his body they buried at the mount of Se'ir.

And it came to pass in the thirty-second year after the children of Israel had gone down into Egypt, that Pharaoh the friend of Joseph died. Joseph was then seventy-one years of age. Before his death, Pharaoh commanded his son who succeeded him, to obey Joseph in all things, and the same instructions he left in writing. This pleased the people of Egypt, for they loved Joseph and trusted implicitly in him. Thus while this Pharaoh reigned over Egypt the country was governed by Joseph's advice and counsel. The Lord was with him, and all his undertakings proved successful. His wisdom seemed to grow greater daily, and all Egypt delighted in showing him honour and respect. For eighty years Joseph ruled Egypt, and his brothers dwelt in Goshen in safety and were fruitful and multiplied exceedingly; and they served the Lord in the manner which their father Jacob had taught them.

Joseph lived in Egypt ninety-three years, being as a prince of the country eighty years of that time; and then the days drew nigh when he felt the hand of death approaching. He sent for his brothers and all their children, and they drew around his bed.

"Behold," said he, "I am going to die, but God will surely visit ye and bring ye out from this land into the land which he hath sworn unto your fathers to give unto ye. And now when the Eternal thus visits ye and leads ye out from Egypt, take my bones away from here with ye."

Joseph made the children of Israel swear, for themselves and their descendants, to carry with them his bones when they should go up out of Egypt.

And Joseph died at the age of one hundred and ten years, in the seventy-first year after the children of Israel had entered Egypt, and his body was embalmed and afterwards laid in the ground near the banks of the river Nile. And all Egypt wept for Joseph seventy days, and his brethren mourned for him seven days as they did for Jacob his father.

Then Pharaoh took the dominion in his own hands, and governed the people wisely and in good faith.

In the same year Zebulun, the son of Jacob, died at the age of one hundred and fourteen years; and five years later Simeon died, aged one hundred and twenty years. Four years after this Reuben died, aged one hundred and twenty-five years; and Dan died the next year one hundred and twenty-four years old. Issachar died a year later, aged one hundred and twenty-two; and Asher followed him aged one hundred and twenty-three. Gad departed the next year, one hundred and twenty-five years old; and Judah the year following at the age of one hundred and twenty-nine years. Naphtali lived one year later, and died at the age of a hundred and thirty-two years; and Levi died the year after, one hundred and thirty-seven years of age, living to a greater age than that reached by any of his brethren.

After the death of Joseph and his brothers, the Egyptians began to afflict the Israelities, and they embittered their lives from that day even until the day when they went up out of the land. They deprived them of the fruitful land which Joseph had given them, and of the houses which they had built, and the homes they had made for themselves. The hand of the Egyptians grew constantly heavier upon the people till their lives became a burden to them.

In the hundred and second year after Israel went down to Egypt. Pharaoh the king and that whole generation of people had died out, and a new king and a new people who knew not Joseph held possession of the land.

Young Pharaoh was forty-nine years of age when he was crowned, and as is customary upon the assumption of authority by a new ruler, his ministers came before him to tell of the doings and progress of his kingdom. And these spoke to him, saying:

"Behold these people, the children of Israel, are greater and mightier than we. Advise us, we pray, that we may destroy them gradually, lest they so increase in the land as to prove a snare and a stumbling-block to us. Perchance if war comes upon us they may add their strength to the ranks of our enemies and drive us out of our own country."

The king answered:

"This is my advice, and I bid ye heed it well. The fortresses, Pithom and Ra'amses, are not strong enough for their purpose of protection, they should be rebuilt and with greater care. Let us deal subtly. Issue a proclamation in my name, saying:

"'A decree of Pharaoh, king of Egypt. Every dutiful citizen is requested to join in the rebuilding and strengthening of the fortresses Pithom and Ra'amses, that we may be prepared for enemies in time of war. Every citizen is called upon to obey this behest, and each day he shall receive from the treasury, wages for the work which he has done.'

"Then at the outset, ye, too, must go to work, and it shall come to pass when the Israelites come and join ye, that ye shall pay them, as we promise, each day their wages. Gradually ye and the other Egyptians may stay away from the work, until the Israelites are prosecuting it alone; then appoint Egyptian taskmasters over them; and, finally, when they come to ye one day for what they have earned, inform them that henceforth they must labour without payment. If they refuse or rebel, be ready, and compel them to submit by force. Obey my words in every particular, and happiness to ye will be the result. Our country will be strengthened and the hard labour will reduce the numerical strength of this people."

This advice pleased the Egyptians greatly, and they followed it implicitly. The proclamation was issued, and all the Israelites, with the exception of the children of Levi, obeyed the orders. Many Egyptians took part in the work also, and daily received their wages, but they were gradually dismissed, until in about three months' time the Israelites were working alone. Then the taskmasters, who had been appointed over them, withheld from them their wages, and when they refused to work, compelled them by force to resume their labour.

Thus all the children of Israel, with the exception of those of the tribe of Levi, who saw the snare of the Egyptians, and who having refused to work for wages could not now be compelled to labour without payment, were kept steadily at this work, strengthening all the strongholds of Egypt, making bricks and labouring in the fields, until the Lord remembered them and delivered them from the land.

But the heavier the burden laid upon the Israelites, the more rapidly they appeared to increase in numbers. And in the hundred and twenty-fifth year after the sons of Jacob had entered Egypt, the inhabitants of the land saw that what they had intended by their oppression had failed; that Israel still increased. The elders and wise men therefore appeared again before the king, and said:

"O king, live for ever! According to the advice which thou didst give us concerning this people Israel, have we done, and yet it has proved unavailing. The more we have oppressed them, the greater has been their increase, and now the land of Goshen is filled with them. To thy wisdom we, with all thy people, look for advice which shall reduce the number of these people."

The king answered:

"Let me hear from some of ye; give ye advice as to what can be done to them."

Then answered Job, from a country in the land of Uz, one of the king's counsellors, and said:

"If it be pleasing to the king, I will venture to speak. The advice which the king did give us concerning this people was good, and the course which we have pursued in its carrying out we will still continue, and the advice which I give now, with permission of the king, is but in addition to the same. Behold, we have been fearing for many years that a war may come upon us; we have been also fearing that the Israelites may so increase in the land and spread throughout it as to drive us from our own country. Now, if it please the king, let a royal order be issued, and let it be written among the laws of Egypt, that it may never be changed. Let this order decree the shedding of the life-blood of every male born to these Hebrews. If we follow this advice and destroy every male, we can have no cause to fear treason from this people in the future."

This advice met with the approbation of the king, his counsellors and wise men, and the king did as Job had recommended. A proclamation was issued throughout the land, dooming every male born to the Hebrews to immediate destruction.

There lived in the land of Egypt a man named Amram; he was the son of Kehath, the Son of Levi, the son of Jacob. This man married Yochebed, the daughter of Levi, his father's sister. And the woman bore a daughter, whom she called *Mir'yam*, for this was in the days when the Egyptians embittered the life of the Hebrews. Afterwards she bore a son, and called him Aaron.

And it came to pass in the one hundred and thirtieth year after Israel had entered Egypt, that Pharaoh, the king of the land, dreamed that he was sitting on his throne, and raising his eyes, saw before him an old man holding in his hand a pair of large balances. The old man hung the balances, and taking all the elders of Egypt, her princes and officers, he bound them together and placed them on one of the balances; on the other he placed a lamb, and lo, to the wonder of the dreaming man, the lamb weighed heavier than all the mighty men of Egypt.

Pharaoh awoke, and sending for his officers, he related to them this dream, which caused them both fear and amazement. Now among the magicians of Egypt there was one whom the king considered especially wise, Bil'am, the son of Be'or. For him the king sent, and desired an explanation of the vision. "A great evil will befall Egypt in the latter days," replied Bil'am, the son of Be'or. "A son will be born in Israel who will destroy Egypt, kill its inhabitants, and carry his people out from among them. Now, oh lord and king, give heed to this matter, and destroy the power of the children of Israel and their future welfare, before this misfortune to Egypt buds."

"What can we do?" inquired Pharaoh; "we have tried many plans without success."

Bil'am answered, "Send for thy two nearest counsellors, and we will consult together."

And Pharaoh sent for Re'uël, the Midianite, and Job, his counsellors, and they appeared before him accordingly. Then said the king, "Ye have all heard my dream and its interpretation; now give me your advice; how may this people Israel be conquered ere this threatened evil falls upon us?"

Re'uël, the Midianite, answered and said:

"Oh king, live for ever! If it be pleasing in thy eyes, oh king, cease to afflict this people. They are the chosen of God from the olden days, and never have they been oppressed with impunity. Pharaoh of old was punished for Sarah's sake, as was also Abimelech the Philistine, for the same cause. Jacob was delivered from the toils both of Esau, his brother, and his uncle, Laban. Thy great-grandfather exalted their great-grandfather, Joseph, because he recognised the wisdom which God had implanted in him, and which saved the people of the land from starvation. Therefore, oh king, remove thy yoke from them and let them go hence to Canaan, the land of the sojournings of their forefathers."

These words of Re'uël, the Midianite, angered Pharaoh, and he sent him in shame from his presence. Re'uël went out from Egypt that day unto his own country, carrying with him the staff of Joseph.

The king then said to Job, his counsellor:

"What is thy opinion concerning these Hebrews?" And Job answered:

"Are not all the inhabitants of Egypt in the hands of the king? Whatever may be most pleasing in thy eyes, that do."

Then spoke Bi'lam, and said:

"None of the means proposed for the subduing of the Hebrews will prove successful. Fire cannot prevail over them, for Abraham was delivered from its power; the sword will fail, for Isaac was delivered from its edge, and a ram killed in his stead; they cannot be exterminated by rigorous labour, for Jacob worked day and night for Laban, and yet prospered. Listen, oh king, to the advice which I shall give thee. By this means only wilt thou be able to prevail over them. Command that all the male children born to these Hebrews be cast into the river, for none of their ancestors ever escaped from the death in the water."

This advice pleased Pharaoh, and his princes and the king did according to the words of Bi'lam. A proclamation was issued, and Pharaoh sent his officers through the land of Goshen where the Israelites dwelt, to see that all the male children were cast into the river on their birth, while the female infants were kept alive.

It came to pass about this time that Miriam, the daughter of Amram, the sister of Aaron, prophesied and said, "A second son will be born to my father and mother, and he will deliver the Israelites from the Egyptian power."

A second son was born to them according to her words, and when his mother saw he was a goodly child of handsome appearance, she hid him for three months in her inner chamber.

Now in those days strict search was made in the houses of the Hebrews for male infants, and many means were used to ascertain the places where their parents concealed them. Egyptian women carried infants into the houses in Goshen, and making these babies cry, the hidden infants would cry also, thus discovering their place of hiding. The women would then report to Pharaoh, and officers would seize the babe which parents had vainly endeavoured to save.

And it came to pass after Yochebed had succeeded in keeping her son concealed for three months, the fact of his birth became known in the above manner, and his mother taking the child quickly, before the officers arrived, hid him in a box made of bulrushes, and concealed the same carefully in the flax which grew along the Nile. She sent Miriam, her daughter, to watch the box from a distance, and observe what might happen to it.

And the day was hot and sultry, and the air oppressive, and many of the people came to find relief from the exhausting heat in the cooling waters of the Nile. Bathia, the daughter of Pharaoh, came with this purpose attended by her maidens, and entering the water she chanced to see the box of bulrushes, and pitying the infant she rescued him from death.

Many were the names given to the infant thus miraculously preserved. Bathia called him "*Moses,*" saying, "I have *drawn* him from out the water;" his father called him "*Heber,*" because he was *reunited*to his family; his mother called him "*Yekuthiel,*" "for," said she, "I *hoped in God,*" his sister called him "*Yarad,*" saying, "I *went down* to the river to watch him;" Aaron, his brother, called him "*Abigedore,*" for God had *repaired the breach* in the house of Jacob, and the Egyptians ceased from that time to cast the infants into the water; his grandfather called him "*Abi Socho,*" saying, "for three months he was *hidden,*" and the children of Israel called him, "*Shemaiah Ben Nethanel,*" because in his day God *heard their groaning* and delivered them from their oppressors.

Moses became even as a son to Bathia, the daughter of Pharaoh, as a child belonging rightly to the palace of the king.

Now it came to pass when Pharaoh saw that the advice of Bi'lam did not prove effective, but that the Israelites, on the contrary, seemed to increase and multiply even more rapidly than before, he laid additional labour upon them, and issued orders that if any man failed in accomplishing his full daily task, his children should be walled up alive in the building in which he worked. This order continued in effect for many years.

About this time, when Moses was three years old, Pharaoh sitting at his banquet table, with his queen upon his right, Bathia at his left, and his two sons, with Bi'lam and the princes of his realm about him, took Moses upon his lap. The child stretched forth his hand, and taking the royal crown from Pharaoh's head placed it upon his own.

In this action the king and the people around him imagined they saw a meaning, and Pharaoh asked:

"How shall this Hebrew boy be punished?"

Then said Bi'lam, the son of Be'or, the magician, "Think not, because the child is young, that he did this thing thoughtlessly. Remember, oh king, the dream which thy servant read for thee; the dream of the balances. The spirit of understanding is already implanted in this child, and to himself he takes thy kingdom. Such, my lord, hath ever been the way of his people, to trample down those who have dealt kindly with them, to deceitfully usurp the power of those who have reared and protected them. Abraham, their ancestor, deceived Pharaoh, saying of Sarah, his wife, 'She is my sister;' Isaac, his son, did the same thing; Jacob obtained surreptitiously the blessing which rightfully belonged to his brother; he travelled to Mesopotamia, married the daughters of his uncle, and fled with them secretly, taking large flocks and herds and immense possessions; the sons of Jacob sold their brother Joseph into slavery; he was afterwards exalted by thy ancestor and made second in Egypt, and when a famine came upon the land, he brought hither his father with all his family to feed upon its substance, while the Egyptians sold themselves for food; and now, my lord, this child arises to imitate their actions. He mocks thee, oh king, thy elders and thy princes. Therefore, let his blood be spilled; for the future welfare of Egypt let this thing be done."

The king replied to the words of Bi'lam:

"We will call our judges together, and if they deem the child deserving of death he shall be executed."

When the judges and wise men assembled according to the order of the king, Jithro, the priest of Midian, came with them. The king related the child's action and the advice which Bi'lam had given him, requesting their opinions on the same.

Then said Jithro, desirous to preserve the child's life:

"If it be pleasing to the king, let two plates be placed before the child, one containing fire, the other gold. If the child stretches forth his hand to grasp the gold, we will know him to be an understanding being, and consider that he acted towards thee knowingly, deserving death. But if he grasps the fire, let his life be spared."

This advice met with the king's approval, and two plates, one containing gold, the other fire, were placed before the infant Moses. The child put forth his hand, and grasping the fire put it to his mouth, burning his tongue, and becoming thereafter "heavy of mouth and heavy of tongue," as mentioned in the Bible. Through this childish action the life of Moses was saved.

Moses grew up, a handsome lad, in the palace of the king; he dressed royally, was honoured by the people, and seemed in all things of royal lineage.

He visited the land of Goshen daily, observing the rigour with which his brethren were treated, and inquiring of them why they laboured and were so oppressed, he learned of all the things which had happened before his birth; all things concerning the children of Israel and all things concerning himself. Learning of Bi'lam's desire to have him destroyed in his infancy, he expressed enmity towards the son of Be'or, who fearing his power and his favour with the king's daughter, fled to Ethiopia.

Moses urged the king of Egypt to grant the men of Goshen one day of rest from their labour, in each week, and the king acceded to his request.

And the Lord was with Moses, and his fame extended through all the land.

When he was about eighteen years old, Moses visited his father and mother in Goshen; and going also where his brethren were working he saw an Egyptian smiting a Hebrew, and he killed the Egyptian and fled from Egypt, as the occurrence is related in the Bible.

It came to pass in those days that the Assyrians rebelled against Kikanus, the king of Ethiopia, to whom they were under tribute. Kikanus, appointing Bi'lam, the son of Be'or, who had fled from Egypt, to be his representative in his absence, marched forth with a large army and subdued the Assyrians, and imposed heavy taxes upon them.

Bi'lam, the son of Be'or, was unfaithful to his trust, and usurping the power he was delegated to protect, he induced the people of Ethiopia to appoint him their king in place of the absent Kikanus. He strengthened the walls of the capital, built huge fortresses, and dug ditches and pits between the city and the river Gichon, which compassed all the land of Ethiopia.

When King Kikanus returned with his army, he was amazed to witness the preparations for defence which had been made during his absence, and he thought that the people had feared an attack from the kings of Canaan while he was away, and had prudently made ready for it. But when the gates of the city were closed against him, and he called in vain to have them opened, he joined battle with the adherents of Bi'lam. For nine years the war between Kikanus and Bi'lam continued, with severe losses to the former.

When Moses fled from Egypt he joined the army of Kikanus, and soon became a great favourite with the king and with all his companions.

And Kikanus became sick and died, and his soldiers buried him opposite the city, rearing a monument over his remains, and inscribing upon it the memorable deeds of his life. Then they said to one another, "What shall we do? For nine years we have been absent from our homes; if we attack the city it is likely we shall be again repulsed, and if we remain here, the kings of Edom, hearing that our leader is dead, will fall upon us and leave none alive. We had best appoint another king in the stead of Kikanus."

So the army appointed Moses to be their king and leader, in the hundred and fifty-seventh year after Israel went down into Egypt.

And Moses found favour in the eyes of the Lord, and he inspired his soldiers with courage by his voice and his example. He attacked the fortresses in mass, with the blowing of trumpets and great enthusiasm, and the city was delivered into his hands; eleven hundred of his opponents being slain in the battle.

But Bi'lam, the son of Be'or, escaped and fled back to Egypt, becoming one of the magicians mentioned in the Scriptures.

And the Ethiopians placed Moses upon their throne and set the crown of state upon his head, and they gave him the widow of Kikanus for a wife. Moses remembered, however, the teachings of his fathers--how Abraham made his servant swear that he would not bring a daughter of the Canaanites to be the wife of Isaac, and how Isaac had said to his son Jacob, "Thou shalt not take a wife from the daughters of the Canaanites, neither shalt thou intermarry with the descendants of Ham;" therefore the widow of Kikanus was a wife to Moses in name only.

When Moses was made king of Ethiopia the Assyrians again rebelled, but Moses subdued them and placed them under yearly tribute to the Ethiopian dynasty.

Now, it happened in the hundred and eightieth year after Israel had gone down into Egypt, that there arose thirty thousand men of the tribe of Ephraim, and formed themselves into companies. And they said:

"The time, mentioned by the Lord to Abraham at the covenant of the pieces (Gen. 15: 13), has arrived; we will go up out of Egypt." And trusting in their own might these men left Egypt.

They did not take any provisions with them, save what was necessary for a day's journey; they took naught but gold and silver, saying, "We shall be able to buy food of the Philistines."

As they travelled towards Gath, they met a party of shepherds and said to them, "Sell us your flocks, for we are hungry."

But the shepherds replied:

"The flocks are ours, and we will not sell them to you."

Then the men of Ephraim seized upon the flocks by force, and the shepherds made a great outcry, which reached the ears of the inhabitants of Gath, who assembled to ascertain its cause. And when the Gathites learned how their brethren had been treated, they armed themselves and marched forth to battle with the wrongdoers; and many fell from both parties. On the second day the men of Gath sent messengers to the cities of the Philistines, saying:

"Come and help us smite these Ephraimites, who have come up from Egypt, seized our flocks, and battled with us for no cause."

And the Philistines marched forth, about forty thousand strong, and they smote the Ephraimites, who were suffering from weariness and hunger, and there escaped from the death dealt out to Ephraim, only ten men.

Thus were the men of Ephraim punished for going up out of Egypt before the time appointed by the Lord.

The bodies of those who fell remained unburied in the valley of Gath, and their bones were the same bones which rose up, endowed with life, in the time of Ezekiel, as his prophecies record.

The ten who escaped returned to Egypt and related to the children of Israel what had occurred to them.

During this time Moses was reigning in Ethiopia in justice and righteousness. But the queen of Ethiopia, Adonith, who was a wife to Moses in name only, said to the people, "Why should this stranger continue to rule over you? Would it not be more just to place the son of Kikanus upon his father's throne, for he is one of you?"

The people, however, would not vex Moses, whom they loved, by such a proposition; but Moses voluntarily resigned the power which they had given him, and departed from their land. And the people of Ethiopia made him many rich presents, and dismissed him with great honours.

Moses being still fearful of returning to Egypt, travelled towards Midian, and sat there to rest by a well of water. And it came to pass that the seven daughters of Re'uël (or Jithro) came to this well to water their flocks. The shepherds of Midian drove them away, designing to keep them waiting until their own flocks had been watered, but Moses interfered in their behalf, and they returned home early to tell their father what had occurred. Re'uël then sent for Moses, and the latter related to him all that had happened them since his flight from Egypt. And Moses lived with Re'uël, and he looked with favour upon Ziporah, the daughter of his host, and married her.

During this time the Lord smote Pharaoh, king of Egypt, with leprosy. The disease was exceedingly grievous, and the king suffered inexpressible agony. And the taskmasters who were placed over the Israelites complained to the king that the latter were neglecting their work and becoming lazy.

"They are taking advantage of my sickness," exclaimed the king, and ordering his chariot, he prepared to ride out himself to upbraid the workmen, and to see that they did not shirk their labour.

And it happened as he rode through a narrow pass his horses lost their footing, the chariot was overturned, the king was thrown into the road, and the wheels of the chariot passed over him. The tender flesh was torn from his body, and the bones, which had grown brittle with his disease, broke. His servants laid him upon a bier and carried him to his palace; but when they laid him upon his bed the king knew that his time to die had come. And his wife and his princes assembled, weeping, around his bed, and Pharaoh wept with them; and his officers requested him to name his successor.

Now Pharaoh had two sons and three daughters. The eldest son was a man of foolish habits and excitable disposition, while the second, who was intelligent and versed in the sciences of his country, was yet a man of wicked imagination, disfigured, and a dwarf. Yet the king, taking into consideration his superior intelligence, named his second son to reign after him.

For three years Pharaoh suffered intense agony, then he died, and was buried in the place of the kings; but he was not embalmed, for his body was in too diseased a state to admit of manipulation.

In the two hundred and sixth year after Israel entered Egypt, this Pharaoh ascended the throne of the land. And he made the burden on the children of Israel heavy and oppressive; he would not continue to allow them the day of rest granted in his father's time, but made idleness during his father's sickness his excuse for depriving them of it.

And the children of Israel sighed in their heavy bondage, and cried unto the Lord. And God heard their voices, and remembered his covenant with Abraham, with Isaac, and with Jacob.

Now while Moses was living with Re'uël, the Midianite, he noticed a staff in the latter's garden, and he took it, to be a walking-stick in his hand. And this was the same staff, the staff of Joseph, which Re'uël carried away with him when he fled from Egypt. This same staff Adam carried with him out of Eden. Noah inherited it, and gave it afterwards to Shem, his son, It passed through the hands of Shem's descendants until it came into the possession of Abraham. When Abraham left all his worldly goods to Isaac this staff was numbered with them, and when Jacob fled from his brother's anger into Mesopotamia, he carried this staff in his hand, and while residing in Egypt he gave it to Joseph, his son.

And it came to pass at the end of two years that the Lord again sent Moses unto Pharaoh to bring out the children of Israel from his land. And Moses spoke to Pharaoh all the words which the Lord had commanded, but Pharaoh would not hearken to them. Therefore the strength of God was wielded against the Egyptians, and He smote Pharaoh and his officers, and his people, with grievous plagues.

Through the hands of Aaron God changed the waters of Egypt into blood. They who drew water from a matting stream, looked into their vessels, and lo, their water was red blood; they who sought to drink and slake their thirst, but filled their mouths with blood, and they who used water in preparing bread, found blood mixed with the dough upon their kneading troughs.

Then the rivers brought forth frogs, and they entered into the houses of the Egyptians, into their feel and into their beds.

And still the Lord's arm was stretched forth in anger over Egypt, and He smote the land with the grievous plague of lice; lice on man and beast, on king and queen, and all the people of the land.

Then God sent against Egypt the wild beasts of the forest. And they entered the inhabited cities and destroyed men and cattle, and made great havoc in the land. And serpents, and scorpions, and all manner of reptiles, with mice. weasels, and all manner of vermin and flies, and hornets, and all manner of insects filled the land of Egypt and fed upon it.

Then God sent a pestilence among the cattle; all but a tenth part of the cattle of the Egyptians died in one night; but the cattle belonging to the Israelites in Goshen were not affected; they lost not a single animal.

Then the bodies of the Egyptians became sore and full of boils, and noxious, and their flesh was greatly inflamed. Yet still the anger of God burned against them and His hand was still raised in wrath.

And God sent a hailstorm which destroyed the vines and trees, and green herbs and growing plants, and the people who ventured out of their houses, and the unsheltered cattle, were killed by the falling stones. Then great swarms of locusts filled the land, destroying all that the hail had spared.

And after this darkness covered all the land, and for three days and three nights the people could not see even their hands before them.

And during this period of darkness God smote those of the Israelites who were rebellious of heart, and who were not desirous of obeying his commands. In the darkness did God do this that the Egyptians might not rejoice thereat.

And after this God commanded Moses and Aaron to prepare the Passover sacrifice, saying, "I will pass over the land of Egypt and slay the first born, both of man and beast." The children of Israel did as they had been commanded, and it came to pass at midnight that the Lord passed over the land and smote the first born of Egypt both of man and beast.

Then there was a great and grievous cry through all the land, for there was not a house without its dead; and Pharaoh and his people rose up in alarm and consuming grief.

And Bathia, the daughter of Pharaoh, went forth to seek Moses and Aaron, and she found them in their dwelling singing praises to the Lord. And Bathia addressed Moses, saying:

"Lo, I have nourished thee in my arms and loved thee in my heart even from thy infancy, and how hast thou rewarded my care and affection! Upon me, upon my people, and upon my father's house, thou hast brought calamity and affliction."

"Have any of the plagues troubled thee?" inquired Moses; "if so, tell me, I pray." And Bathia answered, "No." "Thou art also," continued Moses, "the first born of thy mother, and yet thou art here alive and well before me. Be comforted, not the slightest harm shall come to thee."

And Bathia answered:

"Such comfort cannot profit me, when I see this great misfortune bearing down the king my brother, his servants, and his house."

"They would not hearken to the voice of God," answered Moses, "and therefore is this punishment meted to them."

Then Pharaoh appeared before Moses and Aaron, and he cried to them:

"Arise, take thy brethren, their flocks and herds, and all they have; leave naught behind; go, but entreat the Lord for me."

And the Egyptians sent the children of Israel forth with great wealth, flocks, and herds, and precious things, even as the Lord had promised Abraham in his vision of the "covenant between the pieces."

The children of Israel did not leave Egypt that night, for they said, "We are not men of secret ways, to hurry off at midnight." They waited until morning, obtaining gold and silver vessels from their late oppressors.

Moses took with him the bones of Joseph, and the others of the people carried up with them also the bones of Jacob's other sons.

And the children of Israel journeyed from Raämses to Succoth. Two hundred and ten years after their entrance into Egypt, the Israelites departed therefrom, six hundred thousand men, with wives and children.

For three days after the departure of the Israelites, the Egyptians were occupied in burying their dead, and after this they began to talk together, saying, "Moses and Aaron said to Pharaoh, 'We desire to go a three days' journey into the wilderness, to sacrifice unto the Lord our God;' now let us rise up early and follow after them. If they return to Egypt we shall know them for faithful men, but if they do not intend returning, we will bring them back by force."

A great host of the Egyptians followed after the Israelites, and came up with them while they were encamped before *Pi Hachiroth*, observing the festival of the Lord.

And the Egyptians called out to them:

"Ye have been gone from Egypt five days, and ye promised to return in three; do ye not intend to come back?"

Then Moses and Aaron answered, saying:

"The Lord hath commanded us to keep on our way, even to the land flowing with milk and honey, which He swore unto our ancestors to give to us."

When the Egyptians saw that the Israelites had determined to be independent of them, they arrayed themselves to fight against their fleeing servitors. But God strengthened the hearts of His people, and the princes, of E«n pt fled before them back to their land.

And when Pharaoh learned what had happened to them, and how many of them had been slain, he exclaimed:

"We have acted foolishly in allowing these slaves to leave us. We shall miss their services in the manufacture of bricks, and in building up our fortresses. When our tributaries hear of this tiling, they will rebel against us, unless we take severe measures with these Israelites, for they will say, 'If slaves can successfully rebel against them, how much easier will it be for princes and rulers like ourselves to cast their yoke from off our necks.'"

Therefore Pharaoh assembled his wise men, his magicians, and his elders, and taking counsel together they resolved to pursue and recapture their bondsmen.

And Pharaoh issued a proclamation calling upon every fighting man to hold himself in readiness for the march, and the hosts of Egypt assembled accordingly.

Then Pharaoh opened his treasury and gave presents to every man according to his rank, and he spoke to them in urbane and gracious tones, saying:

"Behold, in wars, the soldier gains the spoil, but it belongs unto his king, such is the law; but in this instance I will divide equally with you.

"The law requires the soldier to advance in battle, even in the front of the conflict, but on this occasion I will lead and ye shall follow me. The law commands the king's servants to prepare his chariot, but see, this day I will pre pare it myself."

The words of Pharaoh pleased the soldiers, and they cheerfully armed themselves with swords and spears, with bows and arrows.

And the Israelites were encamped by the Red Sea, and lifting up their eyes they beheld the Egyptians marching upon their rear. And their hearts became filled with terror, for the waters were before them and their enemies behind, and they cried aloud unto the Lord.

And there was great division of opinion among them. Those who differed divided themselves into four parties, and Moses replied to each of them in a suitable manner.

The first party, composed of the tribes of Reuben, Simeon, and Issachar, wished to throw themselves into the sea, for they could see no hope of escape. But Moses said to them:

"Fear not; stand firm and see the salvation of the Lord that He will do for ye this day."

The tribes of Zebulun, Naphtali, and Benjamin favoured a return to Egypt. To them Moses said:

"As ye have seen the Egyptians this day, ye shall not see them again any more for ever."

The tribes of Judah and Joseph desired to meet the Egyptians and to fight with them. But Moses said:

"Keep your position; the Lord will fight for ye, and ye shall hold your peace."

The fourth party, the tribes of Levi, Gad, and Asher, counselled a sudden attack, a surprise, upon the Egyptians, thinking that it would confuse and weaken them, and to these Moses said:

"Move not; fear nothing; only call upon the Lord to deliver ye out of their hands."

And it came to pass after Moses had spoken these words that he rose up in the midst of the people, and he prayed unto the Lord, saying:

"I beseech thee, oh Lord God of the universe, to save this people which thou hast brought forth from Egypt. Let not the Egyptians triumph, and say vauntingly, 'Our hand is strong.'"

And the Lord said to Moses:

"Wherefore cry unto me? Speak unto the children of Israel and bid them to go forward."

And Moses stretched forth his rod over the sea as God commanded and the waters were divided.

And the children of Israel passed through the Red Sea dryshod, and when they had passed through, the waters returned as before. And the waters closed over the Egyptians, and not one was saved of all their hosts.

Then sang Moses and the children of Israel unto the Lord in tones of gladness

"I will sing unto the Lord, for gloriously hath He triumphed.
The horse and the rider He hath cast into the sea."

PART SECOND. SPECIMENS OF BIBLICAL COMMENTARIES

1. The Deliverance From Egypt

"Moses fled from the face of Pharaoh and tarried in the land of Midian, and sat down by a well."

THREE of the prominent Biblical characters met their wives for the first time by wells of water--namely, Isaac, Jacob, and Moses.

In regard to Isaac we find, "And Isaac came from the road at the well of *Chai roi*" (Gen. 13), in addition to which Eleazer, his father's messenger, met Rebecca by the well. Jacob met Rachel by the well, and Moses met the daughters of Jithro when they came to water their father's flocks.

The Lord hates idolatry. Why then did Moses seek the house of an idolater?

The Rabbis say that Jithro had seen the error of his ways and resigned his position as priest to the idols of Midian before Moses came to him. For this reason the people held aloof from him and his family, holding no intercourse with them, and for this reason the shepherds refused to work for him, and his daughters were obliged to water and attend to his flocks.

"His eyes see, His eyebrow searches the sons of man," says the Psalmist.

"Although His divinity is of heaven," said Rabbi Janaai, "His eyes look upon earth. Even as the king who built high tower in his orchard and dwelt therein. To his labourers he said, 'Look to my orchard that you keep it in good condition, the walks clean, and the trees carefully attended that they may bring forth good fruit. He among ye who is faithful shall receive a just reward, and he who neglects my charge shall meet the punishment he deserves!' The world, vast and immense, is the orchard of the great King of kings, and he has placed man therein to keep his laws and statutes, and to preserve the sweet savour of obedience. They who are faithful will be rewarded, while they who neglect their trust will be dealt with according to their deeds. Therefore the Psalmist says, 'His eyes see, His eyebrow searches the sons of man."

He searches the righteous. How? By judging of the manner in which they attend to the flocks entrusted to their charge.

David, the son of Jesse, He tried in this manner. Before the lambs David set tender grass for food; to the old sheep he gave soft herbs and tender grass, while to the young sheep, able to chew well, he gave the old grass; feeding each according to its wants and strength. Therefore the Lord said, "David, who is able to care for the wants of the flocks entrusted to him, will be able to rule properly over my flock, the people of Israel," even as it is written, "After the young flock He brought Him to rule over Jacob His people."

So did the Lord try Moses. While keeping the flock of his father-in-law in the wilderness a lamb left the flock and ran away. The merciful shepherd pursued it, and found it quenching its thirst at a spring by the roadside. "Poor lamb," said Moses, "I did not know that thou vast thirsty;" and after the lamb had finished drinking, he took it up tenderly in his arms and carried it back to the flock. Then said God, "Moses, merciful Moses, if thy love and care is so great for an animal, how much greater will it be, exerted for thy fellow-being! thou shalt lead my people Israel."

Why did the Lord appear to Moses in a thorn bush? Because the thorn bush is lowly among trees, and Israel was then lowly among the nations of the earth. Roses, the most beautiful of the flowers, grow with thorns, so among Israel both righteous and unrighteous men were numbered. He who thrusts his hand into thorns may do so without hurt, but he cannot draw it forth again without being torn by the brambles. So was it with Israel. When Jacob entered Egypt it was with peace, none noticed, to disturb him; but when his children went out from the land, it was with signs, miracles, and war. And lest Moses might chance to think that the rigour of the Egyptians had already destroyed Israel, God appeared in a burning bush that was not consumed, to typify the state and future of Israel, complete and perfect, despite the fire of persecution.

"And God said, I have greatly seen the affliction of my people who are in Egypt."

When Hagar was dismissed by Abraham, and when her son cried to her for water in the wilderness, she appealed to Heaven, saying, "Merciful Father, thou didst promise me, 'I will multiply thy seed;' and now, behold my son must die of thirst!"

Upon this the angels asked, "What ails thee, Hagar?" &c.

According to Rabbi Simon, the angels opposed the assistance rendered Ishmael, saying, "If he is saved today he will bring evil upon thy children Israel in the future." Then said God, "How has his conduct been to-day?" And when the angels answered, "Innocent and correct," God continued, "He shall be judged to-day only in relation to his actions of to-day."

So was it with the Israelites in Egypt. The Lord knew what their future conduct would be. He said, "I have seen greatly;" not simply "I have seen," but "I have seen greatly;" which means more than limited view or mere observation.

The Lord said to Moses, "Thou seest one thing, but I see two. That the children of Israel will receive the Decalogue upon Mount Sinai is known to thee; but I foresee the event which will follow, the making of the molten calf. Yet still I judge them but by their present conduct. I have heard their cry, and though I know that they will murmur against me in the wilderness, nevertheless will I redeem them. I said to Jacob their progenitor, 'I will go down with thee to Egypt, and I will also surely bring thee up again.' Now I am going to bring my children up as I have promised them, and lead them to the land which I gave unto their fathers. Their cry has reached me, and the last days of their bondage are drawing nigh. Go therefore . . . that thou mayest bring forth my people, the children of Israel, out of Egypt. Thou art the one appointed co redeem them."

And Moses answered:

"When Jacob went down into Egypt didst Thou not say to him, 'I will go down with thee to Egypt, and I myself will surely bring thee up again?' And now Thou sayest, 'Go *thou*.' How can I bring them up? How protect them from the summer's heat and the cold of winter? How can I support an army of six hundred thousand men, with many women and little ones, and some among them who are invalids and crippled, requiring extra care and special food?"

"The unleavened bread which they will carry with them will be sufficient for them all for thirty days," replied the Lord.

Then Moses said:

"When they shall say to me, 'What is His name?' how shall I answer them?"

And God replied:

"I have many names. I am called 'God Almighty' (*El-Shaddai*), 'The Lord of Hosts' (*Adonai Zebaoth*), 'God' (*Elohimn*). When I judge the wicked I am called 'The Lord of Hosts,' and when I rebuke the sinner I am called 'God Almighty.' When I show mercy to my people I am called 'Eternal' (Jehovah)."

Then God said to Moses, "I will be that I will be; this is my name for ever."

God meant by this, "I will be with them in this bondage, and I will be with them in their future captivity."

Then said Moses:

"Why should I mention future captivity to them while they are suffering under their present bondage?"

And God replied:

"Thou hast spoken well; say naught of their future troubles."

"And Moses answered and said, 'But behold they will not believe me.'"

Moses was wrong in making this response, for God had already said, "They will hearken to thy voice."

So God said

"What hast thou in thy hand?"

This was a rebuke, meaning that by the staff which he carried in his hand he deserved punishment for doubting. Why did Moses's staff become a serpent? Because he implied falsehood to the Lord, even as did the serpent in Eden.

A heathen chief said to Rabbi Josah, "My gods are greater than thy gods."

"Why?" asked the sage.

"Because," replied the heathen, "when your God appeared in the thorn bush Moses hid his face, but when he saw the serpent, which is my god, he fled before it."

And Rabbi Josah answered:

"When our God appears we cannot flee from him; He is in the heaven and on earth, on sea and dry land; but if a man flies from thy god, the serpent, a few steps deliver him."

What significance has the serpent in respect to the redemption of Israel? Pharaoh is compared to the serpent, as it is written (Ezekiel 28), "The great serpent." Even as the bite of a serpent to man was the bondage of Pharaoh to Israel.

The Lord said to Moses, "Pharaoh is now as a serpent; thou shalt smite him with thy staff and he shall become powerless as wood. Even as a staff is useless for aggression without man's assistance, motive power, so shall Pharaoh cease to be aggressive." Therefore He said, "Put forth thy hand and grasp it by the tail."

Why was Moses commanded to put his hand into his bosom when it was made white with leprosy? Because slander and falsehood are generally spoken in secret, even as the bosom is hidden.

How did this change to leprosy illustrate the redemption of Israel?

Even as a leper defiles the clean, so did the Egyptian contact defile the Israelites, and as the leprous hand was restored to its purity, so did God design to purify His people.

In the first two miracles which the Lord displayed to Moses the objects regained their original appearance; but in the third, the change from water to blood, the former did not recover its original qualities. So God fore-shadowed that Moses would not be pardoned for his sin at *Meribah*.

Each time when Moses's death is mentioned in the Scriptures, the cause of his death before entering the holy land, his disobedience at *Meribah* is mentioned. Why is this?

Two men were once punished by the civil authorities; one had committed a crime, the other but a slight misdemeanour. The latter requested that the cause of his punishment might be made public, that people might not confound his misdemeanour with the greater crime.

So was it with Moses. God decreed that he should die in the wilderness, and He also decreed that all that generation (save Joshua and Caleb) should also perish. Therefore that Moses might not be classed with hem, as rebellious against the Lord, the special cause for his punishment s mentioned in connexion with his death.

"Moses said to the Lord, Pardon, O Lord! I am not a man of words."

Seven days did the Lord repeat His command to Moses, and still Moses hesitated to obey. "I am not a man of words to-day"--that is one day--"yesterday"--two days "also"--three--"the day before"--four--"also"--five--"nor since"--six. "Thou hast spoken"--seven.

Then God said:

"Even if thou be not a man of words, fear not; have I not created all the mouths which speak? can I not make those who speak dumb, and put words into the mouths of those who are dumb at my pleasure? It is my pleasure that thou shouldst speak to Pharaoh."

And Moses made answer, saying:

"They are the descendants of Abraham those whom thou wouldst redeem. Which is the nearer to a man, his brother's son, or his son's son?
To redeem Lot, his brother's son, Thou didst send angels; and now to redeem his own children, six hundred thousand strong, besides the women and the young, Thou wouldst send me. To Hagar Thou didst send five angels when she fled from Sarah, her mistress; but to sixty thousand of the children of Sarah Thou wouldst send but me."

The Rabbis tell us that Moses was not reluctant to accept this mission through fear or a dread of labour, or a disinclination to obey God, but because he thought it should rightly belong to Aaron, his elder brother. Yet

God was displeased with Moses, and, therefore, He gave the priesthood which He had designed for him, to Aaron, in saying:

"Is there not Aaron thy brother, the Levite?"

When God said "thy brother," the word "Levite" was implied, because Moses being a Levite, his brother must necessarily have been the same; but this was God's meaning:

"I thought to make thee my priest, and continue thy brother, the Levite; but for thy reluctance in obeying my wishes, he shall be the priest and thou the Levite."

"And the lord said to Aaron, 'Go to meet Moses.'"

"Oh that some one would make thee as my brother," is one of the beautiful expressions of Solomon's song.

What kind of a brother? Not as was Cain to Abel, for "Cain rose up against his brother Abel and slew him." Not as Ishmael to Isaac, for Ishmael hated Isaac; neither as Esau, for "Esau hated Jacob." Not as the brothers of Joseph, for "they could not speak peaceably to him;" but even such a brother as Aaron to Moses, as it is written, "And he (Aaron) went and met him (Moses) by the mount of God, and kissed him" (Ex. 4: 27).

"And after that Moses and Aaron went in."

Where were the elders? We find it written, "Thou and the elders of Israel shall come."

The elders started out, but dropped off gradually, through fear; therefore, after this, it is always written simply, "Moses and Aaron went in."

"Thus hath said the Everlasting One," &c.

According to Rabbi Chiyah, it happened at this time that all the neighbouring kings were calling upon Pharaoh to pay their homage to him and bring him presents; and each of the princes brought with him his god. Moses and Aaron stood at the palace gates, and the guard thinking they too were tributaries, bade them enter. Pharaoh looked at them, and seeing them to be strangers he imagined that they also brought him presents, and he wondered why they did not salute him as the others did. He spoke and asked them, "What is your desire?" And they answered, "Thus saith the Lord, let my people go," &c.

And Pharaoh said in angry pride:

"Who is this Lord that I am to obey,--at whose voice I am to let Israel go? He has never made me an offering or appeared before me; I know him not, nor will I let Israel go."

Then he continued:

"Lo, I will consult my records and see if I find there the name of your God. Here I find the names of all the gods; the gods of Amon, the gods of Moab, the gods of Zedin, but the name of your God I cannot find."

And Moses answered:

"Our God is a living God."

And Pharaoh said to him:

"Is he young or old? What is his age; how many cities has he captured; how many countries has he conquered; how long has been his reign?"

Then said Moses:

"His power fills the universe. He was before the world saw light, He will be, when the world exists no more. He formed thee; with His spirit thou breathest."

And Pharaoh further asked, "What are his deeds?" To which the messengers of God replied:

"The voice of the Lord breaketh in pieces the cedars; He stretched out the heavens, He laid the foundation of the earth, rending the mountains and breaking into stones the rocks. His bow is of fire, His arrows are of flame. He formed the mountains and the hills, covered the fields with green, bringing forth fruits and herbs. He removeth kings, and kings He exalteth."

"Ye come to me with falsehoods," returned Pharaoh "ye tell me that your God is the Lord of the world; know then that Egypt is mine, and I have created the great river Nile which floweth in its boundaries."

("Mine is my stream, and I have made it for myself." Ezekiel 19: 3).

Then Pharaoh asked of his magicians, "Have ye ever heard of their God?" And the magicians answered, "We have heard of him. He is the son of wise men, the son of a king of olden time."

"Thou askest now, 'Who is the Lord?' said Moses. "The time will come when thou wilt say, 'The Lord is righteous.' Thou sayest now, 'I know not your Lord.' The time cometh when thou wilt say, 'I have sinned against your Lord.'"

"And they met Moses and Aaron . . . 'to put a sword in their hands to slay us.'"

"Yea," said the overburdened children of Israel to Moses and Aaron, "we are like a lamb which the wolf has carried from its flock, the shepherd strives to take it from him, but between the two the lamb is pulled to pieces; between ye and Pharaoh will we all be killed."

"Then Moses said to the Lord, 'O Lord, wherefore hast Thou let so much evil come upon this people?'"

The Lord had already informed Moses that He would harden Pharaoh's heart, and that he would refuse to let Israel go; therefore God now replied to him, "Thou wilt see now what I am going to do to Pharaoh, but thou wilt not see what I shall do to the three kingdoms of Canaan."

"And I appeared to Abraham," &c.

The Lord said to Moses:

"Woe, woe, that the righteous are no more; I mourn fop the patriarchs. I revealed myself to Abraham, to Isaac, said to Jacob as God Almighty, but not by the name 'Eternal,' as I have done to thee, yet they never murmured either at my commands or at my works. I said to Abraham, 'Arise, walk through the land, its length and breadth, for I will give it to thee;' and when his wife died and he wanted but a grave for her, he was obliged to buy it with money, yet he slid not murmur and reproach me, saying, 'Thou didst promise to give me all this land, and now I am obliged to sue for and purchase but a very small portion.' I said to Isaac, 'Sojourn in this land, for unto thee and thy seed will I give all these countries;' and when he wanted a little water he could get none, for the herdsmen of Gerar did strive with his herdsmen to prevent their digging a well; still Isaac raised not his voice against me. I said to Jacob, 'The ground whereon thou liest, to thee will I give it;' and when he wished to pitch there his tent he was obliged to pay a hundred *kessitah*, yet he did not murmur against the Lord, or even ask of me my name, as thou hast done."

"And the lord spake unto Moses and Aaron, and gave them a charge unto the children of Israel, and unto Pharaoh, the king of Egypt."

A king had a fine and elegant orchard in which he planted trees, both fruitful and unfruitful His servants said to him, "What benefit is there in the planting of barren trees?" And he replied to them, "Fruitful trees and those which bear not, are equally useful; where could we procure wood for our houses, our ships, and our utensils, if we did not have these sturdy trees which bear no fruit?"

Even as the righteous glorify the Lord in their happiness so does the punishment of the wicked glorify the Lord when they proclaim, "Justly have we been punished."

When Aaron performed the miracles with his staff, Pharaoh laughed, and made light of them, saying:

"It is customary for merchants to carry their wares to places wanting them,--why shouldst thou come with such tricks to a country full of magicians as Egypt is?"

He sent for some small children, and even they changed their rods into serpents.

"But Aaron's staff swallowed up their staves."

The swallowing of their staves was not the only miracle, but that Aaron's staff did not grow larger in size thereafter, added to the wonder.

---

2. The Ten Plagues

"Thus hath said the Lord, 'By this thou shalt know that I am the lord; behold I will smile........the waters of the river, and they shall be turned to blood.'"

When a human being designs to injure another, or to take vengeance on an enemy, he comes upon him suddenly and without warning. Not so, however, does God act. He warned Pharaoh of every plague which He brought upon Egypt, in order to give him the opportunity for repentance.

Why were the waters first smitten? Because the Egyptians worshipped the river Nile, and the Lord said, "I will first smite the god and then its nation," according to the proverb, "I will first smite the gods, then the priests will be terrified."

Blood.

Why did the Lord punish the Egyptians with blood? Because they shed the blood of innocent infants, therefore was the water of their rivers turned to blood.

"And the Lord said unto Moses, say to Aaron, Take thy staff and stretch out thy hand over the waters of Egypt."

Why could not Moses himself smite the river?

Because the waters had protected and guarded him when he slumbered, a helpless infant, in the ark of bulrushes, and the wise sayings teach us, "Into the well wherefrom thou drawest water thou shouldst cast no stones."

Frogs.

We are apt to think the frog superfluous, not requisite in the economy of the universe. Not so,--every living thing has its purpose, and the frogs became an instrument in Pharaoh's punishment. The river Nile brought forth frogs in abundance, but they strayed not from its banks. Then God said, "Thou sayest, 'the river is mine,'--verily I will show thee that even thy house is not thy own; the frogs shall enter into it, even into thy kneading trough, they will sit in thy dough and consume it."

The frogs caused the Egyptians morn annoyance than that occasioned by the mere pecuniary loss which they carried with them, for they were very noisy; therefore it is written, "Moses cried (*i.e.*, spoke with a loud voice) to the Lord, on account of the frogs."

Lice.

"Say to Aaron . . . and smite the dust of the earth."

Why did not Moses himself smite the dust?

Because Moses hid in the dust the body of the Egyptian whom he found smiting a Hebrew, and the dust concealed his action. Therefore were the plagues involving the water and the dust wrought through Aaron.

Why were the Egyptians afflicted with this plague?

Because they had forced the Israelites to sweep the streets and to work in mortar, dust, and bricks. Therefore was the dust of the streets turned to lice. The magicians were unable to produce the lice, because they could not imitate articles smaller than a barleycorn; therefore they said, "This is the finger of God."

The Multitude of Beasts.

"Rise up early," &c.

God said to Moses, "This man persists in his obstinacy, despite the plagues already brought upon him; therefore say to him that the next will be more dreadful than the others all combined; bid him let Israel go."

The beasts swarmed first into the house of Pharaoh, because he was the first to oppress Israel, and then into the houses of his servants, because they followed in his lead.

Why were these beasts brought upon the Egyptians? Because they had forced the Israelites to endanger their lives by hunting wild beasts.

We find that the frogs died in the land of Egypt, but that the beasts were removed. Why this difference? Because the frogs were worthless, but the Egyptians might have profited from the furs of the wild beasts.

Pestilence.

Why was this plague brought upon them?

To show that the plagues were directed only against the Egyptians, for as the Bible tells us, "There had not died of the cattle of the Israelites even one." Even cattle belonging to a Hebrew and in the possession of an Egyptian was saved, as was also the cattle owned in shares by an Egyptian and an Israelite.

Boils.

Why did He bring boils upon them?

Because they had compelled the Israelites to clean their houses and courts, thus making their blood impure, and producing boils.

Why were the magicians unable to stand before Moses on account of the inflammation?

Because they had advised that every son born to Israel should be cast into the river.

"The Lord hardened," &'c.

When the Lord saw that the five plagues already brought upon Pharaoh did not cause his repentance, he said, "Even should he wish to repent hereafter, I will harden his heart that he may receive the full measure of his punishment."

Hail.

"Behold, then will I let rain about this time to to-morrow," &c.

Moses made a mark upon the wall of Pharaoh's house, saying, "When the sun shall shine to-morrow upon this spot there will be hail, therefore bring in thy cattle," &c.

Again, the compassion of God is displayed to us. Even in his anger He was still mercifully inclined towards the wicked people and their cattle. He intended the plague of hail to destroy vegetation, not life; therefore He warned the people to keep themselves and their flocks under shelter.

"The lord said . . . Stretch out thy hand towards the heaven," &c.

Although "the heavens are the heavens of the Lord," yet "the earth hath He given to the children of men" (Psalm 120: 16).

An emperor, ruling Rome and Syria, might issue a decree forbidding Romans to visit Syria, and Syrians to visit Rome. So God in creating the world pronounced the heavens "the heavens of the Lord," the residence of godly beings.

"But the earth hath He given to the children of men;" the earth must be the scene of their sojournings. Yet, "whatsoever the Lord willeth hath He done, in the heavens and on the earth; in the seas and in all the deeps" (Psalm 135:16).

He descended upon the earth at Mount Sinai; at the time of the creation He said, "Let the waters gather together in one place," and when it pleased Him so to do, He made the sea dry land, even as it is written, "And the children of Israel walked upon dry land in the midst of the sea."

In the same manner God gave Moses permission to rule over the heavens, to stretch his hands towards them, and bring down a hailstorm over the land of Egypt.

Why were they punished with hail?

Because they had compelled the Israelites to plough their fields, sow their grain, care for their trees, and to perform all the menial labour incidental to the cultivation of the soil. Therefore God sent this hailstorm to destroy the products of the ground, that the Egyptians might reap no profit from the enforced labour of His people. When God saw that they disregarded His warning, and neglected to put their cattle under shelter, He caused the cattle to die from the effects of the storm.

The hailstones were very large, each of them being about the size of an infant's head; and as they touched the ground they burst into flame.

Locusts.

Why did God bring the locusts into Egypt?

The Israelites had sowed the fields with grain, and the locusts were brought to destroy all that had escaped the hail.

This plague was so grievous as to wring from Pharaoh the acknowledgment, "I have sinned against the Lord your God that I did not let Israel go." "And against you" (Moses and Aaron), "that I have driven you out of my house."

Darkness.

"But for all the children of Israel there was light in their dwellings."

Why, is it not written, "There was light in the land of Goshen?"

Because, wherever the Israelites were, there was light for them; but to an Egyptian, even in the same room with an Israelite, all was impenetrable darkness.

The Slaying of the First-Born.

"Thou shalt not see my face any more."

Such were the words of Pharaoh, when Moses appeared before him, to warn him for the last time of the doom awaiting him should he still oppose the exodus of Israel. Moses answered:

"Thou hast spoken well. Nevermore will I come to thee, but thou wilt come to me, and thy servants and thyself will entreat me, bending, to depart from thy country, and then will I go."

Some of the Egyptians, fearing Moses's prophecy, slept that night in the houses of the Israelites. But the death-stroke found them, and the Israelite awakening, found an Egyptian's corpse beside him.

Great was the distress in Egypt. Pharaoh called to Moses and Aaron, and said, "Arise!" They replied, "What would Pharaoh with us? Has he come to us?" "Arise!" he cried, "arise and go."

The Israelites went forth from Egypt on the eve of the fifteenth of Nissan; on this same night, many years later, the army of Sennacherib, encamped before Jerusalem, was slain by the Lord. King Hezekiah, and the inhabitants of the besieged city, celebrated the feast of Passover according to the command of God, and sang praises and hallelujahs to His Holy Name.

But Hezekiah was heavy at heart, and he said:

"To-morrow the city may be taken." Yet, lo, when they arose in the morning, the Lord had again passed over for His people, and the invading army lay dead in its camp.

Before inflicting the last plague, God warned Pharaoh, as it is written, "*I will smite all the first-born of Egypt*."

Had God wished to make this the first, instead of the last of the plagues, He could have done so; but He desired to increase the severity with the number of the plagues, and accordingly the lightest he sent first.

"The Lord will pass through the land of Egypt and smite all the first-born."

A certain king sent his son to a distant country, the people of which received him with great honours, and conferred distinction upon him, finally making him their ruler. When his father heard this, he said:

"What honour shall I do them in return? I will call that country after the name of my son."

After some time had elapsed, he again received news from the distant land; its people had taken away the honours conferred upon his son, and made him a slave He therefore went to war with them and delivered his son.

Joseph went down to Egypt and was made governor. Great respect was also paid to Jacob, for whose death "the Egyptians mourned seventy days."

For this God named Egypt after the garden of Eden, as it is written, "As the garden of the Lord is the land of Egypt." When, however, the Israelites were oppressed and reduced to slavery, God made war upon Egypt, through the medium of the ten plagues, and through the last delivered his "son," Israel, from bondage.

During the night, while the Hebrews sang praises to God, Pharaoh came to the place where Moses and Aaron dwelt, and he cried, "Arise, get thee out," &c. Then the people scattered themselves among the Egyptians, borrowing vessels of gold and silver. But Moses sought the sepulchre of Joseph, and carried forth his bones, according to the charge transmitted to him.

"And it came to pass at the end of four hundred and thirty years," &c.

These years are counted from the time that God appeared to Abraham in the vision known as "The Covenant of the Pieces," and told him that his seed should be "strangers in a land not theirs." They lived in Egypt, however, only two hundred and ten years. Upon the same month and day, as they had entered Egypt, they left it. On that date Joseph was released from prison, and in subsequent years it witnessed the performance of many wonders in behalf of God's people.

In King Hezekiah's time Jerusalem was delivered from Sennacherib; during the Babylonian captivity, Shedrach, Meshach, and Abednego were delivered from the fire of furnace, and Daniel came forth unharmed from the lion's den.

---

3. The Death Of Moses

"The Lord said to Moses, Behold, thy days approach that thou must die."

The death of Moses is alluded to, in the Bible, ten times.

"Thy days approach that thou must die." (Deut. 31: 14.)

"And thou shalt die on the mount." (Deut. 33: 50.)

"For I am going to die."

"For I know that after my death." (Deut. 31: 29.)

"And how much more after my death." (Deut. 31: 27.)

". . . Blessed the children of Israel before his death." (Deut. 33: 1.)

"And Moses was one hundred and twenty years old when he died." (Deut. 34: 7.)

"And it came to pass after the death of Moses." (Josh. I: 1.)

"Moses, my servant, is dead." (Josh. 1: 2.)

Moses himself thought that he had committed but a slight offence, which would be pardoned; for ten times had Israel tempted God's wrath and been forgiven through his intercession, as it is written, "And the Lord said, I have pardoned according to thy word." But when he became convinced that he would not be pardoned, he made the following supplication:

"Sovereign of the Universe, my trouble and my exertion for Israel's sake is revealed and known before Thee. How I have laboured to cause Thy people to know Thee, and to believe in Thy holy Name and practise Thy holy law, has come before Thee. O Lord, as I had shared their troubles and their distress, I hoped to share their happiness. Behold now the time has come when their trials will cease, when they will enter into the land of promised bliss, and Thou sayest to me, 'Thou shalt not pass over this Jordan.' Oh, Eternal, great and just, if Thou wilt not allow me to enter into this goodly land, permit me at least to live on here in this world."

Then God answered Moses, saying:

"If thou wilt not die in this world, how canst thou live in the world to come?"

But Moses continued:

"If Thou wilt not permit me to pass over this Jordan, let me live as the beasts of the field; they eat of the herbs and drink of the waters, and live and see the world; let my life be even as theirs."

And God answered:

"Let it suffice thee; do not continue to speak unto me any more on this matter." (Deut. 3: 26.)

Yet again Moses prayed:

"Let me live even as the fowls; they gather their food in the morning and in the evening they return unto their nests,--let my life be even as theirs."

And again God said:

"Let it suffice thee; do not continue to speak to me any more on this matter."

Then Moses, convinced that his death was determined on, proclaimed:

"He is the Rock; His work is perfect and His ways are just; the God of truth, just and upright is He."

"And Moses died there in the land of Moab, according to the word of the Lord."

Holy Writ testifies to the righteousness of Moses, "And there arose not a prophet since in Israel like unto Moses, whom the Lord knew face to face."

The heavens wept and exclaimed, "The pious one hath departed, there is none upright among men."

When Joshua searched for his friend and teacher and failed to find him, he wept bitterly and cried, "Help me, O Lord! for the pious have ceased to be."

The angels proclaimed, "He executed the justice of the Lord;" and Israel added, "And His judgments with Israel." And together they exclaimed:

"He shall come in peace; they shall rest in their beds every one walking in his uprightness."

Blessed be the memory of the just.

---

4. The Book Of Esther

AND it came to pass when Nebuchadnezzar died, that his son, Evil-Merodach, claimed the kingdom. But the people refused to anoint him as ruler, and they said to him:

"Behold, once before was thy father removed from the vicinity of human beings and compelled to eat herbs and grass like the beasts of the field for seven years. And lo, we deemed him dead and appointed princes in his stead to rule over us, and when he returned he put these princes to death. How can we now make you king? It may be with your father as it was m former days, he may yet return."

Now when the people spoke thus to Evil-Merodach, he went to his father's tomb and removed from the same the corpse of the king. He fastened an iron chain about its feet, and dragged his father's body through the streets of the capital, to prove to the people that he was indeed dead. As it is written in Isaiah:

"But thou, thou art cast out of thy grave like a discarded offshoot." (Isaiah 14: 19.)

Then the people of the country proclaimed Evil-Merodach king.

And Daniel said to the king:

"Thy father, Nebuchadnezzar, never opened the door of his prisons" (meaning when he once incarcerated a person it was for life), "as it is written, 'never opened the prison-house of his prisoners.' (Isaiah 14: 17.) Now when the Israelites were adjudged guilty by God of the many sins which they committed, behold thy father came up and laid the land of Israel desolate. He destroyed our holy temple, and our people he sent captives and exiles to Babel. Among them was Yehoyachim the king of Judah. For thirty-two years he has lain in prison because he neglected to follow the will of God. Now, I pray thee, let him be released. Oh, be not stiff-necked. Remember the punishment of thy father when he became proud and blasphemed, and said, 'There is no king or ruler but myself only,' as it is written, 'I will ascend above the height of the clouds; I will be equal to the Most High.'" (Isaiah 14: 14.)

Then Evil-Merodach listened to the words of Daniel and performed the will of God. He released Yehoyachim, the king of the tribe of Judah, and he opened the doors to the other prisoners and gave them liberty.

And He anointed Yehoyachim, and dressed him in royal garments; "and he ate bread before him continually all the days of his life." (Kings 25: 29.)

And from Evil-Merodach the kingdom descended to Darius of Media, and Ahasuerus, of Persia, was the son of Darius of Media.

From the house of this same Ahasuerus was banished Vashti, the daughter of Evil-Merodach, the son of Nebuchadnezzar. For her iniquity was she banished, for she compelled the Jewish women to labour upon their holy Sabbath.

This same Ahasuerus commanded that the wine of one hundred and twenty-seven provinces should be furnished on his banquet table, that the men of one hundred and twenty-seven provinces might drink, each man of the wine of his own country, of his own province, that he might not consume strange and hurtful drink.

This same Ahasuerus was a foolish king. "My queen shall be sent away," he ordered; "but my decree must never be abolished."

In the time of this same Ahasuerus the people of Israel were sold,--aye, without money; as it is written: "For naught were ye sold." (Isaiah 52: 3.)

And in the time of this same Ahasuerus the words written in the Pentateuch came to pass: "In the morning shall ye say, 'Would that it were evening,' and in the evening, 'Would that the morning were nigh.'" (Deut. 28: 67.)

This was the same Ahasuerus who once dismissed his wife for the sake of his friend, and again killed his friend for the sake of his wife. He sent away Vashti, his wife, in accordance with the advice of Memuchan his friend, and he killed his friend Haman, for the sake of Esther, his wife.

And it came to pass in the days of this Ahasuerus that he desired to sit upon the throne of Solomon. The magnificent throne of Solomon which had been carried from Jerusalem to Egypt by Sheshak the king of Egypt. From his hands it passed to Sennacherib the king of Assyria; from him was it returned to Hezekiah, and again carried away by Pharaoh Nechoh of Egypt. Nebuchadnezzar, the king of Babel, wrenched it from the possession of Pharaoh, and when Cyrus, the king of Media,. conquered the land of Persia, the throne was brought to Shushan and passed into the possession of Ahasuerus.

But he had a new throne made for himself. He sent artisans to Alexandria, and they were two years making for him his throne. "In the third year of his reign, the king Ahasuerus sat upon his own throne, and Solomon's throne was not used any more."

"There was a certain Jew in Shushan, the capital, whose name was Mordecai."

Why was Mordecai called a Jew? He was not of the tribe of Judah, but a descendant of Benjamin? He was called a Jew because he feared the Lord as all Jews should do.

Mordecai was a descendant of Shimï, whose life King David spared when he had incurred the penalty of death for reviling his ruler. For David foresaw the miracle which should be wrought through the instrumentality of Mordecai in years then hidden in the future.

And Mordecai brought up his cousin Hadassah or Esther. She was called Hadassah (meaning "myrtle") because of her sweet disposition and kindly acts, which were compared to the fragrant perfume and ever fresh beauty of the myrtle. In many instances the righteous are compared to the myrtle, as in Isaiah (55: 13), "In place of the thorn the fir tree shall spring forth, and the nettle shall give place to the myrtle."

This sentence is thus construed:

Instead of Haman, the thorn, the fir tree, Mordecai shall spring forth; and in place of Vashti, compared to a nettle, Esther, the myrtle, shall share the Persian throne.

Her name, Esther, was also well chosen; from the Greek, *Estarah*, a bright star. Her pious deeds ceased only with her life, and her beauty was equalled only by her spiritual qualities.

Shortly before Esther's birth her father died, and her mother followed him when the babe drew her first breath. Then Mordecai, her father's nephew, adopted her, and brought her up as his child.

After the king had married Esther he was anxious to learn her descent, and asked her, "Where are thy kindred? Behold, I have prepared a banquet, bid them attend."

And Esther answered him

"Thou art a wise king, and surely thou knowest that my parents are dead; do not sadden me, I pray, my lord, by such inquiries."

'Twas then that the king released the people from the payment of the year's taxes, and gave presents "according to his ability" to all his nobles, declaring that it was done in "Esther's honour."

He imagined that through this the fame of the proceeding and Esther's name would become known throughout the nations, and he might learn thereby of her people.

When this plan failed he called all the beautiful virgins of his provinces together again, thinking that jealousy might induce Esther to tell him of her predecessors, but without avail. Esther mentioned not her people.

"In those days, when Mordecai was sitting in the king's gate, .Bigthana and Theresh became wroth," &c.

Rabbi Johanan said: "God has made servants wroth against their lords for the accomplishment of justice, and He has also made masters wroth with their servants for the same purpose." The latter instance is to be found in the history of Joseph, as it is written, "There was with us in the prison a Hebrew lad," and the former instance is that of Bigthana and Theresh, the chamberlains of the king.

"And the thing became known to Mordecai."

The two officers spoke in a strange language; they thought that Mordecai could not understand them. But Mordecai had been a member of the Sanhedrim; he was a learned man, and what they said was well understood by him.

One officer said to the other:

"Since the king married Esther we have had neither rest nor peace; the coming and the going makes life wearisome it would be better for us if we should remove him from the world."

The other acquiesced with him, but said:

"How is it to be done? I am on guard; I cannot leave."

But the first speaker said:

"Go, and I will attend to both thy guard and mine."

Therefore it is written, "*And the thing was inquired info and found true*;" that is, one of the guards was found absent from his post.

"After these events." What events?

After God had created the remedy before the infliction of the wound; after Mordecai had saved the king's life before the orders for the destruction of his people were promulgated.

After these events the king advanced Haman, the son of Hamdatha, the Agagite, to an illustrious position in the kingdom. He was raised, however, but to be destroyed. His destiny was like to that of the hog in the parable of the horse, the colt, and the hog.

A certain man possessed a horse, a colt, and a hog. For the two former he measured out daily a certain amount of food; so much was their allowance, no more, no less; the hog, however, was allowed to eat according to his own pleasure. Said the colt to the horse, "How is this? Is it just? We work for our food while the hog is a useless animal; surely we should have as much to eat as is given him."

"Wait," answered the horse, "and you will soon see, in the downfall of the hog, the reason."

With the coming of the autumn the hog was killed.

"See," said the horse, "they did not give the hog so much to eat for his own benefit, but in order to fatten him for the killing."

Haman was a direct descendant of Esau. His father, Hamdatha, was the son of Sararch, he of Kuzah, Iphlotas, Joseph, Josim, Pedome, Madé, Belaäkan, Intimrom, Haridom, Shegar, Negar, Parmashtáh, Vayzathah, Agag, Sumki, Amalek, and lastly Eliphaz, the first-born of Esau.

"Why transgressest thou the king's commands?"

The servants of the king's gate said to Mordecai:

"Why wilt thou refuse to bow before Haman, transgressing thus the wishes of the king? Do we not bow before him?"

"Ye are foolish," answered Mordecai, "aye, wanting in reason. Listen to me. Shall a mortal, who must return to dust, be glorified? Shall I bow down before one born of woman, whose days are short? When he is small he cries and weeps as a child; when he grows older sorrow and sighing are his portion; his days are full of wrath and anger, and at the end he returns to dust. Shall I bow to one like to him? No, I prostrate myself before the Eternal God, who lives for ever. He who dwells in Heaven and bears the world in the hollow of His hand. His word changes sunlight to darkness, His command illumines the deepest gloom. His wisdom made the world, He placed the boundaries of the mighty sea; the waters are His, the sweet and the salt; to the struggling waves he says, 'Be still, thus far shalt thou come, no further, that the earth may remain dry for my people.' To Him the great Creator and Ruler of the Universe, and to no other will I bow."

Haman was wroth against Mordecai, and said to him:

"Why art thou so stiff-necked? Did not thy forefather bow down to mine?"

"How?" replied Mordecai; "which of my ancestors bowed before forefather of thine?"

Then Haman answered:

"Jacob, thy forefather, bowed down to Esau, his brother, who was my forefather."

"Not so," answered Mordecai, "for I am descended from Benjamin, and when Jacob bowed to Esau, Benjamin was not yet born. Benjamin never bowed until his descendants prostrated themselves in the holy temple, when the divinity of God rested within its sacred portals, and all Israel united with him. I will not bow before the wicked Haman."

"*In the first month, that is, in the month Nissan (April), they cast the lot before Haman.*" He cast the lot "from day to day." At first he selected the first day of the week as the one for the destruction of the Jews; but then he said, "No; light was created upon that day, which is to their merit. On the second day the heavens were created; also to their merit. On the third day, the Garden of Eden, with all the herbs and trees; on the fourth the sun, moon, stars, and all the hosts of Heaven, also a merit to them. On the fifth day the fowls of the Heaven were created, and among them the pigeon, which the Jews have used for a sacrifice, so that will not answer for their extermination. On the sixth day Adam and Eve were created, and on the seventh day is their Sabbath, the covenant between them and their God."

He then took his chances with the months. In the month of Nissan (April) they were released from the servitude of Egypt, and many miracles were performed in their favour. In the month of Iyar (May) the manna first descended from Heaven, and in that month, too, five calamities were to happen. During the month of Sivan they received the ten commandments, and hold their feast of weeks. Neither of these months would do. The next cast was the Month *Tamuz* (July). But in that month the walls of Jerusalem were destroyed, and Haman, thinking that might prove sufficient punishment for any of their sins in that month, passed it by and cast again. The next lot fell on *Ab* (August). But in that month the last of the generations doomed to wander through the wilderness forty years had perished. The time of their punishment had expired, and in that same month Moses had spoken with God, and prayed to Him, "Show me Thy Glory." This was too great a month to the Israelites to allow its selection for their extermination.

The next month was *Elul* (September). 'Twas in this month that Moses ascended for the third time the mount of God, to receive the second tables of stone. Also, during this month, the walls of Jerusalem were completed, as it is written in Nehemiah 6: 15: "And so was the wall finished on the twenty-and-fifth day of the month Elul."

Tishri (October) would not be favourable to his purpose, because the Day of Atonement, when all Israel would be devout in prayer, occurs within it. Neither would the following month, *Heshvan*, suit his designs, because it was in this month that the waters of the flood were set loose upon the world and Noah and his family saved. During *Kislev* (December) the foundation of the Temple was laid. In*Thebet* (January) Nebuchadnezzar besieged Jerusalem, also a sufficient punishment for that period, And also, during this month, the eleven tribes made peace with Benjamin. Neither was Shebat (February) a month displaying any guilty action deserving of God's wrath on the part of His people. When he came to the month of Adar, however, he said, "Lo, I have thee now, even as the fish of the sea" (the sign of the month's planet being two fish). In this month the lawgiver, Moses, died, and Haman thought it would prove unlucky for Israel. He forgot, however, that Moses was also born in Adar, on the seventh, day of the month.

"Then said Haman unto King Ahasuerus:

"There is a people scattered throughout thy provinces, yet separate and distinct from the nation among which they dwell. They will not intermingle or associate with us. They will not marry with the daughters of our land, neither will they allow our sons to wed their daughters. They do not aid in building up the state, for they have many holy days on which they are idle and refuse to traffic. The first hour of each day they devote to their prayer, 'Hear, O Israel, the Lord is One.' The second hour they also sing praises, and much time they waste in prayers and graces. Each seventh day they make a Sabbath, and pass the time in their synagogues reading from their Pentateuch and their prophets; aye, and in cursing thee, the king. They enter their children into a covenant of the flesh when they are but eight days old, that they may remain a peculiar people for ever. In the month of *Nissan* they hold a feast, which they call the Passover, when they remove all leaven from their houses, and they say, 'As we remove the leaven from our houses, so may the wicked king be removed from our midst.' They have many fasts and feasts, upon all of which they curse the king, and pray for thy death and the downfall of thy kingdom. Lo, there arose once a king, Nebuchadnezzar, who destroyed their temple, despoiled their great city, Jerusalem, and sent the inhabitants thereof into exile. Still their pride and stubborn spirit remained unbroken. Know, also, that their fathers went down into Egypt, seventy men, and when they went up from thence they numbered full six hundred thousand, in addition to their women and little ones. Among this nation there are men, large dealers they buy and they sell, but they execute not the laws of the king and the realm. What profit, then, is it to have such a people scattered through thy provinces?

"Now, if it be pleasing in the eyes of the king, let a decree be published to destroy and exterminate them from our midst."

And Ahasuerus answered:

"We are not able to do this thing. Their God has not deserted them, and they have prevailed over people greater and stronger than ourselves. We cannot accept thy advice in this matter."

Still Haman persisted from time to time to pour complaints against the Jews in the ears of the king, and to urge their complete destruction. Finally Ahasuerus said, "As thou hast troubled me so much about this thing I will call together my officers, counsellors, and wise men, and ask their opinion."

When these sages were called before him the king put the question to them, and asked:

"Now what is your advice, shall this nation be destroyed or not?"

And the wise men answered unanimously, and said:

"Should Israel be stricken from existence the world itself would no longer be; for through the merit of Israel and the law given to them the world exists. Are the people not called near to God (relatives)? 'Unto the children of Israel, a people near to Him.' Not alone this, they are also called children of the Lord, as it is written, 'Ye are the children of the Lord your God' (Dent. 14: r). Who can escape that raises a hand against his children? Pharaoh was punished for his conduct towards them; how shall we escape?"

Then Haman arose and replied to these words:

"The God who caused the death of Pharaoh and his hosts has grown old and feeble; his power leas departed from him. Did not Nebuchednezzar destroy his temple and send his people into exile? Why did he not prevent that if he was all-powerful?"

By such arguments as these Haman altered the opinions and advice of the sages, and the letters ordering the massacre which he desired were prepared according to his command.

When Mordecai ascertained what had been done he rent his garments, clothed himself in sackcloth, and sat in ashes. He wept in his anguish, and said, "Woe, woe to us for this severe decree. Not even a half of our people shall be saved, nor a third part nor a fourth, but the whole body must be rooted out; woe, woe to us!"

Then when the Israelites beheld Mordecai's grief and heard his words, they assembled together, a great multitude of people, and Mordecai addressed them as follows:

"Ye people of Israel, ye chosen ones of our Father in Heaven, know ye not what has happened? Have ye heard naught of the decree against us, that Haman and the king have ordered our destruction from the face of the earth? We have no friendly influence on which to depend, no prophets to pray for us, no city of refuge. We are a flock without a shepherd; we are as a ship at sea without a pilot, as orphans without a father, aye, as sucklings who have lost their mother."

Then they carried the ark in which the scrolls of the law were deposited, into the streets of Shushan, and draped the same in mourning colours. And Mordecai opened the scrolls and read the passage in Deuteronomy (4: 30), "When thou art in tribulation, and all these things have overtaken thee, in the latter end of days, then wilt thou return to the Lord thy God, and be obedient unto His voice. For a merciful God is the Lord thy God."

"People of the house of Israel," said Mordecai, "let us follow the example of the men of Nineveh, at the time when Jonah, the son of Amitai, was sent to proclaim the overthrow of their capital. The king rose from his throne, changed his royal robes for sackcloth and ashes, and caused a fast to be proclaimed. Neither man nor beast, neither herds nor flocks, tasted of food or drank of water. 'God saw their works that they turned from their evil ways, and God bethought Himself of the evil which He had spoken that He would do them and He did it not' (Jonah 3: 7). Let us likewise proclaim a penitential fast; these men were saved, and they were heathens; we are the sons of Abraham, and it behooves us more especially to repent our evil ways and trust to the forgiveness of a merciful God Turn ye, turn ye from your unrighteous paths, oh house of Israel, wherefore will ye die!"

And when he had finished speaking these words, Mordecai went out into the city and cried with a loud and bitter cry.

The house of Israel was filled with dread at the edict of the king. Sorrow crossed the threshold of each Jewish home; a spirit of anguish filled every habitation.

A certain man called on a Persian friend and entreated him to use his influence to save his life and the lives of his family. "I, my wife, and my children will be your slaves," said he, "only save our lives."

The Persian answered:

"How can I do so? The decree stares that any Persian harbouring a Jew shall be put to death with him."

The Israelite departed with a broken spirit. "How truly," said he, "have the words of the Bible been fulfilled? 'Ye will offer yourselves for sale unto your enemies, for bondmen and bondwomen, without any one to buy ye.'" (Deut. 28: 68.)

Each day the people marked the passage of time, by saying, "Thus many days more have the Jews to live," and so was another Biblical passage verified.

"And thy life shall hang in doubt before thee .... In the morning thou wilt say, Who would but grant that it were only evening! And at evening thou wilt say, Who would but grant that it were only morning! From the dread of thy heart which thou wilt experience, and from the sight of thy eyes which thou wilt see." (Deut. 28: 66-67.) And with each day the morning increased and hope seemed still more vain.

If we lose a relation or a dear friend, our grief is at first intense, but with each day it loses its poignancy until we are consoled and comforted. How different was it in the case of the condemned Jews; each day the wailing grew stronger, for each day but brought them nearer to the hour of their destruction.

The act of Ahasuerus in intrusting his ring to Haman, was productive of more repentant feelings in the people of Israel than had been the words of their forty-eight prophets.

The prophets had cautioned Israel against serving idols, and urged upon them the necessity of atonement, and yet their words had been unheeded; but with the transmission of the king's ring to Haman's possession, the great call for repentance made itself immediately heard.

But Haman was to receive his punishment. There is a saying of the Rabbis, "If a stone falls upon a pitcher, the pitcher breaks; if the pitcher falls upon the stone, the pitcher also breaks." Be it as it may, it is bad for the pitcher, and bad similarly for the enemies of Israel; for even when Israel strays from righteousness, the instruments of their chastisement are also punished, as in the instances of Nebuchadnezzar, Titus, Haman, &c.

"Then came the maidens of Esther with her chamberlains, and told it to her (the grief of Mordecai)......And she called Hathach and gave him a charge for Mordecai to know what this was, and why this was......And Mordecai told him all that had happened unto him."

Meaning, a dream, which Mordecai had dreamt in the second year of the reign of King Ahasuerus, he now recollected and told to Hathach. "An earthquake shook the world, and darkness and great storms frightened the inhabitants. Two monsters were engaged in deadly conflict, and the noise of the struggle caused the nations to quake with fear. In the midst of the nations was a small weak people, and the other nations wished to blot it from the world. A great distress oppressed this few people and they cried aloud to God for succour and protection. Then a small spring arose, even between the two monsters that were battling, and it increased in size until it seemed to become as wide and boundless as the sea, even as though it would engulf the world. Then the sun broke forth in brightness o'er the earth, and the weak nation, blessed with peace, dwelt safely, though the ruins of many greater nations were spread about it."

This dream he had previously related to Esther, and now through her messenger, he sent the queen this word:

"Behold, thou wilt recollect the dream which I related to thee in thy youth. Arise, pray to God and beseech from Him mercy; then go before the king and speak bravely for the cause of thy people and thy kindred." And further he sent to Esther these words:

"'Imagine not in thy soul,' and say not 'the king has selected me for his queen; and. therefore I need not pray for mercy to Israel.' Into exile thou wert carried as well as the rest of thy people, and the decree which destroys one, destroys all. Do not imagine that thou alone canst escape, of all the Jews. For the sin of thy great grandfather Saul do we now suffer. If he had obeyed the words of Samuel, the wicked Haman had not descended from him who was of the family of Amalek. If Saul had slain Agag, the son of Hamadatha had not bought us for ten thousand silver talents; the Lord would not have delivered Israel into the hands of the wicked. Yet Moses prayed to the Lord for Israel, and Joshua discomforted Amalek; so arise thou, and pray before thy Father in heaven, and he who did execute justice on Amalek will now do the same to his wicked seed. From three oppressors of Israel does Haman draw his life-blood. First, Amalek, who was the first to fight against Israel, and who was defeated by Joshua. Next, Sisera, who laid a hand of iron upon our ancestors and met his punishment through a woman, Ja'el. Lastly, Goliath, who defied the camp of Israel and was laid low by the son of Jesse. Therefore, let not thy prayers cease, for God has ever listened to the breathings of a contrite heart, and for the sake of our ancestors He will show us favour. They were delivered from their enemies when all seemed hopeless. Pray, therefore, and imagine not that thou alone, of all thy people, shall be able to find safety."

On the day when Mordecai ordered his brethren to fast and humble themselves before God, he uttered the following supplication:

"Our God and God of our fathers, seated on Thy throne of grace! Oh Lord of the universe, Thou knowest that not through the promptings of a proud heart did I refuse to bow before Haman. Thee only I fear, and I am jealous of the glory of Thy presence; I could not give to flesh and blood Thy honour--to the creature that which belongs to the Creator alone. Oh God, deliver us from his hand, and let his feet become entangled in the net which he has spread for us. Let the world know, oh our Redeemer, that Thou hast not forgotten the promise which supports and strengthens us in our dispersion. 'And yet for all that, though they be in the land of their enemies, will I not cast them away, neither will I loath them to destroy them utterly, to break my covenant with them, for I am the Lord their God.'"

When Esther received the message of Mordecai, she too ordered a fast, and replaced her royal apparel with the sackcloth and ashes of mourning; and bowing her face before the Lord, she uttered this heartfelt prayer:

"God of Israel, from the beginning of time Thou hast reigned; the world and all it contains Thy power has created; to Thee, Thy handmaid calls for help! I am alone, oh God, without father and mother. Even as a poor woman, who begs from door to door, do I come before Thee for mercy, from window to window in the house of Ahasuerus. From Thee alone can help and salvation flow. Oh, Father of the fatherless! stand upon the right hand of the orphan, I beseech Thee; give her mercy and favour in the eyes of Ahasuerus, that he may be moved to grant her petition for the lives of her people. 'May the words of my mouth and the meditations of my heart be acceptable before Thee, oh Lord, my Rock and my Redeemer. Amen!'"

"And it came to pass on the third day."

After Esther had fasted three days, on the third day of her fast she arose from the ashes on which she had reposed, removed her garments of sackcloth, arrayed herself in her gorgeous robes of state, wearing her richest ornaments of gold of Ophir and precious stones, and prepared to enter the presence of the king. First, however, in voice broken by sobs and strong emotion, she again in privacy addressed the Most High.

"Before Thee, oh God of Abraham, of Isaac, and of Jacob, before Thee, oh God of Benjamin, my ancestor, I pray. Before Thee I pray, ere I appeal unto my husband, Ahasuerus, the king, to supplicate for Thy people, Israel, whom Thou didst separate from other nations, to whom Thou gayest Thy holy law. Thy chosen people, oh God, who praise Thee three times daily, saying, 'Holy, holy, holy, is the Lord of Hosts; the whole earth is full of His glory.' As Thou didst save Chananyah, Mishael, and Azaryah from the raging furnace, and Daniel from the jaws of the lions, so save us now from the enemies who lie in wait for our destruction. Give me grace, I pray Thee, in the eyes of my lord, the king. Through our sins, oh Lord, are we condemned; yea all of us in whom the blood of Abraham quickens; yet surely the children should not suffer for the father's sin! If we have provoked Thy wrath, why should tender hearts and innocent babes be with us condemned to death? Oh remember the merit of Abraham to our salvation. Ten times didst Thou tempt him and he remained faithful before Thee. Protect the children of Thy beloved friends, Abraham, Isaac, and Jacob; banish from about them the evil with which Haman has encircled them." And Esther wept bitterly, and her tongue refused to utter the words which rose to her lips. "I go now," she said in her heart, "unto the king; oh let Thy angels of mercy precede my footsteps; let the favour of Abraham go before me, and the merit of Isaac support my trembling frame; let the kindness of Jacob be in my mouth, and the purity of Joseph upon my tongue. As Thou didst listen to the voice of Jonah when he called upon Thee, so listen now to me. Oh God, whose eye seest the inmost recesses of the heart, remember the merit of the pious ones who served Thee faithfully, and for their sakes allow not my petition to be rejected. Amen."

And Esther took with her two of her waiting maids and entered the court of the king. On the arm of one she leaned, while the other followed bearing her train, that the golden fabric might not sweep along the ground. She concealed her grief in her heart, and her face was bright and her appearance happy.

It happened, when the king saw Esther standing in the court, that he was very wroth to think that she had overstepped both law and custom. Esther glanced up, and reading his anger in his eyes, became greatly terrified, and leaned heavily upon the handmaid who supported her. God saw her failing motion, and, pitying the distress of the orphan, he gave her grace before the king. The anger vanished from his eyes, and rising from his seat, he advanced to Esther and embraced and kissed her. With his arm about her neck he looked into her eyes, and seeing there her fear, he said, "What wilt thou, Queen Esther? Why art thou alarmed? Our laws are not meant for thee; thou art my friend; wherefore didst thou not speak when thy eyes looked upon me?"

And Esther answered:

"Because, my lord, when first I looked upon thee, thy glory and thy honour terrified me."

*   *   *   *   *

Esther had three objects in inviting Haman to her banquet with the king.

First. She did not wish Haman to think that she knew of his guilt, or was conspiring against him, which he might suspect if he discovered that Hatach carried messages between herself and Mordecai.

Secondly. She desired, in pursuance of her plan, to make the king jealous of Haman. Naturally he would ask himself why she had invited only Haman, thus singling him from, and honouring him above, the other princes.

Thirdly. That Israel might not be too sure of her efforts and so depend upon her altogether. Rather to let them find additional reasons for relying solely on the Lord.

"Then said unto him Zeresh, his wife, with all her friends, 'Let them make a gallows,'" &c.

"Thou canst never prevail against Mordecai by means which have already been brought to bear against his people," said Zeresh to Haman. "Thou canst not kill him with a knife or sword, for Isaac was delivered from the same; neither canst thou drown him, for Moses and the people of Israel walked safely through the sea. Fire will not burn him, for with Chananyah and his comrades it failed; wild beasts will not tear him, for Daniel was rescued from the lions' fangs; neither will a dungeon contain him, for Joseph walked to honour through a prison's gates. Even if we deprive him of sight we can not prevail against him, for Samson was made blind, and yet destroyed thousands of the Philistines. There is but one way left us; we must hang him."

It was in accordance with this advice that Haman built the gallows fifty cubits high. After he had erected this dread instrument of death, he sought the presence of Mordecai, to gloat over his coming triumph. He found the Jew in the college, with his pupils gathered around him. Their loins were girded with sackcloth, and they wept at the words which their teacher was addressing to them.

"To-morrow," said Haman, "I will first destroy these children, and I will then hang Mordecai on the gallows I have prepared."

He remained in the school and saw the mothers of the pupils bring them their meals; but they all refused to eat, saying, "By the life of our teacher, Mordecai, we will neither eat nor drink; fasting will we die."

"In that night sleep fled from the king."

Ahasuerus imagined that Haman was a lover of Esther, because he alone, of all the princes, was invited to her banquet. When he slumbered he dreamed that he saw Haman with a sword in his hand, attempting his life, and awakening in fright, he was unable again to sleep. So he arose and called to Shimshi, his scribe, who was a relative of Haman, and bade him open the book of the chronicles of events which happened during the reigns of the kings of Persia and Media, and read to him from the same. The first page at which Shimshi opened the book contained the record of Mordecai's discovery and disclosure of the treason of Bigthana and Theresh, the king's chamberlains. The scribe did not wish to read this, and was about turning to another portion, when the king saw the action, and commanded him to read from the page which was first spread before him.

"Haman, therefore, said to the king, 'For the man whom the king desireth to honour let them bring a royal apparel,'" &c.

When the king heard this advice his suspicions seemed to him as facts. "He wishes to put on my royal apparel," thought Ahasuerus, "and to place my crown upon his head; then he will destroy me and reign in my stead."

Then said the king to Haman, "Bring from my state wardrobe the garment of purple from Ethiopia, the garment set with precious stones, to each of the four corners of which a golden chain is attached; bring also the ornaments which I wore on the day of my coronation, my hat of Ethiopian manufacture, and my royal cloak, embroidered with pearls from Africa. Go, then, to my stables, and take from thence the best steed which I possess; array Mordecai, the Jew, in the garments, and place him upon the horse."

And Haman answered, "There are many Jews in Shushan who are called Mordecai; which one is to have the honour?"

"Do all this that thou hast spoken," replied the king, "to Mordecai, the Jew, who lives by the king's gates; he who hath spoken well to the king and saved his life."

When Haman heard these words the blood seemed to congeal in his heart; his face grew blanched, his eyes became dim, and his mouth as though paralysed; with great effort he said:

"Oh king, how--how--can I tell which Mordecai thou meanest?"

"I have but just said," returned the king; "he who dwells at my gates."

"But he hates me," exclaims Haman, "me and my ancestors; do not force me to do him this honour, and I will pay ten thousand silver talents into thy treasury."

The king answered:

"Though I should give that ten thousand talents to Mordecai, aye, and give him also thy house to rule over it, yet this honour which thou hast spoken shouldst thou also do to him."

"My ten sons shall run before thy chariot," pleaded Haman; "they shall be thy slaves, if thou wilt but forego this order "

The king answered:

"Though thou, and thy wife, and thy ten sons should be slaves to Mordecai, yet this honour should be also his." But Haman still entreated:

"Lo, Mordecai is but a common subject of the king, appoint him ruler of a city, a province, or a street--let that be the honour paid him."

And again the king replied:

"Though I should appoint him ruler over al my provinces, though I should cause him to command all who owe me obedience on sea and land, still this honour, too, which thou hast spoken, should be done him. Surely he who has spoken to the advantage of his king, he who has preserved the life of his king, deserves all that should belong to the one whom the king most delights to honour."

"But the letters," continued Haman; "the letters which have been sent to all thy provinces, condemning him and his people to death.'

"Peace, peace," exclaimed the king; "though they should be recalled, Mordecai should still be honoured as thou hast spoken. Say no more, Haman; as thou hast spoken, do quickly; leave out nothing of all that thou hast said."

When Haman saw that all appeal was useless, he obeyed the king's orders with a heavy heart. With the garments and the richly caparisoned steed he sought Mordecai, and said, "Arise, oh Mordecai the righteous, descendant of Abraham, Isaac, and Jacob, arise from thy sackcloth and ashes; lo, they have prevailed more than my talents of silver, and thy God has bestowed mercy upon thee. Arise, Mordecai, throw off thy sackcloth and ashes and don these royal garments."

Then Mordecai answered, "Oh, wicked Haman! the time cometh when thou shalt eat wormwood and drink gall, oh son of Amalek."

"Come," returned Haman, "dress and mount the steed; the orders of the king must be obeyed."

Haman anointed Mordecai with sweet perfumes; arrayed him in royal robes, and mounted him upon the king's horse, according to his words and the commands of Ahasuerus. Then a procession was formed. Seventeen thousand soldiers were detailed as escort and divided into two bodies; one preceded and the other followed Mordecai, who was thus in the centre on a horse led by Haman. As they marched through the streets of Shushan the soldiers shouted, "Thus shall be done to the man whom the king desireth to honour."

When the Jews beheld this great procession, and Mordecai honoured in the midst of it, they followed after; and in return to the shouts of the troops they called out loudly, "Thus shall be done to the man who serves the King who created heaven and earth, and whom he desireth to honour." When Esther saw her kinsman thus arrayed, she thanked the Lord and praised Him.

"With the Psalmist I may say," she exclaimed, "'He raiseth up out of the dust the poor, from the dunghill he lifteth up the needy.' (Ps. 113: 7.) 'That he may set him with princes, even with the princes of His people.'"

Mordecai also praised the Lord, and said:

"'Thou hast changed my mourning into dancing for me, Thou hast loosened my sackcloth and girded me with joy; I will extol Thee, oh Lord, for Thou hast lifted me up, and hast not suffered my enemies to rejoice over me.'" (Ibid. 30: 12.)

Four distinct services did Haman render Mordecai. First, he was his hairdresser, for he shaved and anointed him. Secondly, he was his *valet*, for he attended him in the bath. Thirdly, he was his footman, for he led the horse Mordecai rode. Fourthly, he was his trumpeter, for he proclaimed before him: "Thus shall be done to the man whom the king desireth to honour."

"And Haman related to Zeresh his wife," &c.

Haman received but little comfort from his friends. "Thou wilt surely fall," said his wife; "for those who endeavoured to burn Chananyah, Mishael, and Azaryah in the fiery furnace, were themselves consumed in the flames; take heed, for thou wilt surely fall before this Jew."

When the servants of the king saw that Haman was losing prestige, they too turned against him. Charbonyah told the king that Haman had designs against his royal person. "If thou believest not me," said the sycophant, "send to his house and there wilt thou find a gallows fifty cubits high for Mordecai, because he spoke well of thee and saved thy life."

The king said to Mordecai, "Go bring thy enemy Haman and hang him upon the gallows; do to him whatever is pleasing to thee."

Haman appealed to Mordecai and begged to be put to death by the sword, but Mordecai hearkened not to his words.

"Who digs a pit for another deserves to fall therein himself,' said he; "he who rolls a stone against another must not complain if it turn back and crush himself."

The following is the letter sent under the king's seal to counteract the decree issued against the Jews:

"To the noblemen, princes, and inhabitants of all our provinces, peace. Our government cannot prosper unless its people are united; let this find you all living in fraternal harmony. Let all the people of our provinces trade together as one nation; let them have compassion and charity towards all nations and creeds, and honour all peaceful kingdoms of the earth. They who would deceive the king by evil reports concerning any people in our midst, and endeavour to obtain permission to exterminate peaceful, law-abiding persons, deserve death, and should meet with it. Let such as they perish, and the remainder live in harmony, forming a bond of peace never to be broken; aye, of triple thickness, that it may never grow weak. Let no insult be offered to any people.

"Esther is pious, worthy, and our queen, and Mordecai is the wisest of his age; he is without fault, he and his people. Through the advice of Haman, the son of Hamdatha, was our former decree issued, which now is declared null and void. And further we decree that the Jews may arise and protect themselves, aye, and take vengeance on such as raise a bloody hand against them.

"He who created Heaven and Earth has put these words in our heart and in our mouth, and thus we utter and decree them according to the laws of Persia and Media."

---

5. King Solomon, The Wise

"Seest thou a man that is diligent in his work? Before kings may he place himself; let him not place himself before obscure men." (Prov. 22: 29.)

In this verse Solomon alludes to himself. He built the holy temple in seven years, while he occupied fourteen years in erecting his palace. Not because his palace was more elegant or more elaborate in its workmanship than was the temple, but because he was diligent in his work to finish God's house, while his own house could await time and opportunity.

Four cases of comparative righteousness between fathers and children may be noted:

First. A righteous man begets a righteous son.

Second. A wicked man begets a wicked son.

Third. A wicked man begets a righteous son.

Fourth. A righteous man begets a wicked son.

To each of these cases we may find a Biblical allusion; to each of them we may apply a parable and a proverb.

In reference to the righteous father and the righteous son, we find the following verse (Psalm 45: 17): "Instead of thy fathers shall be thy children." And we may apply the parable of the good fig tree which brought forth luscious fruit.

In reference to the wicked father and the wicked son we have in Numbers 32: 14: "And now behold, ye are risen up in your fathers' stead, a new race of sinful men."

Ancient is the proverb, "From the wicked proceedeth wickedness;" and applicable, the parable of the serpent bringing forth an asp.

In the third case, the wicked father begets a righteous son, as it is written, "Instead of the thorn shall come up the fir tree." And to this can we apply the parable of the rose budding on the bramble bush.

Lastly, a righteous man has a wicked son, as it is written, "Instead of wheat, thorns come forth." (Job 21: 40.) And we have also the parable of the attractive peach tree which brought forth bitter fruit.

Solomon was a king, the son of a king; the wise son of a wise father; a righteous man's righteous child. All the incidents in David's life, all his characteristics were paralleled in the life of Solomon.

David reigned for forty years, as it is written, "And the days that David governed Israel were forty years."

Of Solomon it is written, "And Solomon reigned in Jerusalem over all Israel forty years." David expressed himself by "words," as it is written, "And these are the last *words* of David."

Solomon likewise expressed himself by "words."

"The *words* of Koheleth the son of David." (Eccles. 1: 1.)

David said, "All is *vanity*;" as it is written, "For *vanity* only do all men make a noise." (Psalm 39: 7.)

Solomon expressed himself with the same word, "*vanity*."

"*Vanity* of *vanities*, saith Koheleth." (Eccles. 1: 2.)

David wrote books, viz.: the five books of Psalms; and Solomon wrote three books: Proverbs, Ecclesiastes, and the Song of Solomon.

David composed songs: "And David spoke unto the Lord the words of this song." (Samuel 22: I.)

Solomon also composed a song: "The song of songs, which is Solomon's."

He was the wise king alluded to in Proverbs 16: 23, "The heart of the wise maketh his mouth intelligent, and upon his lips increaseth information." Meaning that the heart of the wise is full of knowledge and understanding; but this is shown to the world through the words of his mouth. And, by uttering with his lips the thoughts of his mind (or heart) he increases the information of the people. If a man possessing brilliant diamonds and precious stones, keeps his jewels concealed, no one is aware of their value;

but if he allows them to be seen, their worth becomes known, and the pleasure of ownership is enhanced.

Applying this comparison to the case of Solomon, while his wisdom was locked up in his own breast it was of value to no one; but when he had given to the world his three books, men became acquainted with his great abilities. "The words of his lips increased the information of his people," and so great was his reputation that any one in doubt concerning the meaning of a Biblical passage sought the king for an interpretation.

Not only in sacred lore did he raise the standard of education. He had mastered and taught the sciences of Natural Philosophy, Physiology, Botany, Agriculture, Mathematics in all its branches, Astronomy, Chemistry, and in fact all useful studies. He also taught Rhetoric and the rules of Poesy. In alliterative and alphabetical versification he was an adept.

"And in addition to this that Koheleth was wise, he continually taught the people knowledge."

If what others said interested the people, how much more readily did they listen to Solomon; with how much more ease did they comprehend him!

We may illustrate his method of teaching by the following comparison. There was a basket without ears, filled with fine fruit, but the owner was unable to get it to his home on account of the difficulty in carrying it, until a wise man, seeing the predicament, attached handles to the basket, when it could be carried with great ease.

So did Solomon remove difficulties from the path of the student.

Rabbi Huna further illustrated this same thing. "There was once," he said, "a well of most pure and excellent water; but the well was so deep that the people were not able to reach the water, until a man of wisdom taking a bucket attached to it one rope after another until the whole was long enough to reach to the water. So was it with Solomon's teachings. The Bible is a well of truth, but its teachings are too deep for the understanding of some. Solomon, however, introduced parables and proverbs suited to the comprehension of all, through which means a knowledge of the law became readily obtainable."

Rabbi Simon, the son of Chalafta, related the following parable: "A certain king had an officer to whom he was much attached, and whom he took great delight in honouring. One day he said to this favourite, 'Come, express a wish, anything that I can give thee shall be thine.' Then this officer thought, 'If I ask the king for gold or silver or precious stones, he will give what I ask; even though I desire higher honour and more exalted station he will grant it, yet I will ask him for his daughter, for if he grants that, all the rest will be included.'"

When the Lord appeared to Solomon in Gibon, and said to him in a dream, "What shall I give to thee?" Solomon reflected, "If I ask for gold, silver, or jewels, the Lord will give them to me; I will ask, however, for wisdom; if that is granted me, all other good things are included." Therefore, he replied, "Give to thy servant an understanding heart."

Then said the Lord:

"Because thou hast asked for wisdom, and requested not wealth or dominion over thy enemies; by thy life, wisdom and knowledge shall be thine, and through them thou shalt obtain wealth and power."

"*And Solomon awoke, and behold it was a dream.*" He wandered into the fields, and he heard the voices of the animals; the ass brayed, the lion roared, the dog barked, the rooster crowed, and behold he understood what they said, one to the other.

An ox, even after being killed and dressed, may be made to stand, provided the sinews are uncut; but if they are severed, cords are required to hold the body together. While Solomon remained free from sin his prayers were granted him for his own sake, but when he departed from the righteous way, the Lord said to him, "For the sake of David, my servant, I will not take the kingdom from thee in thy lifetime."

Solomon said, "Vanity of vanities; vanity, even as a shadow." A shadow of what nature? The shadow of a tower or a tree remains the shadow for awhile, and then is lost, but the shadow of a bird flieth away, and there is neither bird nor shadow. David said, "Our days are as a passing shadow," and Rabbi Huna said, "Our days pass quickly from us, even as the shadow of a flying bird."

With the word vanity, Solomon expresses seven stages of a man's life.

The infant he compares to a king; riding in his little coach, and being kissed, admired, and praised by all. The child of three or four years he compares to a pig, fond of the dirt and soiling itself with its food. The child of ten is fond of dress; the youth adorns himself and seeks a wife; the married man is bold as the dog in seeking a livelihood for himself and family; and the old man he likens to an ape.

"God gave wisdom to Solomon."

When Solomon was about building the temple, he applied to the king of Egypt for men to aid him in the work. Pharaoh, consulting his astrologers, selected those men who were to die within the year. When they arrived at Jerusalem the wise king sent them back at once. With each man he sent a shroud, and directed them to say to their master, "If Egypt is too poor to supply shrouds for her dead, and for that purpose sends them to me, behold here they are, the men and the shrouds together; take them and bury thy dead."

He was wiser than all other men, wiser even than Adam, who gave names to all the animals of the world, and even to himself, saying, "From the dust of the ground I was formed, and therefore shall my name be *Adam*." Rabbi Tanchum said, "Where is thy wisdom and thy understanding, oh king Solomon? Thy words not only contradict themselves, but also the words of David, thy father. He said, 'Not the dead can praise the Lord' (Psalm 115: 17), and thou didst say, 'Thereupon praised I the dead that are already dead, more than the living who are still alive.' (Eccles. 4 2.) And thou didst also say, 'For a living dog fareth better than a dead lion.'" (Ibid. 9: 4.)

These seeming contradictions, however, may be readily explained. David said, "Not the dead can praise the Lord," meaning that we should study God's law during life, as after its cessation ’twould be impossible. Solomon said, "Thereupon praised I the dead that are already dead." When the children of Israel sinned in the wilderness, Moses prayed for them for their own sakes, and his prayer was unanswered; but when he said, "Remember Abraham, and Isaac, and Israel, Thy servants," he met with a prompt reply. Therefore did not Solomon speak well in saying, "Praise the dead that are already dead?" Take another instance. A king may decree laws, but many of his subjects may disregard them. Sometimes these laws, even if earnestly observed during the life of the one who made them, may be repealed or become obsolete after his death. Moses, however, made many stringent laws, which have been observed through all generations. Therefore, Solomon said well, "Thereupon will I praise the dead."

Rabbi Judah, in the name of Rab, further explained this verse. He said, "What is the meaning of the following passage? 'Show me a token for good, that they who hate me may see it and be ashamed.' (Psalm 76:17.) David said to God, after his sin with Bathsheba (Samuel 2), 'Sovereign of the Universe, pardon me for my sin.' The Lord answered, 'I will pardon thee.' Then said David, 'Show me the token in my lifetime,' but God said, 'Not in thy lifetime, but in the lifetime of Solomon, thy son, will I show it.' Thus, when Solomon dedicated the temple, though he prayed with fervent devotion, he was not answered until he said, 'O Lord God, turn not away from the face of thy anointed. Remember the pious deeds of David, thy servant.' (2 Chron. 6:42.) Then he was speedily answered, for in the next verse we read, 'And when Solomon had made an end of praying, a fire came down from Heaven and consumed the burnt offering and the sacrifices, and the glory of the Lord filled the house.' Then were the enemies of David put to shame, for all Israel knew that God had pardoned David for his sin. Did not Solomon say well then, 'Thereupon praised I the dead?' For this reason, further on in the chapter we read, 'And on the three-and-twentieth day of the seventh month he dismissed the people unto their tents, joyful and glad of heart, because of the good that the Lord had done for David, and for Solomon, and for Israel, His people."

Solomon said, "For a living dog fareth better than a dead lion."

Expounding this verse, Rabbi Judah said, in the name of Rab, "What is the meaning of the verse, 'Let me know, O Lord, my end, and the measure of my days, what it is; I wish to know when I shall cease to be.' (Psalm 39: 5.)

"David said to God, 'Let me know, O Lord, my end.' God answered, 'I have decreed that for each one his end must be veiled in the future.' Then David said, 'What is the measure of my days?' Again God replied, 'No man may know the measure of his days.' 'I wish to know when I shall cease to be,' continued David; and God answered, 'Thou wilt die on a Sabbath.'

"'Let me die the day after,' entreated David, but the Lord answered, 'No; then the kingdom will be Solomon's, and one reign may not take away from another reign even so much as a hair's breadth.' 'Then let me die the day before,' exclaimed David, 'for a day in Thy courts is better than a thousand elsewhere,' and God said, 'One day spent by thee in studying my law is more acceptable than the thousand burnt offerings thy son Solomon will sacrifice.'

"It was David's custom to pass every Sabbath in the study of the Bible and its precepts, and he was thus engaged upon the Sabbath which was to be his last. Back of the king's palace there was an orchard, and David, hearing a noise therein, walked thither to ascertain its cause. On entering the orchard he fell to the ground, dead.

"The noise in the orchard had been caused by the barking of the king's dogs, who had not that day received their food. Solomon sent a message to the Rabbinical College, saying, 'My father lies dead in his orchard; is it allowable to remove his body on the Sabbath? The dogs of my father are entreating for their food; is it proper to cut meat for them to-day?' This answer was returned by the college: 'Thy father's body should not be removed to-day, but give meat to the dogs.' Therefore said Solomon, 'A living dog fareth better than a dead lion,' justly comparing the son of Jesse to that king of beasts."

Solomon was the chosen of the Lord, who called him, through the mouth of Nathan, the prophet, *Yedidiah* (the beloved one). He was called *Solomon* (peace), because in his days peace reigned, as it is written, "And Judah and Israel dwelt in safety." (Kings 5:5.) He was called *Ithiel* (God with me) because God was his support.

And when Solomon sat upon the throne of his father David, all the nations of the earth feared him; all the people of the earth listened anxiously for his words of wisdom.

Afterwards he had a throne made especially for himself by Hiram, the son of a widow of Tyre. It was covered with gold of Ophir, set with all kinds of precious and valuable stones. The seat of the throne was approached by six broad steps. The right side of the first step was guarded by an ox made of pure gold, and the left side by a lion of the same metal. On the right of the second step stood a bear also of gold, and upon the left a lamb, symbolical of enemies dwelling in peace together. On the right of the third step was placed a golden camel, and on the left an eagle. On the right of the fourth step there was also an eagle with outspread wings, and on the left a bird of prey, all of the same precious metal. On the fifth step to the right a golden cat crouching in position; on the left a chicken. On the right of the sixth step a hawk was fashioned, and on the left side a pigeon, and upon the top of the step a pigeon clutched a hawk in her talons. These animals were designed to typify the time when those of adverse natures shall unite in harmony, as it is written in Isaiah (11: 6), "And the wolf shall then dwell with the sheep."

Over the throne was hung a chandelier of gold with seven branches; it was ornamented with roses, knobs, bowls, and tongs; and on the seven branches the names of the seven patriarchs, Adam, Noah, Shem, Abraham, Isaac, Jacob, and Job, were engraven.

On the second row of the branches of the chandelier were engraven the names of the seven pious ones of the world, Levi, Kehath, Amram, Moses, Aaron, Eldad, and Madad. Above all this hung a golden churn filled with pure olive oil, and on this was engraven the names of Eli, the High Priest, and his two sons, Hophni and Phineas, and on the other side the names of the two sons of Aaron, Nadab and Abihu.

On the right hand of the throne two chairs were placed, one for the High Priest, and the other for the Vice-High Priest, and upon the left side, from the top to the ground, seventy-one chairs were stationed as seats for the members of the Sanhedrim.

The throne was made upon wheels, that it could be moved easily wherever the king might desire it to be.

The Lord gave Solomon the power of understanding the nature and properties of the herbs of the field and the trees of the forest, as it is written, "And he spoke concerning the trees, from the cedar tree that is upon the Lebanon even unto the hyssop that springeth out of the wall. He spoke also concerning the beasts, and concerning the fowls, and concerning the creeping things, and concerning the fishes." (1 Kings 5: 13.)

It is said that Solomon ruled the whole world, and this verse is quoted as proof of the assertion, "And Solomon was ruling over all the kingdoms, which brought presents, and served Solomon all the days of his life." (1 Kings 5: 1.)

All the kingdoms congratulated Solomon as the worthy successor of his father, David, whose fame was great among the nations; all save one, the kingdom of Sheba, the capital of which was called Kitore.

To this kingdom Solomon sent a letter:

"From me, King Solomon, peace to thee and to thy government. Let it be known to thee that the Almighty God has made me to reign over the whole world, the kingdoms of the North, the South, the East, and the West. Lo, they have come to me with their congratulations, all save thee alone.

"Come thou also, I pray thee, and submit to my authority, and much honour shall be done thee; but if thou refusest, behold, I shall by force compel thy acknowledgment.

"To thee, Queen Sheba, is addressed this letter in peace from me, King Solomon, the son of David."

Now when Queen Sheba received this letter, she sent in haste for her elders and counsellors to ask their advice as to the nature of her reply.

They spoke but lightly of the message and the one who sent it, but the queen did not regard their words. She sent a vessel, carrying many presents of different metals, minerals, and precious stones, to Solomon. It was after a voyage of two years' time that these presents arrived at Jerusalem, and in a letter intrusted to the captain the queen said. "After thou hast received the message then I myself will come to thee." And in two years after this time Queen Sheba arrived at Jerusalem.

When Solomon heard that the queen was coming he sent Benayahu, the son of Yehoyadah, the general of his army, to meet her. When the queen saw him she thought he was the king, and she alighted from her carriage.

Then Benayahu asked, "Why alightest thou from thy carriage?" And she answered, "Art thou not his majesty, the king?"

"No," replied Benayahu, "I am but one of his officers."

Then the queen turned back and said to her ladies in attendance, "If this is but one of the officers, and he is so noble and imposing in appearance, how great must be his superior, the king."

And Benayahu, the son of Yehoyadah, conducted Queen Sheba to the palace of the king.

Solomon prepared to receive his visitor in an apartment laid and lined with glass, and the queen at first was so deceived by the appearance that she imagined the king to be sitting in water.

And when the queen had tested Solomon's wisdom, and witnessed his magnificence, she said:

"I believed not what I heard, but now I have come, and my eyes have seen it all; behold, the half has not been told to me. Happy are thy servants who stand before thee continually to listen to thy words of wisdom. Blessed be the Lord thy God, who hath placed thee on a throne to rule righteously and in justice."

When other kingdoms heard the words of the queen of Sheba they feared Solomon exceedingly, and he became greater than all the other kings of the earth in wisdom and in wealth. Solomon was born in the year 2912 A.M., and reigned over Israel forty years. Four hundred and thirty-three years elapsed between the date of Solomon's reign and that of the temple's destruction.

PART THIRD.THE RABBIS, THEIR TEACHINGS AND INCIDENTS IN THEIR LIVES

RABBI JUDAH, THE "CHIEF"

RABBI JUDAH, the holy, sometimes called, by reason of his eminence, simply "Rabbi," received his education in the different colleges and from the various sources of learning open to the student in his early days. He was a man of immense wealth, and when he reached the dignity of chief or patriarch, he expended a great portion of his riches in the assistance and for the benefit of the poor. His authority among his contemporaries was superior to that allowed any of his predecessors. He commanded both their love and respect, and it is said that no man, since the time of Moses, combined such advanced learning with authority and dignity equal to his. He was, too, like Moses, truly modest and careful to avoid all pomp and display of power.

He had his chair placed near the entrance of his lecture-room, to spare his hearers the necessity of rising while he passed among them, an honour exacted by the other chiefs. Through his influence with Antoninus, his people were permitted to study the law publicly and were granted many privileges previously denied them, and immunity from many persecutions under which they had previously suffered. It was while he occupied his high position in favour and affluence, that he collected the opinions and debates of pre-ceding Rabbis, now forming the *Mishna*.

The emperor once sent a valuable diamond to Rabbi Judah, requesting a token of friendship in return. The Rabbi sent him a *Mezuzah*.

"My friend," said the emperor, "this gift of thine is of small value, compared to the rich offering which I despatched to thee."

"There is a difference between my gift and thine," returned the Rabbi. "That which thou gavest to me I must watch and guard lest it be stolen from me; but this which I send will watch and guard over thee, even as it is written, 'When thou walkest it will lead thee, and when thou liest down it will watch over thee.'"

Rabbi Judah desired to wed the widow of Rabbi Eleazer, and he sent a messenger to her charged with his proposals. The answer which she returned thereto was this:

"Shall a vessel once used for holy purposes be now used for those less sacred?" Implying that Rabbi Eleazer, the son of Simon, had been a greater man than was Rabbi Judah. Her answer was of the same import as the proverb, "Shall the shepherd hang his work vessels where the master of the house hung his ornaments?"

On receiving this answer Rabbi Judah sent another message to her.

"You are right," said he; "your husband was a more learned scholar than am I, but in good deeds I am at least his equal."

The widow replied:

"Still we differ; I know not that my husband was more learned than Rabbi Judah, but he was his superior in righteousness."

But was Rabbi Eleazer the superior of Rabbi Judah in learning?

It was the custom in the colleges for the teachers and learned Rabbis to sit upon elevated chairs while the pupils were seated on benches, near the floor. When Rabbi Simon, the son of Gamliel, Rabbi Joshua, the son of Korcha, and other celebrated Rabbis were occupying the chairs, Rabbi Eleazer, the son of Simon, and Rabbi Judah were sitting near the floor. Rabbi Simon, son of Gamliel, the father of Rabbi Judah, desiring that some mark of distinction should be paid to his son, induced the teachers to elevate him to one of the chairs. This was done; and then Rabbi Joshua spoke, saying, "He who hath a father to speak for him may live; but he who hath none, may do the best he can, and die."

On hearing this the Rabbis elevated Rabbi Eleazer, the son of Rabbi Simon, also, but Rabbi Eleazer felt himself slighted and neglected, because the above words were spoken previous to his elevation, and said, "Is Rabbi Judah better than I?"

Never after did he feel friendly towards Rabbi Judah. Previously he had assisted the latter in preparing questions to be laid before the college, but now he made light of Judah's inquiries, saying, "They are not worthy of being considered."

This treatment was very trying to the feelings of Rabbi Judah, and he complained to his father of the insults to which he was subjected.

"Be not displeased, my son," replied the latter, "nor take umbrage at the words of Eleazer. Behold, he is a lion, and the son of a lion (a most learned man, and the son of a most learned man), whilst thou art a lion, but the son of a fox (a learned man thyself; but not possessing a learned father), therefore he is thy superior."

This is probably the reason why Rabbi Judah has said, "The world has seen three meek men,--my father, the sons of Bethéra, and Jonathan, the son of Saul."

The sons of Bethéra vacated their positions as chiefs of the college in favour of Hillel, pronouncing him a man of superior learning, therefore their meekness. Jonathan, the son of Saul, said to David, "Thou shalt reign over Israel, and I shall be a second to thee," therefore his meekness; and Rabbi Simon, the son of Gamliel, because he called himself a fox.

Rabbi Judah suffered greatly from bodily pain for thirteen years previous to his death, and when he felt his end on earth approaching he called his children to him and spoke to them as follows:

"Obey the voice of your mother, oh, my children, and remember the teachings of the Most High. Keep a light burning in my room, and let Joseph, the Ophnite, and Simon, the Ephraimite, faithful servants to me in my life, attend me also in my death. And now, my children, let me see the sages of Israel once more."

When the sages entered, according to his request, he said:

"Let no orations or eulogies be made for me in the cities. Open my college, and continue your holy duties thirty days after my death. Although my son Simon is a man of wisdom and understanding, yet I desire that my son Gamliel shall be my successor. Chaninah, the son of Chamah, shall sit in the second seat, next to the chief. I weep that I may study God's law no more."

Then he raised his two hands towards heaven, and said:

"Oh, Lord God of the universe, Thou knowest whether I have worked faithfully with these hands for Thy glory, to obtain a knowledge of Thy law. May it be acceptable to Thee, oh, Sovereign of the universe, that I may rest in peace."

On the day of the Rabbi's death the Rabbins proclaimed a fast, and a day of prayer, for their beloved chief. They also forbid any announcement of his death to interrupt their devotion, and they continued praying until a signal was thrown from the Rabbi's house; they all experienced a shock, as though a heavy missile had struck them, and ceased praying.

Rabbi Judah was buried on the eve of Sabbath; with him died the meekness among the people, and the fear of God.

It is said that the Rabbi had a servant who was richer than the emperor. He acquired his wealth from the sale of the litter from the Rabbi's stables, which gives some idea of the number of animals Rabbi Judah possessed.

Simon, The Righteous

Simon was performing the functions of High Priest during the triumphal career of Alexander, about the year 3000. The sons of Judah found no cause to oppose this warrior, and when, after his first victories over the Persian army, he came to Syria on his way to Egypt, they joined with the kingdoms which paid him homage.

Simon the Righteous, as representative of the nation, proceeded to the seacoast to greet the conqueror, attired in his priestly robes, and attended by a number of priests and nobles in the full dignity of their costumes.

Alexander at once approached the High Priest and greeted him warmly; and when his officers expressed their astonishment at this mark of condescension, he told them that the form and feature of this same priest, clad in the same robes he now wore, had appeared to him in a dream and promised him success in arms.

Alexander was conducted through the Temple by Simon. On entering, he said, "Blessed be the Lord of this house." He was charmed with the beauty of the structure, and expressed a desire to have a statue of himself erected as a remembrance, between the porch and the altar. Simon informed him that it was not allowable to erect any statue or image within the Temple walls, but promised that, as a remembrance, the males born among his people that year should be called Alexander. That is the manner in which the Rabbis Alexander obtained their names.

Alexander continued well-disposed towards the High Priest, and through his intercessions granted the Jews religious freedom and release from all tributary burden during the Sabbatic year; and the Jews entered Alexander's army, and assisted in his conquests.

This state of affairs lasted unfortunately only until the death of Alexander. In the quarrels among his generals, which followed and continued for two decades, the Jewish people suffered much. The armies of Antigonus and his son Demetrius destroyed the fertile fields, gave wings to blessed peace, and filled the inhabitants of Judea with horror and dismay.

’Twas on the Sabbath that Jerusalem was taken by storm. The mighty walls, impenetrable strongholds since the days of Nehemiah, were again breached and broken, and the city laid open to her enemies.

These occurrences Simon lived to see, and his trust in God as well as his love for his people were sorely tried. Yet he did not waver in his faith. He fortified the Temple, repaired its damaged places, and raised the foundation of the five courts. He enlarged the water reservoir in the Temple to provide against a scarcity during siege times, and ever after that the Temple was well supplied with water; a matter of note considering the climate and the soil of Jerusalem.

Neither did Simon neglect the spiritual interests of his people. He did not lead them to believe that their strength and safety depended only upon earthly means. He remembered well the teachings of his predecessors, "Upon three things does the salvation of Israel depend: on the observance of the law, upon reconciliation with God by means of grace furnished by the Temple worship, and upon deeds of benevolence."

The many wars and disturbances which agitated the period of his life were productive of much and varied evil, and the extremely pious sought, as in the days of the prophets, to withdraw from the world and consecrate themselves to God by Nazarean vows.

Simon did not approve of this, and protested against it in many ways. He made an exception, however, in one case, that of a young and handsome shepherd, whom he found to be really sincere in his desire. When the latter came to him, desiring to become a Nazeer, the High Priest questioned him:

"Why," he asked, "why do you, so young and handsome, with flowing, silken ringlets, why do you wish to hide so much beauty and destroy so much which is pleasant to the eye?"

"Because," replied the youth, "my flowing ringlets have almost enticed me to sin from mere vanity. I saw the reflection of my face in a clear stream, and a proneness to self-deification seemed taking such hold of me, that I desire now at once to consecrate my hair unto the Lord, through the Nazarean vow."

Simon kissed the young shepherd, and said to him:

"Would to God there were in Israel many Nazareans like to thee."

Simon is renowned for his familiarity with the law, for his services as president and member of the great Senate, and for the efficient manner in which he strengthened the religious fervour of the people and participated in all their doings and institutions.

He officiated as High Priest for forty years, and himself announced the approach of his death on completing the services on the Day of Atonement. On entering the Holy of Holies upon this sacred day, he had been used to perceive, every year, an apparition in white garments, which attended all his actions in the performance of his office. On this particular day he failed to see it, and considered this fact a harbinger of his death. He died seven days after the holy day.

Posterity honoured him as the most holy among men, and it has been asserted that during his life visible tokens of God's favour never ceased.

His grandchildren, however, deserted Judaism entirely, and set the example for those actions which brought upon Israel the troublous times of Antiochus Epiphanes.

It was shortly after Simon's death, and in view of the degeneracy of the people, that the pious resolved that only the priests should use the holy name of God. The four letters of the sacred name were substituted for the name itself, and the latter was only uttered by the priests when they concluded the daily sacrificial service, and pronounced a blessing on the people, and by the High Priest on the Day of Atonement.

Rabbi Ishmael, The High Priest

Rabbi Ishmael was one of the most prominent and excellent among the fathers of the Talmudical literature. His doctrines are pure, his ideas sublime, and his explanations clear and concise. He died a martyr to Roman persecution, and this end has set the seal of truth and conviction on all the actions and sayings of his life.

There is an historical immortality, as well as a spiritual immortality; Rabbi Ishmael has attained the former, and he was a firm believer in the latter. They who imagine the doctrine of immortality to be an outgrowth of man's vanity, claiming for himself an imaginary preference above other creatures; they who believe it an ancient fiction, without which no courts of law would be able to check the natural proneness of man towards evil doing, could never rise to the courage and sublimity of martyrdom. To Ishmael, common observation as well as innate principles proved the truth of his belief.

First, no atom of matter, in the whole vastness of the universe, is lost; how, then, can man's soul, which comprises the whole world in one idea, be lost? Secondly, in all nature death is but a transformation; with the soul it is the portal to a new and higher realm. Thirdly, our thoughts and feelings, emanating from the soul, are not of an earthly nature. Rabbi Ishmael also advocated with energy the doctrine of man's free agency.

"When a man enters upon the path of truth and justice," said he, "God helps him forward, but when he chooses the way of sin, God says, 'I gave thee reason and free will, go thy way,' even as the trader will wait upon the customer who purchases a good and pleasant article, while to one who desires pitch or sulphur he says, 'Go, wait upon thyself.'"

Many ask, "Why does God permit so much corruption and evil?" Rabbi Ishmael answers, "Not God, but ye, yourselves, are the creators and supporters of moral evils. When a field is covered by weeds, shall a farmer complain to God? No; let him blame himself for his carelessness and neglect. Noble, indeed, is the feeling of the man who reflects that his virtue is his own work, and truely woful is the profligate who cannot but know that his guilt is his alone. 'To the pure help cometh from on high,' was the sentence which cheered our pious forefathers, and which should encourage us."

His definition of sin, too, is far beyond and above the confused ideas of many theologians.

"Sin is an obstruction in the heart; an inability to feel and comprehend all that is noble, true, and great, and to take part in the good." If man is to be freed from sin, his mind and heart must be opened to the influence of enlightenment. The power of the passions must be subdued, and all prejudice, selfishness, and self complacency be removed. For those who entertain the erroneous opinion that Judaism proclaims God as unforgiving and rancorous, nothing further should be necessary than to enumerate the Rabbi's classification of the effects of the Day of Atonement.

"He who violates an affirmative commandment, and repents, is forgiven immediately.

"He who does that thing which is forbidden, and repents, is forgiven on the Day of Atonement.

"He who commits a sin punishable by extirpation, or the death penalty, may be forgiven through suffering, but nothing save death may atone for the one who profanes the name of God."

What is a profanation of the name of God? According to Rab, he who borrows and does not repay commits that sin. Rabbi Abaya says, "A man who acts so that God's name is not honoured in his mouth."

And Rabbi Jochanan says, "The man who has abased his character."

Why should a violation of the affirmative commandments be so easily expiated, as is generally believed, since they are so important? The Rabbi says that sin committed against man is more grievous in the eyes of God than that committed against Himself.

Rabbi Meir

"All that God made was very good."

Rabbi Simon, the son of Eleazer, uses the words "very good" in reference to sleep. "Man sleeps," says he, "and in a few hours he gains renewed strength." Rabbi Samuel, son of Nachman, said, "The incentive leading man towards women is 'very good,' for thereby households are organised and families are formed." Rabbi Hammuna was of the opinion that no more forcible meaning could be given to the words "very good" than in applying them to the ills of life, which, said he, "more than doctrines and reasonings keep men temperate and dependent on a Higher Power." Rabbi Simon, the son of Abba, applied the words "very good" to retaliation; and Rabbi Simon, the son of Lakish, to political government; but the teaching of Rabbi Meir was, that the death of man is "very good."

Judaism aims not to separate, but to unite mankind, and this was one of the great principles of Rabbi Meir's life.

Concerning the passage, "Man shall observe the law and live in it," he said, "Holy Writ says not Israelites, not Levites, not priests, but *men*; therefore the Gentile who observes the law stands on a level with the High Priest."

"Walk before every man in modesty and humility," he said further. "Not only before your co-religionists, but before every man."

Rabbi Meir was a great allegorist; it is said that he knew three hundred allegories relating to the fox alone. Of these hut three fragments remain to us.

"A fox said to a bear, 'Come, let us go into this kitchen; they are making preparations for the Sabbath, and we shall he able to find food.' The bear followed the fox, but being bulky he was captured and punished. Angry thereat he designed to tear the fox to pieces, under the pretence that the forefathers of the fox had once stolen his food; wherein occurs the first saying, 'The fathers have eaten sour grapes, and the children's teeth are set on edge.'

"' Nay,' said the fox, 'come with me, my good friend; let us not quarrel; I will lead thee to another place where we shall surely find food.' The fox then led the bear to a fountain, where two buckets were fastened together by a rope, like balances. It was night, and the fox pointed to the moon reflected in the water, saying, 'Here is a fine cheese; let us descend and partake of it with an appetite.' The fox entered his pail first, but being too light to balance the weight of the bear he took with him a stone. As soon as the bear had gotten into the other pail, however, the fox threw this stone away, and consequently he rose, while the bear descended to the bottom."

Here he applies his second saying, "The righteous is delivered out of trouble, and the wicked cometh in his stead." Each man must suffer for his own sins, and for his own guilt alone. He who follows the luminary of the night, sensuality, must perish, while the righteous one, though carrying a stone (sin), will throw it away betimes, and be delivered from death.

The libertine Elishah, the son of Abuyah, generally called Acher, a most learned man, was one of Rabbi Meir's teachers, and they frequently conversed on Biblical passages.

The people were not pleased that Rabbi Meir should so associate, and they called him therefore *Acherim*, a word composed of the letters of Meir and Acher. But Rabbi Meir referred them to the proverb, "Incline thy ears to listen to the words of the sages, but direct thy heart to what my thought is."

Rabbi Meir ate the date and threw away the seeds; he found a pomegranate, and partaking of the fruit, he rejected the rind. His generation did not comprehend him.

Acher upon one occasion said to Rabbi Meir, "Why is the law compared to gold and glass?"

"Because," replied Rabbi Meir, "it is as hard to acquire as gold is hard in substance, and forgotten with as much ease as glass is broken."

"No," returned the other, in the name of Rabbi Akiba, "the reason is this: when gold and glass are broken they may be melted and worked over into new shapes. So is it with the student of the law, though he may commit many faulty actions there is still hope and help for him."

Rabbi Meir always favoured benevolence, and a care of self as well as of others. "He only is truly rich," he asserted, "who enjoys his wealth."

The passage in Malachi 26: "Many he withheld from iniquity," he interpreted as referring to Aaron, the first high priest, who was so respected that the mere mention of his name, or the thought of how he might regard a certain action were he present, prevented many from falling into sin.

A heathen once said to Rabbi Meir, "Does it seem credible that God, whose majesty you assert fills the universe, should have spoken from between the two staves in the ark of the sanctuary?"

In answer Rabbi Meir held up before the heathen a large and a small looking-glass, in each of which the inquirer beheld his image.

"Now," said the Rabbi, "in each mirror your body is reduced to correspond with the size of the glass,--should the same thing be impossible to God? The world is his large looking glass, the sanctuary his small one."

In regard to instruction, Rabbi Meir always said, "Teach your pupils concisely?" he also said, "Let your supplications be brief;" and his exhortation to parents was, "Teach thy son an honest handicraft."

His favourite maxim was, "Be resolved to know my ways; be attentive at the doors of the law, and guard the law in thy heart. Before thy eyes be the fear of me; protect thy mouth from sinning; cleanse and sanctify thyself from all guilt and iniquity, and God will be with thee."

From the sentence, "Be attentive at the doors of the law," Rabbi Meir declared that every scholar should have at least three teachers, and that the word "doors" possesses a peculiar idea or meaning. For instance, a person in passing the door of the house in which he passed his honeymoon, or the door of a hall of justice in which he has been convicted or acquitted, or the door of a house in which he has sinned, what different thoughts, feelings, and recollections will be awakened in him. With equal strength should the circumstances under which he studied the law be impressed upon his mind. The Israelites are called the "children of God," and Rabbi Meir never ceased to present this filial relation in its true light, filling to the brim the goblet of family happiness, and displaying it to the eyes of the people. "Jeremiah calls us 'foolish children,'" said he; "in Deuteronomy we are called 'children lacking faith;' but under all circumstances we remain 'the *children* of God.'"

Rabbi Meir's wife was good and pious as her husband. There dwelt in his neighbourhood some co-religionists who were followers of Greek customs, who annoyed the Rabbi very much. In his vexation he would have prayed to God to destroy them, but said Beruryah, his wife:

"Be mindful of the teachings of thy faith. Pray not that sinners may perish, but that the sin itself may disappear and no opportunity for its practice remain."

During the Rabbi's absence from home two of his sons died. Their mother, hiding her grief, awaited the father's return, and then said to him:

"My husband, some time since two jewels of inestimable value were placed with me for safe keeping. He who left them with me called for them to-day, and I delivered them into his hands?"

"That is right," said the Rabbi, approvingly. "We must always return cheerfully and faithfully all that is placed in our care."

Shortly after this the Rabbi asked for his sons, and the mother, taking him by the hand, led him gently to the chamber of death. Meir gazed upon his sons, and realising the truth, wept bitterly.

"Weep not, beloved husband," said his noble wife; "didst thou not say to me we must return cheerfully when ‘tis called for, all that has been placed in our care? God gave us these jewels; He left them with us for a time, and we gloried in their possession; but now that He calls for His own, we should not repine."

Hillel Hannasi

Hillel, "the chief of Israel," was the descendant of a renowned family; his father was of the tribe of Benjamin, while his mother was a lineal descendant of King David. He lived about a hundred years before the destruction of the second temple, and was called Hillel the Babylonian, having been born in Babel.

He was forty years of age before he left his native city to commence his studies of the law; he continued studying under Shemaiah and Abtalyon for forty years, and from then until his death, forty years after, he was chief of the college.

During the period of his life as a student, Hillel was often cramped for means to pursue his studies. There is a generally accepted legend, to the effect that upon one occasion, when he lacked the fee demanded by the porter for entrance to the college, he climbed up upon the window-sill, hoping to hear the lectures through the panes. It chanced to be snowing, and the student became so intensely interested that he was quite covered with the snow without being aware of it, and became insensible through the cold. The attention of those inside was called to his state by the early darkening of the room, and by them he was carried in and restored to consciousness.

Hillel's elevation to the presidency of the college occurred in a remarkable manner. The eve of the Passover fell upon the Sabbath. The two chief Rabbis of Jerusalem were the sons of Bethera, and they were asked to decide whether it would be right and lawful to prepare the paschal lamb upon the Sabbath. They were unable to decide the point, when it was mentioned to them that a man of Babel, who had studied under two renowned teachers, Shemaiah and Abtalyon, was then in the place, and might be able to aid their decision. Hillel was appealed to, and he met the question with such wisdom and clearness that the sons of Bethera exclaimed, "Thou art more worthy and competent to fill the office than we are," and through their means Hillel was elected chief of the college in the year 3728 A.M. Hillel was a man of very mild disposition, but he soon found in Shamai a rival of high and hasty temper. Shamai founded a college, which was called *Beth Shamai*, and between that institution and the *Beth Hillel* the controversies were sharp and prolonged, though in the great majority of the cases Hillel and his disciples had by far the best of the arguments.

Hillel's students numbered eighty; the most noted of whom was Jonathan, the son of Uziël.

Upon one occasion an unbeliever approached Shamai and mockingly requested the Rabbi to teach to him the tenets and principles of Judaism in the space of time he could stand on one foot. Shamai, in great wrath, bade him begone, and the man then applied to Hillel, who said:

"Do not unto others what you would not have others do to you. This is the whole law; the rest, merely commentaries upon it."

Many silly students were fond of asking plaguing questions.

"How many laws are there?" asked one of these.

"Two," replied Hillel, "the oral and the written law."

"In the latter I believe," said the student; "but why should I believe the other?"

Hillel then wrote the Hebrew alphabet upon a card, and pointing to the first letter, he asked;

"What letter is that?"

"*Aleph*," replied the student.

"Good," said Hillel; "now the next," pointing to it.

"Beth."

"Good again; but how knowest thou that this is an '*aleph*' and this a '*beth*?'"

"Because we have learned so from our teachers and our ancestors."

"Well," said Hillel, "as thou acceptest this in good faith, so accept the law."

As an evidence of Hillel's practical mind and his thorough appreciation of the demands and wants of his day, the following enactment is of interest.

According to the Biblical laws, all debts were to be remitted in the Sabbatical year; as it is written: "At the end of every seven years shalt thou make a release; . . . the loan which he hath lent to his neighbour," &c. (Deut. 15: 1-2). This measure, intended to adjust the inequalities of fortune, and well qualified for its purpose under some circumstances, was in the Herodian age the cause of much trouble. The wealthy man was loth to loan his money to those most in need of it, fearing to lose it by the provisions of this law. To remedy this evil, Hillel, without directly abrogating the statute of limitation, ordained that the creditor might make a duly signed deposition before the Sabbatical year, reserving the right to collect his outstanding debts at any time that he might think proper. This enactment was beneficial alike to rich and poor, and became a law with the approval of the elders.

Hillel died about the year 3764.

Rashi

*Ra*bbenu *Sh*elomo *Y*itzchaki (Our teacher, Solomon the son of Isaac), generally known as *Rashi*, from the initial letters of his name, was born about the year 1040 in Troyes, France. As a lad, his progress was remarkable; he mastered the most abstruse studies without difficulty, obtaining, in addition to his great proficiency in philology, philosophy, medicine, astronomy, and civil law, a complete mastery over the wide range of Scriptural and Talmudical lore.

He commenced his commentaries upon the Scriptures very early in life, completing the work, it is said, in his thirty-third year. Before giving it to the public, however, he travelled for seven years, visiting the academies of Italy, Greece, Germany, Palestine, and Egypt, storing up for the benefit of coming ages all that an observant eye, a gifted mind, and a diligent scholar could glean.

Upon his return to France, Rashi published his commentaries on the Bible, a book which has never been superseded, and which is now frequently published in connexion with the Hebrew Bible, and he supplemented the same, shortly after, with a commentary upon twenty-three of the treatises of the Talmud.

Many of his works were never published; but among those given to the world is a book of medicine, and a poem, "The Unity of God."

He died at the age of seventy-five years, leaving three daughters, one of whom became the mother of Samuel den Meier, who edited and added to the works of his grandfather.

His eminence, his piety, and his learning became traditional with succeeding generations, and he became the hero of many legends of that nature, which minds in those early days were so ready to grasp and embellish.

It is said that his monarch sent for him upon one occasion, and said to him:

"I have prepared a hundred thousand chariots and two hundred ships; I desire to capture Jerusalem. My soldiers and officers are superior in skill and courage to those now in possession; what thinkest thou of my prospects for success?"

"Thou wilt capture Jerusalem," returned Rashi; "thou wilt reign over it three days, and thou wilt return to this city with three horses and as many men thereon."

"Take heed then that there be not four horses," exclaimed the monarch, angered at this prediction, "for if I return with even one more than thou hast said, I will give thy flesh to the fowls of the air."

The war lasted for four years. The monarch returned with but four horsemen left of all his army, and as they passed through the gates of the city a stone fell, killing one horse and its rider instantly. This brought to mind the words of Rashi; but when the king sought for him, he found that during his absence the old man had gone the way of all flesh.

It is claimed that the chair which Rashi used in the college is still in existence.

Rashi was also called *Jarchi*, derived from the name of the city in which he lived, "Lunel." *Jerach* being the Hebrew, as lune is the French for moon.

In the words of the Talmud, "A righteous man never dies," and, "Happy the man that hath found wisdom, and he that hath acquired understanding."

Maimonides

Moses Maimonides, one of the greatest of Jewish commentators, and a descendant of Rabbi Judah, the compiler of the *Mishna*, was born in the city of Cordova, Spain, March 30th, 1135. His father was somewhat advanced in life when he married, and it is said that he entered into the conjugal state through having dreamed several successive times that he was wedded to the daughter of a butcher in his neighbourhood; the lady whom he did actually marry.

Moses was the only child of this lady, who died shortly after his birth. His father lamented her demise for about a year, and then married again, several children being the result of this second union.

Moses displayed no love for study in his youth; a fact which grieved his father much. All efforts to induce him to become more studious failed; his brothers called him "the butcher's boy," as a term of reproach for his dulness; and finally, in anger, his father drove him from his home.

While travelling, entirely friendless, Moses fell in with a learned Rabbi, and admired his wisdom and knowledge so much that he resolved to study zealously and emulate such attainments.

Many years after this a new preacher was announced to lecture in the synagogue, at Cordova, upon a designated Sabbath. Numerous rumours of his wonderful learning and eloquence were rife, and all were anxious to hear him. In matter, delivery, earnestness, and effect, the sermon excelled all that the people had before listened to, and to the amazement of Maimonides the elder, and his sons, they recognised in the man all were eager to honour, their outcast relative.

The first commentary of Maimonides is upon the *Mishna*, and it concludes with these words:

"I, Moses, the son of Maymon, commenced this commentary when twenty-three years of age. I have finished it at the age of thirty in the land of Egypt."

Maimonides fled from Spain to Cairo, in Egypt, from fanaticism and persecution. There he studied the Greek and Chaldaic languages, becoming master of both after seven years' attention. His fame spread through the country. His scientific standing and his general knowledge were universally recognised, and his books were not only valued by his brethren in faith, but by all the cultured and enlightened of his day.

It is said that the king of Egypt appointed him as one of his staff of physicians. The enlightened men of the kingdom were divided into seven grades, each grade occupying a corresponding position near the throne of the king on state occasions. The monarch considered Maimonides so much superior to the others that he made for him a special position. This, Moses, a modest man, declined. The other physicians, however, were jealous of his high standing, and being unable to injure him openly, they endeavoured to accomplish his ruin in a secret manner.

The king was taken very sick, and Maimonides attended him. Taking advantage of this, the physicians put poison in the draught which Moses had prepared for him, and then informed the king that the latter designed his death. To prove their words, they gave some of the mixture to a dog, and the animal died.

The king was grieved and surprised, and Maimonides, struck dumb with amazement, was unable to say a word.

"Death is the penalty for one who attempts to assassinate his ruler," said the king. "Choose now the mode of thy punishment."

Moses asked for three days for consideration, which the king granted. During this time he prepared a certain mixture, and instructed his pupils to have it ready and apply it according to his directions, when he should be brought home senseless. He then appeared before the king, and desired to have his veins opened. The vital artery was missed, as he had anticipated, and the result was as he had foreseen. After his recovery, he fled from Egypt, taking refuge in a cave, where he wrote his "*Yad Hazakah*" (the "Strong Hand"), consisting of fourteen divisions, typified by the word *Yad*, which also means fourteen.

Maimonides simplified the Talmudical rules and traditions, making them clear to the comprehension of all. He was the author of an exhaustive work, entitled, "*Mishne Torah*," the "Second Law," which was eagerly copied and extensively disseminated. He also wrote many philosophical treatises levelled against atheism, and designed to prove that God produced the world from naught, and at the age of fifty gave to the world his great work, *Moreh Nebuchim* (Guide of the Perplexed), to which Rabbi Judah Charizi added an appendix.

Maimonides died at the age of seventy years, and his remains were interred at Cairo, Egypt. Both Jews and Gentiles mourned his loss. The lamentation in Jerusalem was intense, a fast was declared, the synagogues were opened, and a portion of the law (Levit. 25: 12 to end), and the fifth chapter of Samuel 1, were made parts of the service of the day.

Rabbi Ammon, Of Metz

During the reign of one of the bishops in Metz, there lived a Jew in that city, who was called Rabbi Amnon. He was of illustrious family, of great personal merit, rich and respected by the Bishop and the people. The Bishop frequently pressed him to abjure Judaism and embrace Christianity, but without the slightest avail. It happened, however, upon a certain day, being more closely pressed than usual, and somewhat anxious to be rid of the Bishop's importunities, he said hastily, "I will consider the subject, and give thee an answer in three days."

As soon as he had left the Bishop's presence, however, his heart smote him, and an unquiet conscience blamed him for admitting, even in this manner, a doubt of the true faith. He reached home overwhelmed with grief; meat was set before him, but he refused to eat; and when his friends visited him and ascertained the cause of his low spirits, he refused their proffered consolation, saying, "I shall go down mourning to the grave for these words." On the third day, while he was still lamenting his imprudent concession, the Bishop sent for him, but he refused to answer the call.

Having refused several of the Bishop's messengers, they were finally ordered to seize him, and bring him by force before the prelate.

"Amnon," said the Bishop, "why didst thou not come to nee, according to thy promise, to inform me of thy decision in regard to my request?"

"Let me," answered Amnon, "pronounce my own doom for this neglect. Let my tongue, which uttered those hasty, doubting words, be cut out; a lie I uttered, for I never intended to consider the proposition."

"Nay," said the Bishop, "I will not cut out thy tongue, but thy feet which refused to cone to me, shall be cut off, and the other parts of thy obstinate body shall be also punished and tormented."

Under the Bishop's eye and order, the toes and thumbs of Rabbi Amnon were then cut off, and after having been severely tortured, he was sent home in a carriage, his mangled members beside him.

Rabbi Amnon bore all this with the greatest resignation, firmly hoping and trusting that this earthly torment would plead his pardon with God.

His life after this was of course to be measured only by days. The Feast of the New Year came .round, while he was living, and he desired to be carried to the synagogue. He was conveyed to the house of God, and during the service he requested to be allowed to utter a prayer. The words, which proved to be his last, were as follows:

"I will declare the mighty holiness of this day, for it is awful and tremendous. Thy kingdom is exalted thereon; Thy throne is established in mercy, and upon it Thou dost rest in truth. Thou art the Judge, who chastiseth, and from Thee naught may be concealed. Thou bearest witness, writest, sealest, recordest, and rememberest all things, aye, those which we imagine long buried in the past. The Book of Records thou openest; the great *shophar* (cornet) is sounded; even the angels are terrified, and they cry aloud, 'The Day of Judgment dawns upon us,' for in judgment they, the angels, are not faultless.

"All who have entered the world pass before Thee, Even as the shepherd causes the flock he numbers to pass under his crook, so Thou, oh Lord, causest every living soul to pass before Thee. Thou numberest, Thou visitest; appointing the limitations of every creature, Thy judgment and Thy sentence.

"On the New Year it is written, on the Day of Atonement it is sealed. Aye, all Thy decrees are recorded. Who is to live and who to die. The names of those to meet death by fire, by water, or by the sword; through hunger, through thirst, and with the pestilence. All is recorded. Those who are to have tranquillity, those who are to be disturbed. Those who are to be troubled, those who are to be blessed with repose. Those who are to be prosperous, those for whom affliction is in store. Those who are to become rich, who poor; who exalted, who cast down; but penitence, prayer, and charity, oh Lord, may avert all evil decrees."

When he had finished this declaration, in which he designed to acknowledge his sin and the justice of his punishment, Rabbi Amnon expired, dying fitly in God's house, among the assembled sons of Israel.

May the righteousness of Rabbi Amnon be a precious remembrance in Israel, and may we endeavour to emulate the same. Amen.

Benevolence

ACCORDING to a proverb of the fathers, benevolence is one of the pillars upon which the world rests. "The world," said they, "is sustained by virtue of three things,--the law, divine worship, and active benevolence." The Pentateuch commences and ends with an act of benevolence, as it is written, "And the Lord God made unto Adam and to his wife coats of skin, and clothed them" (Genesis 3: 20); and also, "And He (God) buried him" (Deut. 34: 6). To do a person a favour, is to act beneficently towards him without any hope or desire of return, and may be practised in two cases,--to oblige a person to whom we are not under obligation, and to accommodate or oblige a person, with more trouble to ourselves and more gain to him than he deserves. The mercy which is mentioned in the Bible is that which is given freely and without desert upon the part of one to whom it is granted; for instance, the benevolence of God is called mercy, because we are in debt to God, and He owes us nothing. Charity is also a species of benevolence, but it can only be applied to the poor and needy; while benevolence itself is both for poor and rich, high and lowly. We may even act benevolently towards the dead, attending to the last rites; this is called mercy and truth. If we oblige a fellow-man, it is possible that he may, in the course of time, repay the same; but benevolence to the dead is the very truth of mercy it cannot be returned. In three instances is benevolence superior to charity. Charity near be practised by means of money; benevolence with or without money. Charity is for the poor alone; benevolence either for the poor or for the rich. Charity we can display but to the living; benevolence to the living or the dead.

"After the Lord your God ye shall walk." How is it possible for us to walk after God? By following his attributes and examples. The Lord clothed the naked, as it is written, "The Lord God made to Adam and his wife coats of skin and clothed them." So we must do the same. The Lord visited the sick. "The Lord appeared to him in the grove of Mamre" (which was immediately after the circumcision). So we must do the same. The Lord comforteth the mourner. "It came to pass after the death of Abraham, God blessed his son Isaac." So we must do the same. The Lord buried the dead, as it is written,

"He (God) buried him." So must we do the same. To attend to the dead, follow to its last resting-place the dust of our fellows, is an act of benevolence both to the living and the dead; the spirit departed and the mourners.

Rabbi Judah said, "If a person weeps and mourns excessively for a lost relative, his grief becomes a murmur against the will of God, and he may soon be obliged to weep for another death." We should justify the decree of God, and exclaim with Job, "The Lord gave and the Lord hath taken; blessed be the name of the Lord."

Hospitality is another attribute of benevolence. It is said of Abraham, "And he planted an orchard." This was not an orchard as we understand the word, but an inn. Abraham opened his house to passing travellers, and entertained them in a hospitable manner. When his guests thanked him for his attention, Abraham replied, "Do not thank me, for I am not the owner of this place; thank God, who created heaven and earth." In this manner he made the name of God known among the heathens. Therefore he gave us an example of hospitality which we should follow, as it is written in the proverbs of the fathers, "Let thy house be open wide as a refuge, and let the poor be cordially received within thy walls." When they enter thy house, receive them with a friendly glance, and set immediately before them thy bread and salt. Perhaps the poor man may be hungry, and yet hesitate to ask for food. Even though there may be much to trouble thee, thou must hide thy feelings from thy guests; comfort them if they need kindly words, but lay not thine own troubles before them. Remember how kindly Abraham acted towards the three angels whom he thought were men; how hospitably he treated them, saying, "My lords, if I have found grace in your eyes, do not pass away from your servant," &c. (Gen. 18: 3.) Be always friendly to thy guests, then when thou shalt call upon the Lord He will answer thee.

God knows whether the hearts which seek Him offer Him all of which they are capable. During the existence of the Temple, the Lord received with equal favour the meat offering of a handful of flour and the sacrifice of a bull. So now, the offering of the poor is just as acceptable as the utmost which the rich man can afford, if their hearts are equally with the Lord.

It was said of Rabbi Tarphon, that though a very wealthy man, he was not charitable according to his means. One time Rabbi Akiba said to him, "Shall I invest some money for thee in real estate, in a manner which will be very profitable?" Rabbi Tarphon answered in the affirmative, and brought to Rabbi Akiba four thousand *denars* in gold, to be so applied. Rabbi Akiba immediately distributed the same among the poor. Some time after this Rabbi Tarphon met Rabbi Akiba, and asked him where the real estate which he had bought for him was situated. Akiba led his friend to the college, and showed him a little boy, who recited for them the 112th psalm. When he reached the ninth verse, "He distributeth, he giveth to the needy, his righteousness endureth for ever:"

"There," said Akiba, "thy property is with David, the king of Israel, who said, 'he distributeth, he giveth to the needy.'"

"And wherefore hast thou done this?" asked Tarphon.

"Knowest thou not," answered Rabbi Akiba, "how Nakdimon, the son of Guryon, was punished because he gave not according to his means?"

"Well," returned the other, "why didst thou not tell me this; could I not have distributed my means without thy aid?"

"Nay," said Akiba, "it is a greater virtue to cause another to give than to give one's self."

From this we may learn that he who is not charitable according to his means will be punished.

Rabbi Jochanan, the son of Lakkai, was once riding outside of Jerusalem, and his pupils had followed him. They saw a poor woman collecting the grain which dropped from the mouths and troughs of some feeding cattle, belonging to Arabs. When she saw the Rabbi, she addressed him in these brief words, "Oh Rabbi, assist me." He replied, "My daughter, whose daughter art thou?"

"I am the daughter of Nakdimon, the son of Guryon," she answered.

"Why, what has become of thy father's money?" asked the Rabbi; "the amount which thou didst receive as a dowry on thy wedding day?"

"Ah," she replied, "is there not a saying in Jerusalem, 'The salt was wanting to the money?'"

"And thy husband's money," continued the Rabbi; "what of that?"

"That followed the other," she answered; "I have lost them both."

The Rabbi turned to his scholars and said:

"I remember, when I signed her marriage contract, her father gave her as a dowry one million golden *denars*, and her husband was wealthy in addition thereto."

The Rabbi sympathised with the woman, helped her, and wept for her.

"Happy are ye, oh sons of Israel," he said; "as long as ye perform the will of God naught can conquer ye; but if ye fail to fulfil His wishes, even the cattle are superior to ye."

He who does not practise charity commits a sin. This is proven in the life of Nachum.

Nachum, whatever occurred to him, was in the habit of saying, "This too is for the best." In his old age he became blind; both of his hands and both of his legs were amputated, and the trunk of his body was covered with a sore inflammation. His scholars said to him, "If thou art a righteous man, why art thou so sorely afflicted?"

"All this," he answered, "I brought upon myself. Once was travelling to the house of my father-in-law, and I had with me thirty asses laden with provisions and all manner of precious articles. A man by the wayside called to me, 'Oh, Rabbi, assist me.' I told him to wait until I unloaded my asses. When that time arrived and I had removed their burdens from my beasts, I found to my sorrow that the poor man had fallen and expired. I threw myself upon his body and wept bitterly. 'Let these eyes, which had no pity on thee, be blind,' I said; 'these hands that delayed to assist thee, let them be cut off, and also these feet, which did not run to aid thee.' And yet I was not satisfied until I prayed that my whole body might be stricken with a sore inflammation. Rabbi Akiba said to me, 'Woe to me that I find thee in this state!' But I replied, 'Happy to thee that thou meetest me in this state, for through this I hope that my iniquity may be forgiven, and all my righteous deeds still remain recorded to gain me a reward of life eternal in the future world.'"

Rabbi Janay upon seeing a man bestowing alms in a public place, said, "Thou hadst better not have given at all, than to have bestowed alms so openly and put the poor man to shame.

"One should rather be thrown into a fiery furnace than be the means of bringing another to public shame."

The Rabbis particularly insist that we are not to confine the exercise of charity to our own people, for the law of Moses inculcates kindness and hospitality towards the stranger within our gates. Even the animals are especially remembered in his most merciful code.

Rabbi Juda said, "No one should sit down to his own meals, until seeing that all the animals dependent upon his care are provided for."

Rabbi Jochanan has said that it is as pleasing in God's sight if we are kind and hospitable to strangers, as if we rise up early to study His law; because the former is in fact putting His law into practice. He also said, "He who is active in kindnesses towards his fellows, is forgiven his sins."

Both this Rabbi and Abba say it is better to lend to the poor than to give to them, for it prevents them from feeling ashamed of their poverty, and is really a more charitable manner of aiding them. The Rabbis have always taught that kindness is more than the mere almsgiving of charity, for it includes pleasant words with the more substantial help.

Meekness

We find in the Bible many instances of the pleasure which meekness and humility in the creature affords the Great Creator. The noblest of our ancestors were those who were free from self-pride.

Abraham, the pure in heart, knew well he was but dust of the earth; and when the sons of Heth addressed him as the "prince of God," he bowed down before them.

Moses and Aaron, the leaders of Israel, exclaimed, "What are we!" And Moses in place of being jealous on hearing that two of his followers were prophesying in the camp, said humbly, "Would that all the Lord's people were prophets." (Numb. 11: 29.) When David dedicated to God's service the costly material he had gathered for the Temple, he meekly said, "Only of Thine own have we given Thee." (Ps. 37: 11.) From the Great Eternal, Himself, we learn humility.

He chose Mount Sinai from which to give His commandments: 'twas not the highest of the mountains.

He called to Moses not from a lofty tree but from a lowly bush. When he spoke to Elijah, he allowed the wind to roar, the earth to tremble, and the fire to flash forth; but for His medium He chose "the still small voice,"

Rabbi Hunnah said, "He who is proud in heart is as sinful as the idolater."

Rabbi Abira said, "He who is proud shall be humbled."

Heskaiah said, "The prayers of a proud hard-hearted man are never heard."

Rabbi Ashi said, "He who hardens his heart with pride, softens his brains with the same."

Rabbi Joshua said, "Meekness is better than sacrifice;" for is it not written, "The sacrifices of God are a broken heart--a broken contrite spirit, Thou, oh Lord, will not despise."

THE FEAR OF GOD

The son of Rabbi Hunnah said, "He who possesses a knowledge of God's law, without the fear of Him, is as one who has been intrusted with the inner keys of a treasury, but from whom the outer ones are withheld."

Rabbi Alexander said, "He who possesses worldly wisdom and fears not the Lord, is as one who designs building a house and completes only the door, for as David wrote in Psalm 111th, 'The beginning of wisdom is the fear of the Lord."

When Rabbi Jochanan was ill, his pupils visited him and asked him for a blessing. With his dying voice the Rabbi said, "I pray that you may fear God as you fear man." "What!" exclaimed his pupils, "should we not fear God more than man?"

"I should be well content," answered the sage, if your actions proved that you feared Him as much. When you do wrong you first make sure that no human eyes see you; show the same fear of God, who sees everywhere, and everything, at all times."

Abba says we can show our fear of God in our intercourse with one another. "Speak pleasantly and kindly to every one;" he says, "trying to pacify anger, seeking peace, and pursuing it with your brethren and with all the world, and by this means you will gain that 'favour and good understanding in the sight of God and man,' which Solomon so highly prized." (Prov. 3: 9.)

Rabbi Jochanan had heard Rabbi Simon, son of Jochay, illustrate by a parable that passage of Isaiah which reads as follows: "I, the Lord, love uprightness; but hate robbery (converted) into burnt-offering."

A king having imported certain goods upon which he laid a duty, bade his officers, as they passed the custom-house, to stop and pay the usual tariff.

Greatly astonished, his attendants addressed him thus: "Sire! all that is collected belongs to your majesty; why then give what must be eventually paid into thy treasury?"

"Because," answered the monarch, "I wish travellers to learn from the action I now order you to perform, how abhorrent dishonesty is in my eyes."

Even so is it regarding the dealings of the Almighty with us, pilgrims on earth. Though all we possess belongs to Him, yet He adds to it continually, in order to increase our temporal enjoyment. Should any one imagine, therefore, that to defraud man in order to present to God, what is solely His own, might be allowable, he would be rebuked by the teachings of Holy Writ, for the just God condemns the act, and calls it hateful.

From this we may then infer, for instance, that palm-branches, stolen in order to perform therewith the prescribed rites at the Feast of Tabernacles, are unfit for use by reason of the unlawful manner in which they were obtained.

Rabbi Eleazer said: "He who is guided by righteousness and justice in all his doings, may justly be asserted to have copied God in His unbounded beneficence. For of Him (blessed be His name) we read, 'He loveth righteousness and justice;' that is, 'The earth is filled with the loving kindness of God.'" Might we think that to follow such a course is an easy task? No! The virtue of beneficence can be gained only by great efforts. Will it be difficult, however, for him that has the fear of God constantly before his eyes to acquire this attribute? No; he will easily attain it, whose every act is done in the fear of the Lord.

"A crown of grace is the hoary head; on the way of righteousness can it be found."

So taught Solomon in his Proverbs. Hence various Rabbis, who had attained an advanced age, were questioned by their pupils as to the probable cause that had secured them that mark of divine favour. Rabbi Nechumah answered that, in regard to himself, God had taken cognisance of three principles by which he had endeavoured to guide his conduct.

First, he had never striven to exalt his own standing by lowering that of his neighbour. This was agreeable to the example set by Rabbi Hunna, for the latter, while bearing on his shoulders a heavy spade, was met by Rabbi Choana Ben Chanilai, who, considering the burden derogatory to the dignity of so great a man, insisted upon relieving him of the implement and carrying it himself. But Rabbi Hunna refused, saying, "Were this your habitual calling I might permit it, but I certainly shall not permit another to perform an office which, if clone by myself, may be looked upon by some as menial."

Secondly, he had never gone to his night's rest with a heart harbouring ill-will against his fellow-man, conformably with the practice of Mar Zutra, who, before sleeping, offered this prayer: "O Lord! forgive all those who have done me injury."

Thirdly, he was not penurious, following the example of the righteous Job, of whom the sages relate that he declined to receive the change due him after making a purchase.

Another Rabbi, bearing also the name of Nechumah, replied to Rabbi Akiba, that he believed himself to have been blessed with long life because, in his official capacity, he had invariably set his face against accepting presents, mindful of what Solomon wrote, "He that hateth gifts will live." Another of his merits he conceived to be that of never resenting an offence; mindful of the words of Rabba, "He who is indulgent towards others' faults, will be mercifully dealt with by the Supreme Judge."

Rabbi Zera said that the merit of having reached an extreme age was in his case due, under Providence, to his conduct through life. He governed his household with mildness and forbearance. He refrained from advancing an opinion before his superiors in wisdom. He avoided rehearsing the word of God in places not entirely free from uncleanliness. He wore the phylacteries all day, that he might be reminded of his religious duties. He did not make the college where sacred knowledge is taught, a place of convenience, as, for instance, to sleep there, either occasionally or habitually. He never rejoiced over the downfall of a fellow-mortal, nor would he designate another by a name objectionable to the party personally, or to the family of which he was a member.

HONOUR THY PARENTS

The Bible makes man's parents equally deserving, with the Most High, of his honour and reverence. "*Honour* thy father and thy mother," is one of the precepts of the Decalogue, and it is also written, "*Honour* God from thy wealth." "*Fear* thy father and mother," and "The Lord thy God shalt thou *fear*," are also divine inculcations, while the penalty for the blasphemous child, who sins against either his earthly parents or the great Father of the Universe, is the same, even as it is written, "Who *curses* his father and his mother shall be put to death," and "Every man who *blasphemes* God shall carry his death."

"Three friends," said the Rabbis, "has man." God, his father, and his mother. "He who honours his parents," says God, "honours me, even as though I lived among them."

Rabbi Judah said, "Known and revealed are the ways of man. A mother coaxes a child with kind words and gentle ways, gaining honour and affection; therefore, the Bible says, 'Honour thy father,' before 'honour thy mother.' But in regard to fearing, as the father is the preceptor of the child, teaching it the law, the Bible says, 'Every man shall fear his mother,' before the word 'father.'"

Rabbi Ulah was once asked, "How extended should be this honour due to parents?"

He replied:

"Listen, and I will tell ye how thoroughly it was observed by a heathen, Damah, the son of Nethina. He was a diamond merchant, and the sages desired to purchase from him a jewel for the ephod of the high priest. When they reached his house, they found that the key of the safe in which the diamond was kept was in the possession of Damah's father, who was sleeping. The son absolutely refused to wake his father, to obtain the key, even when the sages in their impatience offered him a much larger sum for the jewel than he had demanded. And further, when his father awoke, and he delivered the diamond to the purchasers, and they offered him the larger sum which they had named, he took from it his first price, returning the balance to them, with the words, 'I will not profit by the honour of my father.'"

Man cannot always judge of man, and in the respect paid to parents by their children, earthly eyes cannot always see the truth. For instance, a child may feed his parents on dainties, and yet deserve the punishment of a disrespectful son; while another may send his father to labour, and yet deserve reward. How may this be?

A certain man placed dainty food before his father, and bade him eat thereof. When the father had finished his meal, he said:

"My son, thou hast prepared for me a most delicious meal. Wherefrom didst thou obtain these delicacies?" And the son replied, insultingly:

"Eat as the dogs do, old man, without asking questions."

That son inherited the punishment of disrespect.

A certain man, a miller, had a father living with him, at the time when all people not working for themselves were obliged to labour a certain number of days for the government. When it came near the time when this service would be required of the old man, his son said to him, "Go thou and labour for me in the mill, and I will go and work for the government."

He said this because they who laboured for the government were beaten if their work proved unsatisfactory, and he thought "it is better for me to run the chance of being beaten than to allow my father to risk it." Therefore, he deserved the reward of the son who "honours his father."

Rabbi Chiyah asserted that God preferred honour shown to parents, to that displayed towards Himself. "It is written," said he, "'Honour the Lord from thy wealth.' How? Through charity, good deeds, putting the *mezuzah* upon thy doorposts, making a tabernacle for thyself during Succoth, &c.; all this if thou art able. If thou art poor the omission is not counted a sin or a neglect. But it is written, 'Honour thy father and thy mother,' and the duty is demanded alike of rich and poor; aye, even shouldst thou be obliged to beg for them from door to door."

Rabbi Abahu said, "Abini, my son, hath obeyed this precept even as it should be observed."

Abini had five children, but he would not allow any of them to open the door for their grandfather, or attend to his wants when he himself was at home. Even as he desired them in their lives to honour him, so he paid respect to his father. Upon one occasion his father asked him for a glass of water. While he was procuring it the old man fell asleep, and Abini, re-entering the room, stood by his father's side with the glass in his hand until the latter awoke.

"What is fear?" and "What is honour?" ask the Rabbis.

Fear thy mother and thy father, by sitting not in their seats and standing not in their places; by paying strict attention to their words and interrupting not their speech. Be doubly careful not to criticise or judge their arguments or controversies.

Honour thy father and thy mother, by attending to their wants; giving them to eat and to drink; put their raiment upon them, and tie their shoes if they are not able to perform these services for themselves.

Rabbi Eleazer was asked how far honour towards parents should be extended, and he replied: "Cast all thy wealth into the sea; but trouble not thy father and thy mother."

Simon, the son of Jochai, said: "As the reward to those who honour their parents is great, so is the punishment equally great for those who neglect the precept."

Each precept of the Bible states what the reward for its observance will be, and with this one we are told, "In order that thy days may be prolonged, and in order that it may go well with thee."

That thy days may be prolonged, not only in this world, but also in the world to come.

The Law And Its Study

"The Lord created me as the beginning of his way" (Prov. 8: 22). This means that God created the law before he created the world. Many sages have made their lives as black as the raven, that is, cruel to themselves as the raven is to her children, by means of continual study, day and night.

Rabbi Johanan said, "It is best to study by night, when all is quiet; as it is written, 'Shout forth praises in the night.'"

Reshbi Lakish said, "Study by day and by night; as it is written, 'Thou shalt meditate therein day and night.'"

Rabbi Chonan, of Zepora, said, "The study of the law may be compared to a huge heap of dust that is to be cleared away. The foolish man says, 'It is impossible that I should be able to remove this immense heap, I will not attempt it;' but the wise man says, 'I will remove a little to-day, some more to-morrow, and more the day after, and thus in time I shall have removed it all.'

"It is the same with studying the law. The indolent pupil says, 'It is impossible for me to study the Bible. Just think of it, fifty chapters in Genesis; sixty-six in Isaiah, one hundred and fifty Psalms, &c. I cannot do it but the industrious student says, 'I will study six chapters every day, and so in time I shall acquire the whole.'"

In Proverbs 24: 7, we find this sentence: "Wisdom is too high for a fool."

"Rabbi Jochanan illustrates this verse with an apple depending from the ceiling. The foolish man says, 'I cannot reach the fruit, it is too high;' but the wise man says, 'It may be readily obtained by placing one step upon another until thy arm is brought within reach of it.' The foolish man says, 'Only a wise man can study the entire law;' but the wise man replies, 'It is not incumbent upon thee to acquire the whole.'"

Rabbi Levi illustrates this by a parable.

A man once hired two servants to fill a basket with water, One of them said, "Why should I continue this useless labour? I put the water in one side and it immediately leaks out of the other; what profit is it?"

The other workman, who was wise, replied, "We have the profit of the reward which we receive for our labour."

It is the same in studying the law. One man says, "What does it profit me to study the law when I must ever continue it or else forget what I have learned." But the other man replies, "God will reward us for the will which we display even though we do forget."

Rabbi Ze-irah has said that even a single letter in the law which we might deem of no importance, if wanting, would neutralise the whole law. In Deuteronomy 22: 17, we read, "Neither shall he take to himself many wives, that his heart may turn away." Solomon transgressed this precept, and it is said by Rabbi Simon that the angels took note of his ill-doing and addressed the Deity: "Sovereign of the world, Solomon has made Thy law even as a law liable to change and diminution. Three precepts he has disregarded, namely, 'He shall not acquire for himself many horses;' 'neither shall he take to himself many wives;' 'nor shall he acquire to himself too much silver and gold.'" Then the Lord replied, "Solomon will perish from the earth; aye, and a hundred Solomons after him, and yet the smallest letter of the law shall not be dispensed with."

The Rabbis have often applied in a figurative sense, various passages of Holy Writ, among others the opening verse of the 55th chapter of Isaiah. "Ho, every one of ye that thirsteth, come ye to the water, and he, too, that hath no money; come ye, buy and eat; yea, come, buy without money and without price, wine and milk."

The three liquids which men are thus urged to procure are considered by the sages of Israel as typical of the law.

One Rabbi asked, "Why is the word of God compared to water?"

To this question the following answer was returned: "As water runs down from an eminence (the mountains), and rests in a low place (the sea), so the law, emanating from Heaven, can remain in the possession of those only who are humble in spirit."

Another Rabbi inquired, "Wherefore has the Word of God been likened to wine and milk?" The reply made was, "As these fluids cannot he preserved in golden vessels, but only in those of earthenware, so those minds will be the best receptacles of learning which are found in homely bodies."

Thus, for instance, Rabbi Joshua ben Chaninah, who was very homely in appearance, possessed great wisdom and erudition; and one of his favourite sayings was, that "though many have exhibited a vast amount of knowledge, notwithstanding their personal attractions, yet had they been less handsome, their acquirements might have beet more extensive."

There is another reason for comparing the Word of God to the last-mentioned liquids, namely, that they demand watching, lest they be spilled or spoiled, and in the same manner our acquaintance with the Bible and the traditions requires constant cultivation, else it will be lost.

The precepts are compared to a lamp; the law of God to a light. The lamp gives light only so long as it contains oil. So he who observes the precepts receives his reward while performing them. The law, however, is a light perpetual; it is a protection for ever to the one who studies it, as it is written:

"When thou walkest, it (the law) will guide thee; when thou liest down, it will watch over thee; and when thou awakenest, it will converse with thee."

When thou walkest, it will guide thee--in *this* world; when thou liest down, it will watch over thee--in the grave; when thou awakenest, it will converse with thee--in the *life to come.*

A traveller upon his journey passed through the forest upon a dark and gloomy night. He journeyed in dread; he feared the robbers who infested the route he was traversing; he feared that he might slip and fall into some unseen ditch or pitfall on the way, and he feared, too, the wild beasts, which he knew were about him. By chance he discovered a pine torch, and lighted it, and its gleams afforded him great relief. He no longer feared brambles or pitfalls, for he could see his way before him. But the dread of robbers and wild beasts was still upon him, nor left him till the morning's dawn, the coming of the sun. Still he was uncertain of his way, until he emerged from the forest, and reached the cross-roads, when peace returned unto his heart.

The darkness in which the man walked was the lack of religious knowledge. The torch he discovered typifies God's precepts, which aided him on the way until he obtained the blessed sunlight, compared to God's holy word, the Bible. Still, while man is in the forest (the world), he is not entirely at peace; his heart is weak, and he may lose the right path; but when he reaches the cross-roads (death), then may we proclaim him truly righteous, and exclaim:

"A good name is more fragrant than rich perfume, and the day of death is better than the day of one's birth."

Rabbi Jochanan, the son of Broka, and Rabbi Eleazer, the son of Chismah, visited their teacher, Rabbi Josah, and he said to them:

"What is the news at the college; what is going on?" "Nay," they answered, "we are thy scholars; it is for thee to speak, for us to listen."

"Nevertheless," replied Rabbi Josah, "no day passes without some occurrence of note at the college. Who lectured to-day?"

"Rabbi Eleazer, the son of Azaryah."

"And what was his subject?"

"He chose this verse from Deuteronomy," replied the scholar:

"'Assemble the people together, the men, the women, and the children;' and thus he expounded it:

"'The men came to learn, the women to listen; but wherefore the children? In order that those who brought them might receive a reward for training their children in the fear of the Lord.'

"He also expounded the verse from Ecclesiastes;

"'The words of the wise are like goads, and like nails fastened (are the words of) the men of the assemblies, which are given by one shepherd.'

"'Why is the law of God compared to a goad?' he said. 'Because the goad causes the ox to draw the furrow straight, and the straight furrow brings forth a plenty of good food for the life of man. So does the law of God keep man's heart straight, that it may produce good food to provide for the life eternal. But lest thou shouldst say, "The goad is movable, so therefore must the law be," it is also written, "*as nails*," and likewise, as "*nails fastened*," lest thou shouldst argue that nails pounded into wood diminish from sight with each stroke, and that therefore by this comparison God's law would be liable to diminution also. No; as a nail fastened or planted, as a tree is planted to bring forth fruit and multiply.

"'The *men of assemblies* are those who gather in numbers to study the law. Frequently controversies arise among them, and thou mightest say, "With so many differing opinions how can I settle to a study of the law?" Thy answer is written in the words *which are given by one shepherd*. From one God have all the laws proceeded. Therefore make thy ears as a sieve, and incline thy heart to possess all these words.'"

Then said Rabbi Josah, "Happy the generation which Rabbi Eleazer teaches."

The sages of the academy in Jabnah expressed their regard for all human beings, learned and unlearned, in this manner:

"I am a creature of God and so is my neighbour. He may prefer to labour in the country; I prefer a calling in the city. I rise early for my personal benefit; he rises early to advance his own interests. As he does not seek to sup plant me, I should be careful to do naught to injure his business. Shall I imagine that I am nearer to God because my profession advances the cause of learning and his does not? No. Whether we accomplish much good or little good, the Almighty will reward us in accordance with our righteous intentions."

Abaygeh offered the following as his best advice:

". . . Let him be also affable and disposed to foster kindly feelings between all people; by so doing he will gain for himself the love both of the Creator and His creatures."

Rabba always said that the possession of wisdom and a knowledge of the law necessarily lead to penitence and good deeds. "For," said he, "it would be useless to acquire great learning and the mastery of Biblical and traditional law and act irreverently towards one's parents, or towards those superior on account of age or more extensive learning."

"The fear of the Lord is the beginning of wisdom; a good understanding have all those who do God's commands."

Rabba said, "Holy Writ does not tell us that to *study* God's commands shows a good understanding, but to *do* them. We must learn, however, before we can be able to perform; and he who acts contrary through life to the teachings of the Most High had better never have been born."

"The wise man is in his smallest actions great: the fool is in his greatest actions small."

A pupil once inquired of his teacher, "What is real wisdom?" The teacher replied, "To judge liberally, to think purely, and to love thy neighbour." Another teacher answered, "The greatest wisdom is to know thyself."

"Beware of conceit and pride of learning; learn thy tongue to utter, 'I do not know.'"

If a man devotes himself to study, and becomes learned, to the delight and gratification of his teachers, and yet is modest in conversation with less intelligent people, honest in his dealings, truthful in his daily walks, the people say, "Happy is the father who allowed him to study God's law; happy the teachers who instructed him in the ways of truth; how beautiful are his ways; how meritorious his deeds! Of such an one the Bible says, 'He said to me, Thou art my servant; oh, Israel, through thee am I glorified.'"

But when a man devotes himself to study, and becomes learned, yet is disdainful with those less educated than himself, and is not particular in his dealings with his fellows, then the people say of him, "Woe to the father who allowed him to study God's law; woe to those who instructed him; how censurable is his conduct; how loathsome are his ways! 'Tis of such an one the Bible says, 'And from his country the people of the Lord departed.'"

When souls stand at the judgment-seat of God, the poor, the rich, and the wicked each are severally asked what excuse they can offer for not having studied the law. If the poor man pleads his poverty he is reminded of Hillel. Though Hillel's earnings were small he gave half each day to gain admittance to the college.

When the rich man is questioned, and answers that the care of his fortune occupied his time, he is told that Rabbi Eleazer possessed a thousand forests and a thousand ships, and yet abandoned all the luxuries of wealth, and journeyed from town to town searching and expounding the law.

When the wicked man pleads temptation as an excuse for his evil course, he is asked if he has been more tempted than Joseph, more cruelly tried than he was, with good or evil fortune.

Yet though we are commanded to study God's law, we are not to make of it a burden; neither are we to neglect for the sake of study any other duty or reasonable recreation. "Why," once asked a pupil, "is 'thy shalt gather in thy corn in its season' a Scriptural command? Would not the people gather their corn when ripe as a matter of course? The command is superfluous."

"Not so," replied the Rabbis "the corn might belong to a man who for the sake of study would neglect work, Work is holy and honourable in God's sight, and He would not have men fail to perform their daily duties even for the study of His law."

PRAYER

Bless God for the good as well as for the evil. When you hear of a death say, "Blessed is the righteous Judge."

Prayer is Israel's only weapon, a weapon inherited from its fathers, a weapon proved in a thousand battles. Even when the gates of prayer are shut in heaven, those of tears are open.

We read (Ex. 17: 11) that in the contest with Amalek, when Moses lifted up his arms Israel prevailed. Did Moses's hands affect the war, to make it or to break it? No; but while the ones of Israel look upward with humble heart to the Great Father in Heaven, no evil can prevail against them.

"And Moses made a serpent of brass and put it upon a pole; and it came to pass that if a serpent had bitten any man, when he beheld the serpent of brass he lived" (Numb. 21: 9).

Had the brazen serpent the power of killing or of giving life? No; but while Israel looks upward to the Great Father in Heaven, He will grant life.

"Has God pleasure in the meat and blood of sacrifices?" ask the prophets.

No. He has not so much ordained as permitted them. "It is for yourselves," He says; "not for me, that ye offer."

A king had a son whom he daily discovered carousing with dissolute companions, eating and drinking.

"Eat at my table," said the king; "eat and drink, my son, even as pleaseth thee; but let it be at my table, and not with dissolute companions."

The people loved sacrificing, and they made offerings to strange gods; therefore, God said to them: "If ye will sacrifice, bring your offerings at least to me."

Scripture ordains that the Hebrew slave who loves his bondage shall have his ears pierced against the doorpost. Why?

Because that ear heard from Sinai's heights these words: "They are my servants; they shall not be sold as bondsmen." My servants, and not my servant's servants; therefore, pierce the ear of the one who loves his bondage and rejects the freedom offered him.

He who sacrifices a whole offering shall be rewarded for a whole offering; he who offers a burnt-offering shall have the reward of a burnt-offering; but he who offers humility to God and man shall receive as great a reward as though he had offered all the sacrifices in the world.

The God of Abraham will help the one who appoints a certain place to pray to the Lord.

Rabbi Henah said, "When such a man dies they will say of him, 'A pious man, a meek man, hath died; he followed the example of our father Abraham'"

How do we know that Abraham appointed a certain place to pray?

"Abraham rose early in the morning and went to the place where he stood before the Lord."

Rabbi Chelboh said, "We should not hurry when we leave a place of worship."

"This," said Abayyeh, "is in reference to leaving a place of worship; but we should certainly hasten on our way thither, as it is written, 'Let us know and hasten to serve the Lord.'"

Rabbi Zabid said, "When I used to see the Rabbis hurrying to a lecture in their desire to obtain good seats, I thought to myself, 'they are violating the Sabbath.' When, however, I heard Rabbi Tarphon say, 'One should always hasten to perform a commandment even on the Sabbath,' as it is written, 'They shall follow after the Lord when He roareth like a lion,' I hurried also, in order to be early in attendance."

That place wherein we can best pray to God is His house; as it is written:

"To listen to the praises and prayers which Thy servant prays before Thee." Alluding to the service in the house of God.

Said Rabin, the son of Ada, "Whence do we derive the tradition, that when ten men are praying in the house of God the Divine Presence rests among them?

"It is written, 'God stands in the assembly of the mighty.' That an assembly or congregation consists of not less than ten, we learn from God's words to Moses in regard to the spies who were sent out to view the land of Canaan. 'How long,' said he, 'shall indulgence be given to this evil congregation?' Now the spies numbered twelve men; but Joshua and Caleb being true and faithful, there remained but ten to form the 'evil congregation.'"

"Whence do we derive the tradition that when even one studies the law, the Divine Presence rests with him?"

"It is written, 'In every place where I shall permit my name to be mentioned, I will come unto thee and I will bless thee.'"

Four Biblical characters offered up their prayers in a careless, unthinking manner; three of them God prospered; the other met with sorrow. They were, Eleazer, the servant of Abraham; Caleb, the son of Ye Phunneh; Saul, the son of Kish; and Jephtah the Giladite.

Eleazer prayed, "Let it come to pass that the maiden to whom I shall say, 'Let down thy pitcher, I pray thee, that I may drink;' and she shall say, 'Drink, and to thy camels also will I give drink;' shall be the one Thou hast appointed for Thy servant Isaac."

Suppose a slave had appeared and answered all the requirement which Eleazer proposed, would Abraham and Isaac have been satisfied? But God prospered his mission, and "Rebecca came out."

Caleb said, "He that will smite *Kiryath-sepher*, and capture it, to whom will I give 'Achsah, my daughter, for wife" (Judges I: 12).

Would he have given his daughter to a slave or a heathen?

But God prospered him, and "Othniel, the son of Kenaz, Caleb's younger brother, conquered it, and he gave him 'Achsah, his daughter, for wife."

Saul said, "And it shall be that the man who killeth him (Goliath) will the king enrich with great riches, and his daughter will he give him" (1 Samuel 17).

He ran the same risk as Caleb, and God was good to him also; and David, the son of Jesse, accomplished that for which he had prayed.

Jephtah expressed himself thus:

"If thou wilt indeed deliver the children of Amon into my hand, then shall it be that whatsoever cometh forth out of the doors of my house to meet me when I return in peace from the children of Amon, shall belong to the Lord, and I will offer it up for a burnt-offering" (Judges 11: 31).

Supposing an ass, or a dog, or a cat, had first met him upon his return, would he have sacrificed it for a burnt-offering? God did not prosper this risk, and the Bible says,

"And Jephtah came to Mizpah unto his house, and behold his daughter came out to meet him."

Said Rabbi Simon ben Jochai, "The requests of three persons were granted before they had finished their prayers--Eleazer, Moses, and Solomon.

"In regard to Eleazer we learn, 'And before he had yet finished speaking that, behold Rebecca came out.'

"In regard to Moses, we find, 'And it came to pass when he had made an end of speaking all these words, that the ground that was under them was cloven asunder, and the earth opened her mouth and swallowed them.'" (Korach and his company.)

"In regard to Solomon, we find, 'And just when Solomon had made an end of praying, a fire came down," &c.

The Sabbath

Rabbi Jochanan said, in the name of Rabbi Joseh, "To those who delight in the Sabbath shall God give inheritance without end. As it is written, 'Then shalt thou find delight in the Lord,' &c. 'And I will cause thee to enjoy the inheritance of Jacob, thy father.' Not as it was promised to Abraham, 'Arise and walk through the land to its length and breadth.' Not as it was promised to Isaac, 'I will give thee all that this land contains;' but as it was promised to Jacob, 'And thou shalt spread abroad, to the West, and to the East, to the North, and to the South.'"

Rabbi Jehudah said that if the Israelites had strictly observed the first Sabbath, after the command to sanctify the seventh day had been given, they would have been spared captivity; as it is written, "And it came to pass on the seventh day, that there went out some of the people to gather (the Mannah), but they found nothing." And in the next chapter we find, "Then came Amalek, and fought with Israel in Rephidim."

The following is one of the many tales designed to show that the observance of the Sabbath is rewarded:

One Joseph, a Jew, who honoured the Sabbath, had a very rich neighbour, who was a firm believer in astrology. He was told by one of the professional astrologers that his wealth would become Joseph's. He therefore sold his estate, and bought with the proceeds a large diamond, which he sewed in his turban, saying, "Joseph can never obtain this." It so happened, however, that while standing one day upon the deck of a ship in which he was crossing the sea, a heavy wind arose and carried the turban from his head. A fish swallowed the diamond, and being caught and exposed for sale in the market, was purchased by Joseph to supply his table on the Sabbath eve. Of course, upon opening it he discovered the diamond.

Rabbi Ishmael, the son of Joshua, was asked, "How did the rich people of the land of Israel become so wealthy?" He answered, "They gave their tithes in due season, as it is written, 'Thou shalt give tithes, in order that thou mayest become rich." "But," answered his questioner, "tithes were given to the Levites, only while the holy temple existed. What merit did they possess while they dwelt in Babel, that they became wealthy there also?" "Because," replied the Rabbi, "they honoured the Holy Law by expounding it." "But in other countries, where they did not expound the Law, how did they deserve wealth?" "By honouring the Sabbath," was the answer.

Rabbi Achiya, the son of Abah, said, "I sojourned once in Ludik, and was entertained by a certain wealthy man on the Sabbath day. The table was spread with a sumptuous repast, and the dishes were of silver and gold. Before making a blessing over the meal the master of the house said, 'Unto the Lord belongeth the earth, with all that it contains.' After the blessing he said, 'The heavens are the heavens of the Lord, but the earth hath He given to the children of men.' I said to my host, 'I trust you will excuse me, my dear sir, if I take the liberty of asking you how you have merited this prosperity?' He answered, 'I was formerly a butcher, and I always selected the finest cattle to be killed for the Sabbath, in order that the people might have the best meat on that day. To this, I believe firmly, I owe my prosperity.' I replied, 'Blessed be the Lord, that He hath given thee all this.'"

The Governor Turnusrupis once asked Rabbi Akiba, "What is this day you call the Sabbath more than any other day?" The Rabbi responded, "What art thou more than any other person?" "I am superior to others," he replied, "because the emperor has appointed me governor over them."

Then said Akiba, "The Lord our God, who is greater than your emperor, has appointed the Sabbath day to be holier that the other days."

Beautiful is the legend of the Sabbath eve.

When man leaves the synagogue for his home an angel of good and an angel of evil accompany him. If he finds the table spread in his house, the Sabbath lamps lighted, and his wife and children in festive garments ready to bless the holy day of rest, then the good angel says:

"May the next Sabbath and all thy Sabbaths be like this. Peace unto this dwelling, peace;" and the angel of evil is forced to say, "Amen!"

But if the house is not ready, if no preparations have been made to greet the Sabbath, if no heart within the dwelling has sung, "Come, my beloved, to meet the bride; the presence of the Sabbath let us receive;" then the angel of evil speaks and says:

"May all thy Sabbaths be like this;" and the weeping angel of goodness, responds, "Amen!"

Rewards And Punishments

Samson sinned against the Lord through his *eyes*, as it is written, "I have seen a woman of the daughters of the Philistines.......This one take for me, for she pleaseth in my *eyes*" (Judges 14: 3). Therefore through his *eyes* was he punished, as it is written, "And the Philistines seized him, and put out his eyes."

Abshalom was proud of his *hair*. "And like Abshalom there was no man as handsome in all Israel, so that he was greatly praised; from the sole of his foot up to the crown of his head there was no blemish on him. And when he shaved off the hair of his head, and it was at the end of every year that he shaved it off, because it was too heavy do him so that he had to shave it off, he weighed the hair of his head at two hundred shekels by the king's weight," Therefore by his *hair* was he hanged.

Miriam *waited* for Moses one hour (when. he was in the box of bulrushes). Therefore the Israelites *waited* for Miriam seven days, when she became leprous. "And the people did not set forward until Miriam was brought in again."

Joseph buried his father. "And Joseph went up to bury his father." There was none greater among the children of Israel than Joseph. Moses excelled him afterwards, however; therefore we find, "And Moses took the bones of Joseph with him." But the world has seen none greater than Moses, therefore 'tis written, "And He (God) buried him in the valley."

When trouble and sorrow become the portion of Israel, and the fainthearted separate from their people, two angels lay their hands upon the head of him who withdraws, saying, "This one shall not see the comfort of the congregation."

When trouble comes to the congregation it is not right for a man to say, "I will go home; I will eat and drink; and things shall be peaceful to me;" 'tis of such a one that the holy book speaks, saying, "And behold these is gladness and joy; slaying of oxen, and killing of sheep; eating of flesh, and drinking of wine. 'Let us eat and drink, for to-morrow we must die.' And it was revealed in my ears by the Lord of Hosts; surely the iniquity shall not be forgiven ye until ye die" (Isaiah 22: 13).

Our teacher, Moses, always bore his share in the troubles of the congregation, as it is written, "They took a stone and put it under him" (Exodus 17: 12). Could they not have given him a chair or a cushion? But then he said, "Since the Israelites are in trouble (during the war with Amalek) lo, I will bear my part with them, for he who bears his portion of the burden will live to enjoy the hour of consolation. Woe to the one who thinks, 'Ah, well, I will neglect my duty; who can know whether I bear my part or not;' even the stones of his house, aye, the limbs of the trees, shall testify against him, as it is written, 'For the stones will cry from the wall, and the limbs of the trees will testify.'"

TRADES

Rabbi Meir said, "When a man teaches his son a trade, he should pray to the Possessor of the world, the Dispenser of wealth and poverty; for in every trade and pursuit of life both the rich and the poor are to be found. It is folly for one to say, 'This is a bad trade, it will not afford me a living;' because he will find many well to do in the same occupation. Neither should a successful man boast and say, 'This is a great trade, a glorious art, it has made me wealthy because many working in the same line as himself have found but poverty. Let all remember that everything is through the infinite mercy and wisdom of God."

Rabbi Simon, the son of Eleazer, said, "Hast thou ever noted the fowls of the air and beasts of the field how easily their maintenance is provided for them; and yet they were only created to serve me. Now should not I find a livelihood with even less trouble, for I was made to serve my fellow-creatures? But, alas! I sinned against my Creator, therefore am I punished with poverty and obliged to labour."

Rabbi Judah said, "Most mule-drivers are cruel. They beat their poor beasts unmercifully. Most camel-drivers are upright. They travel through deserts and dangerous places, and have time for meditation and thoughts of God. The majority of seamen are religious. Their daily peril makes them so. The best doctors are deserving of punishment. In the pursuit of knowledge they experiment on their patients, and often with fatal results. The best of butchers deserve to be rated with the Amalekites, they are accustomed to blood and cruelty; as it is written of the Amalekites, 'How he met thee by the way and smote the hindmost of thee, and that were feeble behind thee, when thou vast faint and weary.'"

Death

Man is born with his hands clenched; he dies with his hands wide open. Entering life he desires to grasp everything; leaving the world, all that he possessed has slipped away.

Even as a fox is man; as a fox which seeing a fine vineyard lusted after its grapes. But the palings were placed at narrow distances, and the fox was too bulky to creep between them. For three days he fasted, and when he had grown thin he entered into the vineyard. He feasted upon the grapes, forgetful of the morrow, of all things but his enjoyment; and lo, he had again grown stout and was unable to leave the scene of his feast. So for three days more he fasted, and when he had again grown thin, he passed through the palings and stood outside the vineyard, meagre as when he entered.

So with man; poor and naked he enters the world, poor and naked does he leave.

Very expressive is the legend, one of many woven around the name of Alexander.

He wandered to the gates of Paradise and knocked for entrance,

"Who knocks?" demanded the guardian angel.

"Alexander."

Who is Alexander?"

"Alexander--*the* Alexander--Alexander the Great--the conqueror of the world."

"We know him not," replied the angel; "this is the Lord's gate, only the righteous enter here."

Alexander begged for something to prove that he had reached the gates of Paradise, and a small piece of a skull was given to him. He showed it to his wise men, who placed it in one scale of a balance. Alexander poured gold and silver into the other scale, but the small bone weighed heavier; he poured in more, adding his crown jewels, his diadem; but still the bone outweighed them all. Then one of the wise men, taking a grain of dust from the ground placed that upon the bone, and lo, the scale flew up.

The bone was that which surrounds the eye of man; the eye of man which naught can satisfy save the dust which covers it in the grave.

When the righteous dies 'tis earth that meets with loss. The jewel will ever be a jewel, but it has passed from the possession of its former owner. Well may the loser weep.

Life is a passing shadow, say the Scriptures. The shadow of a tower or a tree; the shadow which prevails for a time? No; even as the shadow of a bird in its flight, it passeth from our sight, and neither bird nor shadow remains.

Funeral Sermon Over A Dead Rabbi

"My lover goes down into his garden, to the beds of spices, to wander about in the garden and pluck roses" (Song of Songs).

The world is the garden of my lover, and he my lover is the King of kings. Like a bed of fragrant spices is Israel, the sweet savour of piety ascends on high, the perfume of learning lingers on the passing breeze, and the, bed of beauty is fenced round by gentle peace. The plants flourish and put forth leaves, leaves giving grateful shelter to those who suffer from the heats and disappointment of life, and my lover seeking the most beautiful blossom, plucks the roses, the students of the law, whose belief is their delight.

When the devouring flames seize upon the cedar, shall not the lowly hyssop fear and tremble? When anglers draw the great leviathan from his mighty deeps, what hope have the fish of the shallow pond? When the fishing-line is dropped into the dashing torrent, can they feel secure, the waters of the purling brook?

Mourn for those who are left; mourn not for the one taken by God from earth. He has entered into the eternal rest, while we are bowed with sorrow.

RABBI AKIBA

IT is man's duty to thank God for the occurrence of evil even as for the occurrence of good, as it is written, "And thou shalt love the Lord thy God with all thy heart, with all thy soul, and with all thy might."

"With all thy heart." With thy propensities towards good and towards evil.

"With all thy soul." Even though he should demand thy life.

"With all thy might." All thy personal possessions. No matter what measure be meted to thee, for good and for evil, be sincerely thankful.

Rabbi Akiba was once travelling through the country, and he had with him an ass, a rooster, and a lamp.

At nightfall he reached a village where he sought shelter for the night without success.

"All that God does is done well," said the Rabbi, and proceeding towards the forest he resolved to pass the night there. He lit his lamp, but the wind extinguished it. "All that God does is done well," he said. The ass and the rooster were devoured by wild beasts; yet still he said no more than "All that God dues is well done."

Next day he learned that a troop of the enemy's soldiers had passed through the forest that night. If the ass had brayed, if the rooster had crowed, or if the soldiers had seen his light he would surely had met with death, therefore he said again, "All that God does is done well."

It happened once when Rabbi Gamliel, Rabbi Eleazer, the son of Azaria, Rabbi Judah, and Rabbi Akiba were walking together, they heard the shouts and laughter and joyous tones of a multitude of people at a distance. Four of the Rabbis wept; but Akiba laughed aloud.

"Akiba," said the others to him, "wherefore laugh? These heathens who worship idols live in peace, and are merry, while our holy city lies in ruins; weep, do not laugh." '

"For that very reason I laugh, and am glad," answered Rabbi Akiba. "If God allows these who transgress His will to live happily on earth, how infinitely great must be the happiness which He has stored up in the world to come for those who observe His commands."

Upon another occasion these same Rabbis went up to Jerusalem. Whey they reached Mount Zophim and saw the desolation about them they rent their garments, and when they reached the spot where the Temple had stood and saw a fox run out from the very site of the holy of holies four of them wept bitterly; but again Rabbi Akiba appeared merry. His comrades again rebuked him for this, to them, unseemly state of feeling.

"Ye ask me why I am merry," said he; "come now, tell me why ye weep?"

'Because the Bible tells us that a stranger (one not descended from Aaron) who approaches the holy of holies shall be put to death, and now behold the foxes make of it a dwelling-place. Why should we not weep?"

"Ye weep," returned Akiba, "from the very reason which causes my heart to be glad. Is it not written, 'And testify to me, ye faithful witnesses, Uriah, the priest, and Zachariah, the son of Berachiahu?' Now what hath Uriah to do with Zachariah? Uriah lived during the existence of the first Temple, and Zachariah during the second. Know ye not that the prophecy of Uriah is compared to the prophecy of Zachariah. From Uriah's prophecy we find, 'Therefore for your sake Zion will be ploughed as is a field, and Jerusalem will be a desolation, and the mount of Zion shall be as a forest;' and in Zachariah we find, 'They will sit, the old men and women, in the streets of Jerusalem?' Before the prophecy of Uriah was accomplished I might have doubted the truth of Zachariah's comforting words; but now that one has been accomplished, I feel assured that the promises to Zachariah will also come to pass, therefore am I glad."

"Thy words comfort us, Akiba," answered his companions. "May God ever provide us comfort."

Still another time, when Rabbi Eleazer was very sick and his friends and scholars were weeping for him, Rabbi Akiba appeared happy, and asked them why they wept. "Because," they replied, "our beloved Rabbi is lying between life and death." "Weep not, on the contrary be glad therefor," he answered. "If his wine did not grow sour, if his flag was not stricken down, I might think that on earth he received the reward of his righteousness; but now that I see my teacher suffering for what evil he may have committed in this world, I rejoice. He hath taught us that the most righteous among us commits some sin, therefore in the world to come he will have peace."

While Rabbi Eleazer was sick, the four elders, Rabbi Tarphon, Rabbi Joshua, Rabbi Eleazer, the son of Azoria and Rabbi Akiba, called upon him.

"Thou art better to Israel than the raindrops to earth, or the raindrops are for this world only, whilst thou, my teacher, have helped the ripening of fruit for this world and the next," said Rabbi Tarphon.

"Thou art better to Israel than the sun, for the sun is for this world alone; thou hast given light for this world and the next," said Rabbi Joshua.

Then spoke Rabbi Eleazer, the son of Azoria:

"Thou art better to Israel," said he, "than father and mother to man. They bring him into the world, but thou, my teacher, showest him the way into the world of immortality."

Then said Rabbi Akiba:

"It is well that man should be afflicted, for his distresses atone for his sins."

"Does the Bible make such an assertion, Akiba?" asked his teacher.

"Yes," answered Akiba. "'Twelve years old was Manassah when he became king, and fifty-and-five years did he reign in Jerusalem, and he did what was evil in the eyes of the Lord' (Kings). Now, how was this? Did Hezekiah teach the law to the whole world and not to his son Manassah? Assuredly not; but Manassah paid no attention to his precepts, and neglected the word of God until he was afflicted with bodily pain, as it is written (Chron. 33: 10), 'And the Lord spoke to Manassah and to his people, but they listened not, wherefore the Lord brought over them the captains of the armies belonging to the king of Assyria, and they took Manassah prisoner with chains, and bound him with fetters, and led him off to Babylon; and when he was in distress he besought the Lord his God, and humbled himself greatly before the God of his fathers. And he prayed to Him, and He permitted Himself to be entreated by him and heard his supplication, and brought him back to Jerusalem unto his kingdom. Then did Manassah feel conscious that the Lord is indeed the (true) God.'

"Now, what did the king of Assyria to Manassah? He placed him in a copper barrel and had a fire kindled beneath it, and while enduring great torture of his body, Manassah was further tortured in his mind. 'Shall I call upon the Almighty?' he thought. 'Alas! His anger burns against me. To call upon my idols is to call in vain,--alas, alas, what hope remains to me!'

"He prayed to the greatest of his idols, and waited in vain for a reply. He called to the lesser gods, and remained unanswered. Then with trembling heart he addressed the great Eternal.

"'O Eternal! God of Abraham, Isaac, and Jacob, and their descendants, the heavens and the earth are the works of Thy hand. Thou didst give to the sea a shore, controlling with a word the power of the mighty deep. Thou art merciful as Thou art great, and Thou hast promised to accept the repentance of those who return to Thee with upright hearts. As numerous are my sins as the sands which cover the seashore. I have done evil before Thee, committing abominations in Thy presence and acting wickedly. Bound with fetters I come before Thee, and on my knees I entreat Thee, in the name of Thy great attributes of mercy, to compassionate my suffering and my distress. Pardon me, oh Lord, forgive me. Do not utterly destroy me because of my transgressions. Let not my punishment eternally continue. Though I am unworthy of Thy goodness, O Lord, yet save me in Thy mercy. Henceforth will I praise Thy name all the days of my life, for all Thy creatures delight in praising Thee, and unto Thee is the greatness and the goodness for ever and ever, Selah!"

"God heard this prayer, even as it is written, 'And He permitted Himself to be entreated by him, and brought him back to Jerusalem unto his kingdom.'"

"From which we may learn," continued Akiba, "that affliction is an atonement for sin."

Said Rabbi Eleazer, the great, "It is commanded 'thou shalt love the Lord thy God with all thy soul and with all that is loved by thee.'

"Does not 'with all thy soul' include 'with all that is loved by thee?'

"Some people love themselves more than they love their money; to them 'tis said, 'with all thy soul;' while for those who love their money more than themselves the commandment reads, 'with all that is loved by thee.'"

But Rabbi Akiba always expounded the words, "with all thy soul," to mean "even though thy life be demanded of thee."

When the decree was issued forbidding the Israelites to study the law, what did Rabbi Akiba?

He installed many congregations secretly, and in secret lectured before them.

Then Papus, the son of Juda, said to him:

"Art not afraid, Akiba? Thy doings may be discovered, and thou wilt be punished for disobeying the decree."

"Listen, and I will relate to thee a parable," answered Akiba. "A fox, walking by the river side, noticed the fishes therein swimming and swimming to and fro, never ceasing; so he said to them, 'Why are ye hurrying, what do ye fear?'

"'The nets of the angler,' they replied.

"'Come, then,' said the fox, 'and live with me on dry land.'

"But the fishes laughed.

"'And art thou called the wisest of the beasts?' they exclaimed; 'verily thou art the most foolish. If we are in danger even in our element, how much greater would be our risk in leaving it.'

"It is the same with us. We are told of the law that it is 'our life and the prolongation of our days.' This is it when things are peaceful with us; how much greater is our need of it then in times like these?"

It is said that it was but shortly after this when Rabbi Akiba was imprisoned for teaching the law, and in the prison in which he was incarcerated he found Papus, who had been condemned for some other offence.

Rabbi Akiba said to him:

"Papus, what brought thee here?"

And Papus replied:

"Joy, joy, to thee, that thou art imprisoned for studying God's law; but woe, woe is mine that I am here through vanity."

When Rabbi Akiba was led forth to execution, it was just at the time of the morning service.

"'Hear, oh Israel! the Lord our God, the Lord is one,'" he exclaimed in a loud and firm voice.

The torturers tore his flesh with pointed cards, yet still he repeated, "The Lord is one."

"Always did I say," he continued, "that 'with all thy soul,' meant even though life should be demanded of thee, and I wondered whether I should ever be able to so observe it. Now see, to-day, I do so; 'the Lord is one.'"

With these words he died.

Happy art thou, Rabbi Akiba, that thy soul went out in purity for the happiness of all futurity is thine.

Elishah Ben Abuyah

Elishah ben Abuyah, a most learned man, became in after-life an apostate. Rabbi Meir had been one of his pupils, and he never failed in the great love which he bore for his teacher.

It happened upon one occasion when Rabbi Meir was lecturing in the college, that some students entered and said to him:

"Thy teacher, Elishah, is riding by on horseback on this holy Sabbath day."

Rabbi Meir left the college, and overtaking Elishah walked along by his horse's side. The latter saluted him, and asked:

"What passage of Scripture hast thou been expounding?"

"From the book of Job," replied Rabbi Meir. "'The Lord blessed the latter days of Job more than the beginning.'"

"And how didst thou explain the verse?" said Elishah.

"That the Lord increased his wealth twofold."

"But thy teacher, Akiba, said not so," returned Elishah.

"He said that the Lord blessed the latter days of Job with twofold of penitence and good deeds."

"How," inquired Rabbi Meir, "wouldst thou explain the verse, 'Better is the end of a thing than the beginning thereof.' If a man buys merchandise in his youth and meets with losses, is it likely that he will recover his substance in old age? Or, if a person studies God's law in his youth and forgets it, is it probable that it will return to his memory in his latter days?"

"Thy teacher, Akiba, said not so," replied Elishah; "he explained the verse, 'Better is the end of a thing when the beginning was good My own life proves the soundness of this explanation. On the day when I was admitted into the covenant of Abraham, my father made a great feast. Some of his visitors sang, some of them danced, but the Rabbis conversed upon God's wisdom and His laws. This latter pleased my father, Abuyah, and he said,

'When my son grows up ye shall teach him and he shall become like ye; he did not cause me to study for God's sake but only to make his name famous through me.' Therefore, in my latter days have I become wicked and an apostate; and now, return home."

"And wherefore?"

"Because, on the Sabbath day, thou art allowed to go so far and no farther, and I have reckoned the distance thou hast travelled with me by the footsteps of my horse."

"If thou art so wise," said Rabbi Meir, "as to reckon the distance I may travel by the footsteps of thy horse, and so particular for my sake, why not return to God and repent of thy apostacy?"

Elishah answered:

"It is not in my power. I rode upon horseback once on the Day of Atonement; yea, when it fell upon the Sabbath, and when I passed the synagogue I heard a voice crying, 'Return, oh backsliding children, return to me and I will return to ye; except Elishah, the son of Abuyah, he knew his Master and yet rebelled against Him.'"

What caused such a learned man as Elishah to turn to evil ways?

It is reported that once while studying the law in the vale of Genusan, he saw a man climbing a tree. The man found a bird's-nest in the tree, and taking the mother with the young ones he still departed in peace. He saw another man who finding a bird's-nest followed the Bible's command and took the young only, allowing the mother to fly away; and yet a serpent stung him as he descended and he died. "Now," thought he, "where is the Bible's truth and promises? Is it not written, 'And the young thou mayest take to thyself, but the mother thou shalt surely let go, that it may he well with thee and that thou mayest live many days.' Now, where is the long life to this man who followed the precept, while the one who transgressed it is unhurt?"

He had not heard how Rabbi Akiba expounded this verse, that the days would be long in the future world where all is happiness.

There is also another reason given as the cause for Elishah's backsliding and apostacy.

During the fearful period of religious persecution, the learned Rabbi Judah, whose life had been passed in the study of the law and the practice of God's precepts, was delivered into the power of the cruel torturer. His tongue was placed in a dog's mouth and the dog bit it off.

So Elishah said, "If a tongue which uttered naught but truth be so used, and a learned, wise man be so treated, of what use is it to avoid having a lying tongue and being ignorant. Lo, if these things are allowed, there is surely no reward for the righteous, and no resurrection for the dead."

When Elishah waxed old he was taken sick, and Rabbi Meir, learning of the illness of his aged teacher, called upon him.

"Oh return, return unto thy God," entreated Rabbi Meir.

"What!" exclaimed Elishah, "return! and could He receive my penitence, the penitence of an apostate who has so rebelled against Him?"

"Is it not written," said Meir, "'Thou turnest man to contrition?' (Psalm 90: 3). No matter how the soul of man may be crushed, he can still turn to his God and find relief."

Elishah listened to these words, wept bitterly and died. Not many years after his death his daughters came, poverty stricken, asking relief from the colleges. "Remember," said they, "the merit of our father's learning, not his conduct."

The colleges listened to the appeal and supported the daughters of Elishah.

Rabbi Simon

Rabbi Judah, Rabbi Joseh, and Rabbi Simon were conversing one day, when Judah ben Gerim entered the apartment and sat down with the three. Rabbi Judah was speaking in a complimentary strain of the Gentiles (Romans). "See," said he, "how they have improved their cities, how beautiful they have made them, and how much they have done for the comfort and convenience of the citizens; bath-houses, bridges, fine broad streets, surely much credit is due them."

"Nay," answered Rabbi Simon, "all that they have done has been from a selfish motive. The bridges bring them in a revenue, for all who use them are taxed; the bath-houses are for their personal adornment--'tis all selfishness, not patriotism."

Judah ben Gerim repeated these remarks to his friends, and finally they reached the ears of the emperor. He would not allow them to pass unnoticed. He ordered that Judah, who had spoken well of the nation, should be advanced in honour; that Joseh, who had remained silent instead of seconding the assertions, should be banished to Zipore; and that Simon, who had disputed the compliment, should be put to death.

The latter with his son fled and concealed himself in the college when this at became known to him. For some time he remained there comparatively safe, his wife bringing his meals daily. But when the officers were directed to make diligent search he became afraid, lest through the indiscretion of his wife his place of concealment might be discovered.

"The mind of woman is weak and unsteady," said he, "perhaps they may question and confuse her, and thus may death come upon me."

So leaving the city, Simon and his son took refuge in a lonely cave. Near its mouth some fruit trees grew, supplying them with food, and a spring of pure water bubbled from rocks in the immediate vicinity. For thirteen years Rabbi Simon lived here, until the emperor died and his decrees were repealed. He then returned to the city.

When Rabbi Phineas, his son-in-law, heard of his return, he called upon him at once, and noticing an apparent neglect in the mental and physical condition of his relative, he exclaimed, "Woe, woe! that I meet thee in so sad a condition!"

But Rabbi Simon answered:

"Not so; happy is it that thou findest me in this condition, for thou findest me no less righteous than before. God has preserved me, and my faith in Him, and thus hereafter shall I explain the verse of Scripture, 'And Jacob came perfect.' Perfect in his physical condition, perfect in his temporal condition, and perfect in his knowledge of God."

Antoninus, in conversing with Rabbi Judah, said to him:

"In the future world, when the soul comes before the Almighty Creator for judgment, may it not find a plea of excuse for worldly wickedness in saying, 'Lo, the sin is the body's; I am now free from the body; the sins were not mine?'"

Rabbi Judah answered, "Let me relate to thee a parable. A king had an orchard of fine figs, which he prized most highly. That the fruit might not be stolen or abused, he paced two watchers in the orchard, and that they themselves might not he tempted to partake of the fruit, he chose one of them a blind man, and the other one lame. But lo, when they were in the orchard, the lame man said to his companion, 'I see very fine figs; they are luscious and tempting; carry me to the tree, that we may both partake of them."

"So the blind man carried the lame man, and they ate of the figs.

"When the king entered the orchard he noticed at once that his finest figs were missing, and he asked the watchers what had become of them.

"The blind man answered:

'I know not. I could not steal them; I am blind; I cannot even see them.'

"And the lame man answered:

"'Neither could I steal them; I could not approach the tree.'

"But the king was wise, and he answered:

'Lo, the blind carried the lame,' and he punished them accordingly.

"So is it with us. The world is the orchard in which the Eternal King has placed us, to keep watch and ward, to till its soil and care for its fruit. But the soul and body are the man; if one violates the precepts so does the other, and after death the soul may not say, 'It is the fault of the body to which I was tied that I committed sins;' no, God will do as did the owner of the orchard, as it is written:

'He shall call from the heaven above, and to the earth to judge his people' (Psalms).

"He shall call from the 'heaven above,' which is the soul, and to the 'earth below,' which is the body, mixing with the dust from whence it sprung."

A heathen said to Rabbi Joshua, "Thou believest that God knows the future?"

"Yes," replied the Rabbi.

"Then," said the questioner, "wherefore is it written, 'The Lord said, I will destroy everything which I have made, because it repenteth me that I have made them?' Did not the Lord foresee that man would become corrupt?"

Then said Rabbi Joshua, "Hast thou children?"

"Yes," was the answer.

"When a child was born, what didst thou?"

"I made a great rejoicing."

"What cause hadst thou to rejoice? Dost thou not know that they must die?"

"Yes, that is true; but in the time of enjoyment I do not think of the future."

"So was it with God," said Rabbi Joshua. "He knew that men would sin; still that knowledge did not prevent the execution of his beneficent purpose to create them."

One of the emperors said to Rabon Gamliel:

"Your God is a thief, as it is written, 'And the Lord God caused a deep sleep to fall upon Adam, and he slept. And He took a rib from Adam.'"

The Rabbi's daughter said, "Let me answer this aspersion. Last night robbers broke into my room, and stole therefrom a silver vessel: but they left a golden one in its stead."

The emperor replied, "I wish that such thieves would come every night."

Thus was it with Adam; God took a rib from him, but placed a woman instead of it.

Rabbi Joshua, of Saknin, said in the name of Rabbi Levi, "The Lord considered from what part of the man he should form woman; not from the head, lest she should be proud; not from the eyes, lest she should wish to see everything; not from the mouth, lest she might be talkative; nor from the ear, lest she should wish to hear everything; nor from the heart, lest she should be jealous; nor from the hand, lest she should wish to find out everything; nor from the feet, in order that she might not be a wanderer; only from the most hidden place, that is covered even when a man is naked--namely, the rib."

The scholars of Rabbi Simon ben Jochai once asked him:

"Why did not the Lord give to Israel enough manna to suffice them for a year, at one time, instead of meting it out daily?"

The Rabbi replied:

"I will answer ye with a parable. There was once a king who had a son to whom he gave a certain yearly allowance, paying the entire sum for his year's support on one appointed day. It soon happened that this day on which the allowance was due, was the only day in the year when the father saw his son. So the king changed his plan, and gave his son each day his maintenance for that day only, and then the son visited his father with the return of each day's sun.

"So was it with Israel; each father of a family, dependent upon the manna provided each day by God's bounty, for his support and the support of his family, naturally had his mind devoted to the Great Giver and Sustainer of life"

When Rabbi Eleazer was sick his scholars visited him, and said, "Rabbi, teach us the way of life, that we may inherit eternity."

The Rabbi answered, "Give honour to your comrades. Know to whom you pray. Restrain your children from frivolous conversation, and place them among the learned men, in order that they may acquire wisdom. So may you merit life in the future world."

When Rabbi Jochanan was sick his scholars also called upon him. When he beheld them he burst into tears.

"Rabbi!" they exclaimed, "Light of Israel! The chief pillar! Why weep?"

The Rabbi answered, "Were I to be brought before a king of flesh and blood, who is here to-day and to-morrow in the grave; who may be angry with me, but not for ever; who may imprison me, but not for ever; who may kill me, but only for this world; whom I may sometimes bribe; even then I would fear. But now, I am to appear before the King of kings, the Most Holy One, blessed be He, who lives through all eternity. If He is wroth, it is for ever; if He imprisons me, it is for ever; if He slays me, it is for the future world; and I can bribe Him neither with words nor money. Not only this, two paths are before me, one leading to punishment, the other to reward, and I know not which one I must travel. Should I not weep?"

The scholars of Rabbi Johanan, the son of Zakai, asked of their teacher this question:

"Wherefore is it, that according to the law, the punishment of a highwayman is not as severe as the punishment of a sneak thief? According to the Mosaic law, if a man steals an ox or a sheep, and kills it or sells it, he is required to restore five oxen for the one ox, and four sheep for the one sheep (Exodus 21: 37); but for the highwayman we find, 'When he hath sinned and is conscious of his guilt, he shall restore that he hath taken violently away; he shall restore it and its principal, and the fifth part thereof he shall add thereto.' Therefore, he who commits a highway robbery pays as punishment one-fifth of the same, while a sneak thief is obliged to return five oxen for one ox, and four sheep for one sheep. Wherefore is this?"

"Because," replied the teacher, "the highway robber treats the servant as the master. He takes away violently in the presence of the servant, the despoiled man, and the master--God. But the sneak thief imagines that God's eye is not upon him; He acts secretly, thinking, as the Psalmist says, 'The Lord doth not see, neither will the God of Jacob regard it' (Ps. 94: 5). Listen to a parable. Two men made a feast. One invited all the inhabitants of the city, and omitted inviting the king. The other invited neither the king nor his subjects. Which one deserves condemnation? Certainly the one who invited the subjects and not the king. The people of the earth are God's subjects. The sneak thief fears their eyes, yet he does not honour the eye of the king, the eye of God, which watches all his actions."

Rabbi Meir says, "This law teaches us how God regards industry. If a person steals an ox he must return five in its place, because while the animal was in his unlawful possession it could not work for its rightful owner. A lamb, however, does no labour, and is not profitable that way; therefore he is only obliged to replace it fourfold."

Rabbi Nachman dined with his teacher, Rabbi Yitzchak, and, upon departing after the meal, he said, "Teacher, bless me!"

"Listen," replied Rabbi Yitzchak. "A traveller was once journeying through the desert, and when weary, hungry, and thirsty, he happened upon an oasis, where grew a fruitful tree, wide-branched, and at the foot of which there gushed a spring of clear, cool water.

"The stranger ate of the luscious fruit, enjoying and resting in the grateful shade, and quenching his thirst in the sparkling water which bubbled merrily at his feet.

"When about to resume his journey, he addressed the tree and spoke as follows:

"'Oh, gracious tree, with what words can I bless thee, and what good can I wish thee? I cannot wish thee good fruit, for it is already thine; the blessing of water is also thine, and the gracious shade thrown by thy beauteous branches the Eternal has already granted thee, for my good and the good of those who travel by this way. Let me pray to God, then, that all thy offspring may be goodly as thyself.'

"So it is with thee, my pupil. How shall I bless thee? Thou art perfect in the law, eminent in the land, respected, and blessed with means. May God grant that all thy off spring may prove goodly as thyself."

A wise man, say the Rabbis, was Gebiah ben Pesisah. When the children of Canaan accused the Israelites of stealing their land, saying, "The land of Canaan is ours, as it is written, 'The land of Canaan and its boundaries belong to the Canaanites,'" and demanded restitution, Gebiah offered to argue the case before the ruler.

Said Gebiah to the Africans, "Ye bring your proof from the Pentateuch, and by the Pentateuch will I refute it, 'Cursed be Canaan; a servant of servants shall he be unto his brethren' (Gen. 9: 25). To whom does the property of a slave belong? To his master. Even though the land belonged to ye, through your servitude it became Israel's." "Answer him," said the ruler.

The accusers asked for three days' time to prepare their reply, but at the end of the three days they had vanished.

Then came the Egyptians, saying, "'God gave the Israelites favour in the eyes of the Egyptians, and they lent them gold and silver.' Now return us the gold and silver which our ancestors lent ye."

Again Gebiah appeared for the sages of Israel.

"Four hundred and thirty years," said he, "did the children of Israel dwell in Egypt. Come, now, pay us the wages of six hundred thousand men who worked for ye foe naught, and we will return the gold and silver."

Then came the children of Ishmael and Ketura, before Alexander of Mukdon, saying, "The land of Canaan is ours, as it is written, 'These are the generations of Ishmael, the son of Abraham;' even as it is written, 'These are the generations of Isaac, the son of Abraham.' One son is equal to the other; come, give us our share."

Again Gebiah appeared as counsel for the sages.

From the Pentateuch, which is your proof, will I confound ye," said he. "Is it not written, 'Abraham gave all that he had to Isaac, but unto the sons of the concubines that Abraham had, Abraham gave gifts.' The man who gives his children their inheritance during his life does not design to give it to them again after his death. To Isaac Abraham left all that he had; to his other children he gave gifts, and sent them away."

Truly a good man, say the Rabbis, was King Munmaz, a descendant of the Hashmonites. During a period of famine he gave to the poor the contents of his treasury and the treasury of his father.

His relatives upbraided him for his liberality. "What thy father saved," they exclaimed, "thou hast thrown away."

Then answered Munmaz:

"My father laid up treasure here on earth; I gather it in the heavens above. 'The truth comes forth from the earth, but beneficence looks down from heaven.' My father hoarded it where hands might have been stretched forth for it; I have placed it beyond the reach of human hands. 'Thy throne is established in justice and beneficence.' For my father it produced no fruit, but for me it is bringing forth many fold. 'Say to the righteous it is good; the fruit of their labour they may eat.' My father saved money; I saved life. 'The fruit of the righteous is the tree of life. Who saves lives is a wise man.' My father saved for others; I save for myself; my father saved for this world, but I save for the next. 'Thy beneficence will go before thee; the glory of the Lord will gather thee.'

PART FOURTH. PROVERBS AND SAYINGS OF THE RABBIS, LEGENDS, ETC

Sayings Of The Rabbis

WOE to the children banished from their father's table.

A handful of food will not satisfy the lion, neither can a pit be filled again with its own dust.

Pray to God for mercy until the last shovelful of earth is cast upon thy grave.

Cease not to pray even when the knife is laid upon thy neck.

Open not thy mouth to speak evil.

To be patient is sometimes better than to have much wealth.

The horse fed too liberally with oats becomes unruly.

Happy the pupil whose teacher approves his words.

When the cucumbers are young we may tell whether they will become good for food.

Do not to others what you would not have others do to you.

The ass complains of the cold even in July (Tamuz). First learn and then teach.

Few are they who see their own faults.

A single light answers as well for a hundred men as for one.

Victuals prepared by many cooks will be neither hot nor cold.

The world is a wedding.

Youth is a wreath of roses.

A myrtle even in the desert remains a myrtle.

Teach thy tongue to say, "I do not know."

The house which opens not to the poor will open to the physician.

The birds of the air despise a miser.

Hospitality is an expression of Divine worship.

Thy friend has a friend, and thy friend's friend has s friend; be discreet.

Do not place a blemish on thine own flesh.

Attend no auctions if thou hast no money.

Rather skin a carcass for pay, in the public streets, than lie idly dependent on charity.

Deal with those who are fortunate.

What is intended for thy neighbour will never be thine.

The weakness of thy walls invites the burglar.

The place honours not the man, ‘tis the man who gives honour to the place.

The humblest man is ruler in his own house.

If the fox is king bow before him.

If a word spoken in its time is worth one piece of money, silence in *its* time is worth two.

Tobias committed the sins and his neighbour received the punishment.

Poverty sits as gracefully upon some people as a red saddle upon a white horse.

Drain not the waters of thy well while other people may desire them.

The doctor who prescribes gratuitously gives a worthless prescription.

The rose grows among thorns.

The wine belongs to the master, but the waiter receives the thanks.

He who mixes with unclean things becomes unclean himself; he whose associations are pure becomes more holy with each day.

No man is impatient with his creditors.

Make but one sale, and thou art called a merchant.

Mention not a blemish which is thy own, in detraction of thy neighbour.

If certain goods sell not in one city, try another place.

He who reads the letter should execute the message.

A vessel used for holy purposes should not be put to uses less sacred.

Ornament thyself first, then magnify others.

Two pieces of coin in one bag make more noise than a hundred.

Man sees the mote in his neighbour's eye, but knows not of the beam in his own.

The rivalry of scholars advances science.

If thou tellest thy secret to three persons, ten know of it.

When love is intense both find room enough upon one board of the bench; afterwards they may find themselves cramped in a space of sixty cubits.

When wine enters the head the secret flies out.

When a liar speaks the truth he finds his punishment in the general disbelief.

The camel desired horns, and his ears were taken from him.

Sorrow for those who disappear never to be found.

The officer of the king is also a recipient of honours.

He who studies cannot follow a commercial life; neither can the merchant devote his time to study.

There is no occasion to light thy lamp at noontide,

Let the fruit pray for the welfare of the leaf.

Meat without salt is fit only for the dogs.

Trust not thyself until the day of thy death.

Woe to the country which hath lost its leader; woe to the ship when its captain is no more.

He who increaseth his flesh but multiplieth food for the worms.

The day is short, the labour great, and the workman slothful.

Be yielding to thy superior; be affable towards the young; be friendly with all mankind.

Silence is the fence round wisdom.

Without law, civilisation perishes.

Every man will surely have his hour.

Rather be the tail among lions than the head among foxes.

Into the well which supplies thee with water cast no stones.

Many a colt's skin is fashioned to the saddle which its mother bears.

Truth is heavy, therefore few care to carry it.

Say little and do much.

He who multiplieth words will likely come to sin.

Sacrifice thy will for others, that they may be disposed to sacrifice their wills for thee.

Study to-day, delay not.

Look not upon thy prayers as on a task; let thy supplications be sincere.

He who is loved by man is loved by God.

Honour the sons of the poor; they give to science its splendour.

Do not live near a pious fool.

A small coin in a large jar makes a great noise.

Use thy noble vase to-day; to-morrow it may break.

The cat and the rat make peace over a carcass.

He who walks each day over his estate finds a coin daily.

The dog follows thee for the crumbs in thy pocket.

The soldiers fight, and the kings are heroes.

When the ox is down many are the butchers.

Descend a step in choosing thy wife; ascend a step in choosing thy friend.

Beat the gods and their priests will tremble.

The sun will set without thy assistance.

Hold no man responsible for his utterances in times of grief.

One man eats, another says grace.

He who curbs his wrath merits forgiveness for his sins.

Commit a sin twice and it will not seem to thee a crime.

While our love was strong we lay on the edge of a sword, now a couch sixty yards wide is too narrow for us.

Study is more meritorious than sacrifice.

Jerusalem was destroyed because the instruction of the young was neglected.

The world is saved by the breath of school children.

Even to rebuild the Temple, the schools must not be closed.

Blessed is the son who has studied with his father, and blessed the father who has instructed his son.

Avoid wrath and thou wilt avoid sin; avoid intemperance and thou wilt not provoke Providence.

When others gather, do thou disperse; when others disperse, gather.

When thou art the only purchaser, then buy; when other buyers are present, be thou nobody.

The foolish man knows not an insult, neither does a dead man feel the cutting of a knife.

The cock and the owl both await daylight. "The light," says the cock," brings me delight; but what in the world art thou waiting for?"

The thief who finds no opportunity to steal, considers himself an honest man.

A Galilean said, "When the shepherd is angry with his flock, he appoints for its leader a blind bellwether."

Though it is not incumbent upon thee to complete the work, thou must not therefore cease from pursuing it. If the work is great, great will be thy reward, and thy Master is faithful in His payments.

There are three crowns: of the law, the priesthood, and the kingship; but the crown of a good name is greater than them all.

Who gains wisdom? He who is willing to receive instruction from all sources. Who is the mighty man? He who subdueth his temper. Who is rich? He who is content with his lot. Who is deserving of honour? He who honoureth mankind.

Despise no man and deem nothing impossible; every man hath his hour and every thing its place.

Iron breaks stone; fire melts iron; water extinguishes fire; the clouds consume water; the storm dispels clouds; an withstands the storm; fear conquers man; wine banishes fear; sleep overcomes wine, and death is the master of sleep; but "charity," says Solomon, "saves even from death."

How canst thou escape sin? Think of three things: whence thou comest, whither thou goest, and before whom thou must appear. The scoffer, the liar, the hypocrite, and the slanderer can have no share in the future world of bliss. To slander is to commit murder.

Repent the day before thy death.

Ten measures of wisdom came into the world; the law of Israel received nine measures, and the balance of the world one. Ten measures of beauty came into the world; Jerusalem received nine measures, and the rest of the world one.

Rabbi Simon said:

"The world stands on three pillars: law, worship, and charity."

Rabbi Ada said:

"When he who attends the synagogue regularly is prevented from being present, God asks for him."

Rabbi Simon, the son of Joshua, said:

"His enemies will humble themselves before the one who builds a place of worship."

Rabbi Lakish said:

"He who is able to attend synagogue, and "neglects to do so, is a bad neighbour."

Rabbi José said:

"One need not stand upon a high place to pray, for it is written, 'Out of the depths have I called unto Thee, oh Lord'" (Ps. 30: 1). The same Rabbi prohibits moving about or talking during the progress of prayers, enlarging on Solomon's advice, "Keep thy foot when thou goest into the house of the Lord, and be more ready to hear than to offer the sacrifice of fools" (Feel. 5: 1).

Rabbi Chia, the son of Abba, said:

"To pray loudly is not a necessity of devotion; when we pray we must direct our hearts towards heaven."

When our ancestors in the wilderness were saved from death by gazing upon the brazen serpent, it was not the serpent which killed or preserved. It was the trustful appeal to the Father in heaven.

Say the Rabbis, "Praise the Lord for the evil as for the good;" and David is given as an example when he said, "I had met with distress and sorrow, I then called on the name of the Lord" (Ps. 116).

Rabbi Ashi said:

"Charity is greater than all."

Rabbi Eliazar said:

"Who gives charity in secret is greater than Moses."

He finds authority for this saying in the words of Moses (Deut. 9: 19), "For I was afraid of the anger," and the words of Solomon (Prov. 21: 14), which he presents as an answer, "A gift given in secret pacifieth anger."

Rabbi Joshua said:

"A miser is as wicked as an idolater."

Rabbi Eliazar said:

"Charity is more than sacrifices."

Rabbi Jochanan said:

"He who gives (charity) becomes rich," or as it is written, "A beneficent soul will be abundantly gratified."

One day a philosopher inquired of Rabbi Akiba, "If your God loves the poor, why does He not support them?"

"God allows the poor to be with us ever," responded Akiba, "that the opportunities for doing good may never fail."

"But," returned the philosopher, "how do you know that this virtue of charity pleases God? If a master punishes his slaves by depriving them of food and clothing, does he feel pleased when others feed and clothe them?"

"But suppose, on the other hand," said the Rabbi, "that the children of a tender father, children whom he could no longer justly assist, had fallen into poverty, would he be displeased if kind souls pitied and aided them? We are not the slaves of a hard master. God calls us His children, and Himself we call our Father."

Rabbah said:

"When one stands at the judgment-seat of God these questions are asked:

"'Hast thou been honest in all thy dealings?'

"'Hast thou set aside a portion of thy time for the study of the law?'

"'Hast thou observed the first commandment?'

"'Hast thou, in trouble, still hoped and believed in God?'

"'Hast thou spoken wisely?'"

"All the blessings of a household come through the wife, therefore should her husband honour her."

Rab said:

"Men should be careful lest they cause women to weep, for God counts their tears.

"In cases of charity, where both men and women claim relief, the latter should be first assisted. If there should not be enough for both, the men should cheerfully relinquish their claims.

"A woman's death is felt by nobody as by her husband.

"Tears are shed on God's altar for the one who forsakes his first love.

"He who loves his wife as himself, and honours her more than himself, will train his children properly; he will meet, too, the fulfilment of the verse, 'And thou shalt know that there is peace in thy tent, and thou wilt look over thy habitation and shall miss nothing'" (Job 5: 24).

Rabbi Jose said:

"I never call my wife 'wife,' but 'home,' for she, indeed, makes my home.

"He who possesses a knowledge of God, and a knowledge of man, will not easily commit sin.

"The Bible was given us to establish peace.

"He who wrongs his fellow-man, even in so small a coin as a penny, is as wicked as if he should take life.

"He who raises his hand against his fellow in passion is a sinner.

"Be not the friend of one who wears the cloak of a saint to cover the deformities of a fool."

Rabbi Simon said:

"One who gives way to passion is as bad as an idolater.

"Hospitality is as great a virtue as studying the law."

"Never put thyself in the way of temptation," advised Rabbi Judah; "even David could not resist it."

Rabbi Tyra, on being asked by his pupils to tell them the secret which had gained him a happy, peaceful old age, replied, "I have never cherished anger with my family; I have never envied those greater than myself, and I have never rejoiced in the downfall of any one."

"Unhappy is he who mistakes the branch for the tree, the shadow for the substance.

"Thy yesterday is thy past; thy to-day thy future; thy to-morrow is a secret.

"The best preacher is the heart; the best teacher is time; the best book is the world; the best friend is God.

"Life is but a loan to man; death is the creditor who will one day claim it.

"Understand a man by his own deeds and words. The impressions of others lead to false judgment."

Rabbi Jacob said:

"He through whose agency another has been falsely punished stands outside of heaven's gates."

Rabbi Isaac said:

"The sins of the bad-tempered are greater than his merits."

Rabbi Lakish said:

"The man who sins is foolish as well as wicked."

Rabbi Samuel said:

"The good actions which we perform in this world take form and meet us in the world to come.

"Better to bear a false accusation in silence, than by speaking to bring the guilty to public shame.

"He who can feel ashamed will not readily do wrong.

"There is a great difference between one who can feel ashamed before his own soul and one who is only ashamed before his fellow-man."

Rabbi Akiba said:

"God's covenant with us included work; for the command, 'Six days shalt thou work and the seventh shalt thou rest,' made the 'rest' conditional upon the 'work.'"

Rabbi Simon said, on the same subject:

"God first told Adam to dress the Garden of Eden, and to keep it (Gen. 2: 15), and then permitted him to eat of the fruit of his labour."

Rabbi Tarphon said:

"God did not dwell in the midst of Israel till they had worked to deserve His presence, for he commanded, 'They shall make me a sanctuary, and then I will dwell in the midst of them.'"

When Jerusalem was in the hands of the Romans, one of their philosophers asked of the Rabbis:

"If your God dislikes idolatry, why does He not destroy the idols and so put temptation out of the way?"

The wise men answered:

"Would you have the sun and the moon destroyed because of the foolish ones who worship them? To change the course of nature to punish sinners, would bring suffering to the innocent also."

In Ecclesiastes 9: 14, we find this verse:

"There was a little city and the men therein were few, and there came against it a great king, and built around it great works of siege; but there was found in it a poor wise man, and he delivered the city by his wisdom."

The sages interpret this verse most beautifully. The "little city" is man, and the "few men" are his different qualities. The "king" who besieged it is evil inclination, and the "great bulwarks" he built around it are "evil deeds." The "poor wise man" who saved the city is the "good actions" which the poorest may readily perform.

Rabbi Judah said:

"He who refuses to teach a precept to his pupil is guilty of theft, just as one who steals from the inheritance of his father; as it is written, 'The law which Moses commanded us is the inheritance of the congregation of Jacob.' (lieut.) But if he teaches him, what is his reward?"

Raba says, "He will obtain the blessing of Joseph."

Rabbi Eleazer said:

"That house where the law is not studied by night should be destroyed.

"The wealthy man who aids not the scholar desirous of studying God's law will not prosper,

"He who changes his word, saying one thing and doing another, is even as he who serveth idols."

Rabbi Chamah, the son of Papa, said:

"He who eats or drinks and blesses not the Lord, is even as he who stealeth, for it is said, 'The heavens are the heavens of the Lord, and the earth hath He given to the children of men.'"

Rabbi Simon, the son of Lakish, said:

"They who perform one precept in this world will find it recorded for their benefit in the world to come; as it is written, 'Thy righteousness will go before thee, the glory of the Lord will gather thee in.' And the same will be the case, in contrast, with those who sin. For the Bible says, 'Which I commanded thee this day to do them,' to 'do them,' the precepts, to-day, though the reward is not promised to-day; but in the future, ordinances obeyed, will testify in thy favour, for 'thy righteousness will go before thee.'"

The Rabbis pronounced those the "friends of God," who being offended thought not of revenge; who practised good through love for God, and who were cheerful under suffering and difficulties. Of such Isaiah wrote, "They shall shine forth like the sun at noonday."

Love thy wife as thyself; honour her more than thyself. He who lives unmarried, lives without joy. If thy wife is small, bend down to her and whisper in her ear. He who sees his wife die, has, as it were, been present at the destruction of the sanctuary itself. The children of a man who marries for money will prove a curse to him.

He who has more learning than good deeds is like a tree with many branches but weak roots; the first great storm will throw it to the ground. He whose good works are greater than his knowledge is like a tree with fewer branches but with strong and spreading roots, a tree which all the winds of heaven cannot uproot.

Better is the curse of the righteous man than the blessing of the wicked. Better the curse of Achia, the Shelonite, than the blessing of Bil'am, the son of Beor. Thus did Achia curse the Israelites, "And the Lord will smite Israel as the reed is shaken in the water" (Kings 14: 15). The reed bends but it breaks not, for it groweth by the water, and its roots are strong. Thus did Bil'am bless Israel, "As cedar trees beside the waters." Cedars do not grow beside the waters; their roots are weak, and when strong winds blow they break in pieces.

THE DESERT ISLAND

A very wealthy man, who was of a kind, benevolent disposition, desired to make his slave happy. He gave him, therefore, his freedom, and presented him with a shipload of merchandise.

"Go," said he, "sail to different countries, dispose of these goods, and that which thou mayest receive for them shall be thy own."

The slave sailed away upon the broad ocean, but before he had been long upon his voyage a storm overtook him; his ship was driven on a rock and went to pieces; all on board were lost, all save this slave, who swam to an island shore near by. Sad, despondent, with naught in the world, he traversed this island, until he approached a large and beautiful city; and many people approached him joyously, shouting, "Welcome! welcome! Long live the king!" They brought a rich carriage, and placing him therein, escorted him to a magnificent palace, where many servants gathered about him, clothing him in royal garments, addressing him as their sovereign, and expressing their obedience to his will.

The slave was amazed and dazzled, believing that he was dreaming, and all that he saw, heard, and experienced was mere passing fantasy. Becoming convinced of the reality of his condition, he said to some men about him for whom he experienced a friendly feeling

"How is this? I cannot understand it. That you should thus elevate and honour a man whom you know not, a poor, naked wanderer, whom you have never seen before, making him your ruler, causes me more wonder than I can readily express."

"Sire," they replied, "this island is inhabited by spirits. Long since they prayed to God to send them yearly a son of man to reign over them, and He has answered their prayers. Yearly he sends them a son of man, whom they receive with honour and elevate to the throne; but his dignity and power ends with the year. With its close his royal garments are taken from him, he is placed on board a ship and carried to a vast and desolate island, where, unless he has previously been wise and prepared for this day, he will find neither friend nor subject, and be obliged to pass a weary, lonely, miserable life. Then a new king is selected here, and so year follows year. The kings who preceded thee were careless and indifferent, enjoying their power to the full, and thinking not of the day when it should end. Be wiser thou; let our words find rest within thy heart."

The newly-made king listened attentively to all this, and felt grieved that he should have lost even the time he had already missed for making preparations for his loss of power,

He addressed the wise man who had spoken, saying, "Advise me, oh, spirit of wisdom, how I may prepare for the days which will come upon me in the future."

"Naked thou earnest to us and naked thou wilt be sent to the desolate island of which I have told thee," replied the other. "At present thou art king, and may do as pleaseth thee; therefore send workmen to this island; let them build houses, till the ground, and beautify the surroundings. The barren soil will be changed into fruitful fields, people will journey there to live, and thou wilt have established a new kingdom for thyself, with subjects to welcome thee in gladness when thou shalt have lost thy power here. The year is short, the work is long; therefore be earnest and energetic."

The king followed this advice. He sent workmen and materials to the desolate island, and before the close of his temporary power it had become a blooming, pleasant, and attractive spot. The rulers who had preceded him had anticipated the day of their power's close with dread, or smothered all thought of it in revelry; but he looked forward to it as a day of joy, when he should enter upon a career of permanent peace and happiness.

The day came; the freed slave, who had been made king, was deprived of his authority; with his power he lost his royal garments; naked he was placed upon a ship, and its sails set for the desolate isle.

When he approached its shores, however, the people whom he had sent there came to meet him with music, song, and great joy. They made him a prince among then, and he lived with them ever after in pleasantness and peace.

The wealthy man of kindly disposition is God, and the slave to whom He gave freedom is the soul which He, gives to man. The island at which the slave arrives is the world; naked and weeping he appears to his parents, who are the inhabitants that greet him warmly and make him their king. The friends who tell him of the ways of the country are his "good inclinations." The year of his reign is his span of life, and the desolate island is the future world, which he must beautify by good deeds, "the workmen and material," or else live lonely and desolate for ever.

THE EMPEROR AND THE AGED MAN

The Emperor Adrian, passing through the streets of Tiberias, noticed a very old man planting a fig tree, and pausing, said to him:

"Wherefore plant that tree? If thou didst labour in thy youth, thou shouldst now have a store for thy old age, and surely of the fruit of this tree thou canst not hope to eat."

The old man answered:

"In my youth I worked, and I still work. With God's good pleasure I may e'en partake of the fruit of this tree I plant. I am in His hands."

"Tell me thy age," said the emperor.

"I have lived for a hundred years."

"A hundred years old, and still expect to eat from the fruit of this tree?"

"If such be God's pleasure," replied the old man; "if not, I will leave it for my son, as my father left the fruit of his labour for me."

"Well," said the emperor, "if thou dost live until the figs from this tree are ripe, I pray thee let me know of it."

The aged man lived to partake of that very fruit, and remembering the emperor's words, he resolved to visit him So, taking a small basket, he filled it with the choicest figs from the tree, and proceeded on his errand. Telling the palace guard his purpose, he was admitted to the sovereign's presence.

"Well," asked the emperor, "what is thy wish?" The old man replied:

"Lo, I am the old man to whom thou didst say, on the day thou sawest him planting a fig tree, 'If thou livest to eat of its fruit, I pray thee let me know;' and behold I have come and brought thee of the fruit, that thou mayest partake of it likewise."

The emperor was very much pleased, and emptying the man's basket of its figs, he ordered it to be filled with gold coins.

When the old man had departed, the courtiers said to the emperor:

"Why didst thou so honour this old Jew?"

"The Lord hath honoured him, and why not I?" replied the emperor.

Now next door to this old man there lived a woman, who, when she heard of her neighbour's good fortune, desired her husband to try his luck in the same quarter. She filled for him an immense basket with figs, and bidding him put it on his shoulder, said, "Now carry it to the emperor; he loves figs and will fill thy basket with golden coin."

When her husband approached the gates of the palace, he told his errand to the guards, saying, "I brought these figs to the emperor; empty my basket I pray, and fill it up again with gold."

When this was told to the emperor, he ordered the old man to stand in the hallway of the palace, and all who passed pelted him with his figs. He returned home wounded and crestfallen to his disappointed wife.

"Never mind, thou hast one consolation," said she; "had they been cocoanuts instead of figs thou mightest have suffered harder raps."

Proving A Claim

A citizen of Jerusalem travelling through the country was taken very sick at an inn. Feeling that he would not recover, he sent for the landlord and said to him, "I am going the way of all flesh. If after my death any party should come from Jerusalem and claim my effects, do not deliver them until he shall prove to thee by three wise acts that he is entitled to them; for I charged my son before starting upon my way, that if death befell me he would be obliged to prove his wisdom before obtaining my possessions."

The man died and was buried according to Jewish rites, and his death was made public that his heirs might appear. When his son learned of his father's decease he started from Jerusalem for the place where he had died. Near the gates of the city he met a man who had a load of wood for sale. This he purchased and ordered it to be delivered at the inn towards which he was travelling. The man from whom he bought it went at once to the inn, and said, "Here is the wood."

"What wood?" returned the proprietor; "I ordered no wood."

"No," answered the woodcutter, "but the man who follows me did; I will enter and wait for him."

Thus the son had provided for himself a welcome whey he should reach the inn, which was his first wise act.

The landlord said to him, "Who art thou?"

"The son of the merchant who died in thy house," he replied.

They prepared for him a dinner, and placed upon the table five pigeons and a chicken. The master of the house, his wife, two sons, and two daughters sat with him at the table.

"Serve the food," said the landlord.

"Nay," answered the young man; "thy art master, it is thy privilege."

"I desire thee to do this thing; thou art my guest, the merchant's son; pray help the food."

The young man thus entreated divided one pigeon between the sons, another between the two daughters, gave the third to the man and his wife, and kept the other two for himself. This was his second wise act.

The landlord looked somewhat perplexed at this mode of distribution, but said nothing.

Then the merchant's son divided the chicken. He gave to the landlord and his wife the head, to the two sons the legs, to the two daughters the wings, and took the body for himself. This was his third wise act.

The landlord said:

"Is this the way they do things in thy country? I noticed the manner in which thou didst apportion the pigeons, but said nothing; but the chicken, my dear sir! I must really ask thee thy meaning."

Then the young man answered:

"I told thee that it was not my place to serve the food, nevertheless when thou didst insist I did the best I could, and I think I have succeeded. Thyself, thy wife, and one pigeon make three; thy two sons and one pigeon make three; thy two daughters and one pigeon make three; and myself and two pigeons make three also, therefore is it fairly done. As regards the chicken, I gave to thee and thy wife the head, because ye are the heads of the family; I gave to each of thy sons a leg, because they are the pillars of the family, preserving always the family name; I gave to each of thy daughters a wing, because in the natural course of events they will marry, take wing, and fly away from the home-nest. I took the body of the chicken because it looks like a ship, and in a ship I came here and in a ship I hope to return. I am the son of the merchant who died in thy house; give me the property of my dead father."

"Take it and go," said the landlord. And giving him his father's possessions the young man departed in peace.

A Payment With Interest

A certain man, a native of Athina (a city near Jerusalem), visited the city of Jerusalem, and after leaving it, ridiculed the place and its inhabitants. The Jerusalemites were very wroth at being made the subjects of his sport, and they induced one of their citizens to travel to Athina, to induce the man to return to Jerusalem, which would give them an opportunity to punish his insolence.

The citizen thus commissioned reached Athina, and very shortly fell in with the man whom he had come to meet. Walking through the streets together one day, the man from Jerusalem said, "See, the string of my shoe is broken; take me, I pray, to the shoemaker."

The shoemaker repaired the string, and the man paid him a coin more in value than the worth of the shoes.

Next day, when walking with the same man, he broke the string of his other shoe, and going to the shoemaker, he paid him the same large sum for repairing that.

"Why," said the man of Athina, "shoes must be very dear in Jerusalem, when thou payest such a price but for repairing a string."

"Yes," answered the other; "they bring nine ducats, and even in the cheapest times from seven to eight."

"Then it would be a profitable employment for me to take shoes from my city and sell them in thine."

"Yes, indeed; and if thou wilt but let me know of thy corning I will put thee in the way of customers."

So the man of Athina, who had made merry over the Jerusalemites, bought a large stock of shoes and set out for Jerusalem, informing his friend of his coming. The latter started to meet him, and greeting him before he came to the gates of the city, said to him:

"Before a stranger may enter and sell goods in Jerusalem, he must shave his head and blacken his face. Art thou ready to do this?"

"And why not," replied the other, "as long as I have a prospect of large profits; why should I falter or hesitate at so slight a thing as that?"

So the stranger, shaving the hair from his head and blackening his face (by which all Jerusalem knew him as the man who had ridiculed the city), took up his place in the market, with his wares spread before him.

Buyers paused before his stall, and asked him:

"How much for the shoes?"

"Ten ducats a pair," he answered; "or I may sell for nine; but certainly for not less than eight."

This caused a great laugh and uproar in the market, and the stranger was driven from it in derision and his shoes thrown after him.

Seeking the Jerusalemite who had deceived him, he said

"Why hast thou so treated me? did I so to thee in Athina?"

"Let this be a lesson to thee," answered the Jerusalemite. "I do not think thou wilt be so ready to make sport of us in the future."

The Weasel And The Well

A young man, upon his journeys through the country, fell in with a young woman, and they became mutually attached. When the young man was obliged to leave the neighbour-hood of the damsel's residence, they met to say "good-by." During the parting they pledged a mutual faith, and each promised to wait until, in the course of time, they might be able to marry. "Who will be the witness of our betrothal?" said the young man. Just then they saw a weasel run past them and disappear in the wood. "See," he continued, "this weasel and this well of water by which we are standing shall be the witnesses of our betrothal;" and so they parted. Years passed, the maiden remained true, but the youth married. A son was born to him, and grew up the delight of his parents. One day while the child was playing he became tired, and lying upon the ground fell asleep. A weasel bit him in the neck, and he bled to death. The parents were consumed with grief by this calamity, and it was not until another son was given them that they forgot their sorrow. But when this second child was able to walk alone it wandered without the house, and bending over the well, looking at its shadow in the water, lost its balance and was drowned. Then the father recollected his perjured vow, and his witnesses, the weasel and the well. He told his wife of the circumstance, and she agreed to a divorce. He then sought the maiden to whom he had promised marriage, and found her still awaiting his return. He told her how, through God's agency, he had been punished for his wrongdoing, after which they married and lived in peace.

The Lawful Heir

A wise Israelite, dwelling some distance from Jerusalem, sent his son to the Holy City to complete his education. During his son's absence the father was taken ill, and feeling that death was upon him he made a will, leaving all his property to one of his slaves, on condition that he should allow the son to select any one article which pleased him for an inheritance.

As soon as his master died, the slave, elated with his good fortune, hastened to Jerusalem, informed his late master's son of what had taken place, and showed him the will.

The young man was surprised and grieved at the intelligence, and after the allotted time of mourning had expired, he began to seriously consider his situation. He went to his teacher, explained the circumstances to him, read him his father's will, and expressed himself bitterly on account of the disappointment of his reasonable hopes and expectations. He could think of nothing that he had done to offend his father, and was loud in his complaints of in-justice.

"Stop," said his teacher; "thy father was a man of wisdom and a loving relative. This will is a living monument to his good sense and far-sightedness. May his son prove as wise in his day."

"What!" exclaimed the young man. "I see no wisdom in his bestowal of his property upon a slave; no affection in this slight upon his only son."

"Listen," returned the teacher. "By his action thy father hath but secured thy inheritance to thee, if thou art wise enough to avail thyself of his understanding. Thus thought he when he felt the hand of death approaching, 'My son is away; when I am dead he will not be here to take charge of my affairs; my slaves will plunder my estate, and to gain time will even conceal my death from my son, and deprive me of the sweet savour of mourning.' To prevent these things he bequeathed his property to his slave, well knowing that the slave, believing in his apparent right, would give thee speedy information and take care of the effects, even as he has done."

"Well, well, and how does this benefit me?" impatiently interrupted the pupil.

"Ah!" replied the teacher, "wisdom I see rests not with the young. Dost thou not know that what a slave possesses belongs but to his master? Has not thy father left thee the right to select one article of all his property for thy on? Choose the slave as thy portion, and by possessing him thou wilt recover all that was thy father's. Such was his wise and loving intention."

The young man did as he was advised, and gave the slave his freedom afterwards. But ever after he was wont to exclaim:

"Wisdom resides with the aged, and understanding in length of days."

Nothing In The World Without Its Use

David, King of Israel, was once lying upon his couch and many thoughts were passing through his mind.

"Of what use in this world is the spider?" thought he; "it but increases the dust and dirt of the world, making places unsightly and causing great annoyance."

Then he thought of an insane man:

"How unfortunate is such a being. I know that all things are ordained by God with reason and purpose, yet this is beyond my comprehension; why should men be born idiots, or grow insane?"

Then the mosquitoes annoyed him, and the king thought:

"What can the mosquito be good for? why was it created in the world? It but disturbs our comfort, and the world profits not by its existence."

Yet King David lived to discover that these very insects, and the very condition of life, the being of which he deplored, were ordained even to his own benefit.

When he fled from before Saul, David was captured in the land of the Philistines by the brothers of Goliath, who carried him before the king of Gath, and it was only by pretending idiocy that he escaped death, the king deeming it impossible that such a man could be the kingly David; as it is written, "And he disguised his reason before their eyes, and played the madman in their hands, and scribbled on the doors of the gate, and let his spittle run down upon his beard" (Sam. 12-16).

Upon another occasion David hid himself in the cave of Adullam, and after he had entered the cave it chanced that a spicier spun a web over the opening thereto. His pursuers passed that way, but thinking that no one could have entered the cave protected by the spider's web without destroying it, they continued on their way.

The mosquito also was of service to David when he entered the camp of Saul to secure the latter's weapon. While stooping near Abner, the sleeping man moved and placed his leg upon David's body. If he moved, he would awake Abner and meet with death, if he remained in that position morning would dawn and bring him death; he knew not what to do, when a mosquito alighted upon Abner's leg; he moved it quickly, and David escaped.

Therefore sang David:

"All my bones shall say, O Lord, who is like unto Thee."

The Reward Of Faith

The Israelites were commanded to visit Jerusalem on three festivals. It happened upon one occasion that there was a scarcity of water in the city. One of the people called upon a certain nobleman who was the owner of three wells, and asked him for the use of the water which they contained, promising that they should be refilled by a stated date, and contracting in default of this to pay a certain large amount in silver as forfeit. The day came, there had been no rain, and the three wells were dry. In the morning the owner of the wells sent for the promised money. Nakdemon, the son of Gurion, the man who had undertaken this burden for his people's sake, replied, "The day is but begun; there is yet time."

He entered the Temple and prayed that God might send rain and save him all his fortune which he had ventured. His prayer was answered. The clouds gathered and the rain fell. As he passed out of the Temple with a grateful heart, he was met by his creditor, who said:

"True, the rain has refilled my wells, but it is dark; the day has gone, and according to our agreement thou must still pay me the promised sum."

Once more Nakdemon prayed, and lo, the clouds lifted and the sinking sun smiled brightly on the spot where the men stood, showing that the sunlight of day was still there, though the rain-clouds had temporarily obscured its gleams.

Abtinoss And Garmah

There was a certain family, the family of Abtinoss, the members of which were learned in the art of preparing the incense used in the service. Their knowledge they refused to impart to others, and the directors of the Temple, fearing that the art might die with them, discharged them from the service, and brought other parties from Alexandria, in Egypt, to prepare the sweet perfume. These latter were unable to afford satisfaction, however, and the directors were obliged to give the service back into the hands of the family of Abtinoss, who on their part refused to accept it again, unless the remuneration for their services was doubled. When asked why they so persistently refused to impart their skill to others, they replied that they feared they might teach some unworthy persons, who would afterwards use their knowledge in an idolatrous worship. The members of this family were very particular not to use perfume of any kind themselves, lest the people should imagine that they put the sweet spices used in the manufacture of the incense to a baser use.

An exactly similar case to the above occurred with the family of Garmah, which had the monopoly of the knowledge of preparing the show-bread used in the services of the Temple.

It was in reference to these cases that the son of Azai said, "In thy name they shall call thee, and in thy city they shall cause thee to live, and from thy own they will give thee," meaning that trustful persons should not fear that others might steal their occupations; "for in thy name they will call thee," as with the families of Abtinoss and Garmah; "and from thy own they will give thee," meaning that what a man earns is his own, and cannot be taken away.

Trust In God

Rabbi Jochanan, the son of Levi, fasted and prayed to the Lord that he might be permitted to gaze on the angel Elijah, he who had ascended alive to heaven. God granted his prayer, and in the semblance of a man Elijah appeared before him.

"Let me journey with thee in thy travels through the world," prayed the Rabbi to Elijah; "let me observe thy doings, and gain in wisdom and understanding."

"Nay," answered Elijah; "my actions thou couldst not understand; my doings would trouble thee, being beyond thy comprehension."

But still the Rabbi entreated:

"I will neither trouble nor question thee," he said; "only let me accompany thee on thy way."

"Come, then," said Elijah; "but let thy tongue be mute. With thy first question, thy first expression of astonishment, we must part company."

So the two journeyed through the world together. They approached the house of a poor man, whose only treasure and means of support was a cow. As they came near, the man and his wife hastened to meet them, begged them to enter their cot, and eat and drink of the best they could afford, and to pass the night under their roof. This they did, receiving every attention from their poor but hospitable host and hostess. In the morning Elijah rose up early and prayed to God, and when he had finished his prayer, behold the cow belonging to the poor people dropped dead. Then the travellers continued on their journey.

Much was Rabbi Jochanan perplexed. "Not only did we neglect to pay them for their hospitality and generous services, but his cow we have killed;" and he said to Elijah, "Why didst thou kill the cow of this good man, who "

"Peace," interrupted Elijah; "hear, see, and be silent! If I answer thy questions we must part."

And they continued on their way together.

Towards evening they arrived at a large and imposing mansion, the residence of a haughty and wealthy man. They were coldly received; a piece of bread and a glass of water were placed before them, but the master of the house did not welcome or speak to them, and they remained there during the night unnoticed. In the morning Elijah remarked that a wall of the house required repairing, and sending for a carpenter, he himself paid the money for the repair, as a return, he said, for the hospitality they had received.

Again was Rabbi Jochanan filled with wonder, but he said naught, and they proceeded on their journey.

As the shades of night were falling they entered a city which contained a large and imposing synagogue. As it was the time of the evening service they entered and were much pleased with the rich adornments, the velvet cushions, and gilded carvings of the interior. After the completion of the service, Elijah arose and called out aloud, "Who is here willing to feed and lodge two poor men this night?" none answered, and no respect was shown to the travelling strangers. In the morning, however, Elijah re-entered the synagogue, and shaking its members by the hands, he said, "I hope that you may all become presidents."

Next evening the two entered another city, when the *Shamas* (sexton) of the synagogue, came to meet them, and notifying the members of his congregation of the coming of two strangers, the best hotel of the place was opened to them, and all vied in showing them attention and honour.

In the morning, on parting with them, Elijah said, "May the Lord appoint over you but one president."

Jochanan could resist his curiosity no longer. "Tell me," said he to Elijah, "tell me the meaning of all these actions which I have witnessed. To those who have treated us coldly thou hast uttered good wishes; to those who have been gracious to us thou hast made no suitable return. Even though we must part, I pray thee explain to me the meaning of thy acts."

"Listen," said Elijah, "and learn to trust in God, even though thou canst not understand His ways. We first entered the house of the poor man, who treated us so kindly. Know that it had been decreed that on that very day his wife should die. I prayed unto the Lord that the cow might prove a redemption for her; God granted my prayers, and the woman was preserved unto her husband. The rich man, whom next we called up, treated us coldly, and I repaired his wall. I repaired it without a new foundation, without digging to the old one. Had he repaired it himself he would have dug, and thus discovered a treasure which lies there buried, but which is now for ever lost to him. To the members of the synagogue who were inhospitable I said, 'May you all be presidents,' and where many rule there can be no peace; but to the others I said, 'May you have but one president;' with one leader no misunderstanding may arise. Now, if thou seest the wicked prospering, be not envious; if thou seest the righteous in poverty and trouble, be not provoked or doubtful of God's justice. The Lord is righteous, His judgments all are true; His eyes note all mankind, and none can say, 'What dost thou?'"

With these words Elijah disappeared, and Jochanan was left alone.

The Bride And Bridegroom

There was once a man who pledged his dearest faith to a maiden, beautiful and true. For a time all passed pleasantly, and the maiden lived in happiness. But then the man was called from her side, he left her; long she waited, but he did not return. Friends pitied her and rivals mocked her; tauntingly they pointed at her, and said, "He has left thee; he will never come back." The maiden sought her chamber, and read in secret the letters which her lover had written to her, the letters in which he promised to be ever faithful, ever true. Weeping she read them, but they brought comfort to her heart; she dried her eyes and doubted not.

A joyous day dawned for her; the man she loved returned, and when he learned that others had doubted and asked her how she had preserved her faith, she showed his letters to him, declaring her eternal trust.

Israel, in misery and captivity, was mocked by the nations; her hopes of redemption were made a laughing-stock; her sages scoffed at; her holy men derided. Into her synagogues, into her schools went Israel; she read the letters which her God had written, and believed in the holy promises which they contained.

God will in time redeem her; and when He says:

"How could you alone be faithful of all the mocking nations?"

She will point to the law and answer:

"Had not Thy law been my delight, I should long since have perished in my affliction" (Psalm 119).

Truth

When God was about to create man the angels gathered about him. Some of them opening their lips exclaimed, "Create, oh God, a being who shall praise Thee from earth even as we in heaven sing Thy glory."

But others said:

"Hear us, Almighty King, create no more! The glorious harmony of the heavens which Thou hast sent to earth will be by man disturbed, destroyed."

Then silence fell upon the contesting hosts as the Angel of Mercy appeared before the throne of grace on bended knees.

Sweet was the voice which said entreatingly:

"Oh, Father, create Thou man; make him Thine own noble image. With heavenly pity will I fill his heart, with sympathy towards every living thing impress his being; through him will they find cause to praise Thee."

Then the Angel of Mercy ceased, and the Angel of Peace with tearful eyes spoke thus:

"O God, create him not! Thy peace he will disturb, the flow of blood will follow sure his coming. Confusion, horror, war, will blot the earth, and Thou wilt no longer find a pleasant place among Thy. works on earth."

Then spoke in stern tones the Angel of Justice: "And Thou wilt judge him, God; he shall be subject to my sway."

The Angel of Truth approached, saying: "Cease! Oh God of truth, with man Thou sendest falsehood to the earth."

Then all were silent, and out of the deep quietness the Divine words came:

"Thou, oh Truth, shalt go to earth with him, and yet remain a denizen of heaven; 'twixt heaven and earth to float, connecting link between the two."

The Destruction Of Bithar

It was customary in Bithar when a child was born for the parents to plant a young cedar tree, to grow up with the infant. It happened upon one occasion when the daughter of the emperor was riding through the city, that her chariot broke down, and her attendants pulled up a young cedar tree to use in repairing it. The man who had planted the tree, seeing this, attacked the servants and beat them severely. This action incensed the emperor, who immediately despatched an army of eighty thousand men against the city. These captured it and killed the inhabitants, men, women and children. The rivers ran red with blood, and 'tis said that the ground was rich and prolific to the farmers for seven years, from the bodies of those who perished, said to be four hundred thousand Israelites.

THE DESTRUCTION OF JERUSALEM

When the guilt of the Israelites grew too great for the forbearance of the Most High, and they refused to listen to the words and warnings of Jeremiah, the prophet left Jerusalem and travelled to the land of Benjamin. While he was in the holy city, and prayed for mercy on it, it was spared; but while he sojourned in the land of Benjamin, Nebuchadnezzar laid waste the land of Israel, plundered the holy Temple, robbed it of its ornaments, and gave it a prey to the devouring flames. By the hands of Nebuzaradan did Nebuchadnezzar send (while he himself remained in Riblah) to destroy Jerusalem.

Before he ordered the expedition he endeavoured by means of signs, in accordance with the superstition of his age, to ascertain the result of the attempt. He shot an arrow from his bow, pointing to the west, and the arrow turned towards Jerusalem. Then he shot again, pointing towards the east, and the arrow sped towards Jerusalem. Then he shot once more, desiring to know in which direction lay the guilty city which should be blotted from the world, and for the third time his arrow pointed towards Jerusalem.

When the city had been captured, he marched with his princes and officers into the Temple, and called out mockingly to the God of Israel, "And art thou the great God before whom the world trembles, and we here in thy city and thy Temple!"

On one of the walls he found the mark of an arrow's head, as though somebody had been killed or hit near by, and he asked, "Who was killed here?"

"Zachariah, the son of Yehoyadah, the high priest, answered the people; "he rebuked us incessantly on account of our transgressions, and we tired of his words, and put him to death."

The followers of Nebuchadnezzar massacred the inhabitants of Jerusalem, the priests and the people, old and young, women, and children who were attending school, even babies in the cradle. The feast of blood at last shocked even the leader of the hostile heathens, who ordered a stay of this wholesale murder. He then removed all the vessels of gold and silver from the Temple, and sent them by his ships, to Babel, after which he set the Temple on fire.

The high priest donned his robe and ephod, and saying, "Now that the Temple is destroyed, no priest is needed to officiate," threw himself into the flames and was consumed. When the other priests who were still alive witnessed this action, they took their harps and musical instruments and followed the example of the high priest. Those of the people whom the soldiers had not killed were bound in iron chains, burdened with the spoils of the victors, and carried into captivity. Jeremiah the prophet returned to Jerusalem and accompanied his unfortunate brethren, who went out almost naked. When they reached a place called *Bet Kuro*, Jeremiah obtained better clothing for them. And he spoke to Nebuchadnezzar and the Chaldeans, and said, "Think not that of your own strength you were able to overcome the people chosen of the Lord; ‘tis their iniquities which have condemned them to this sorrow."

Thus the people journeyed on with crying and moaning until they reached the rivers of Babylon. Then Nebuchadnezzar said to them, "Sing, ye people,--play for me,--sing the songs ye were wont to sing before your great Lord in Jerusalem."

In answer to this command, the Levites hung their harps upon the willow trees near the banks of the river, as it is written, "Upon the willows in her midst had we hung up our harps" (Ps. 137: 2). Then they said, "If we had but performed the will of God and sung His praises devoutly, we should not have been delivered into thy hands. Now, how can we sing before thee the prayers and hymns that belong only to the One Eternal God?" as it is said, "How should we sing the song of the Lord on the soil of the stranger?" (Ibid. 4).

Then said the officers of the captors, "These men are men of death; they refuse to obey the order of the king; let them die."

But forth stepped Pelatya, the son of Yehoyadah, and thus he addressed Nebuchadnezzar:

"Behold, if a flock is delivered into the hands of a shepherd, and a wolf steals a lamb from the flock, tell me, who is responsible to the owner of the lost animal?"

"Surely the shepherd," replied Nebuchadnezzar.

"Then listen to thine own words," replied Pelatya. "God has given Israel into thy hands; to Him art thou responsible for those who are slain."

The king ordered the chains to be removed from the captives, and they were not put to death.

SECOND DESTRUCTION OF JERUSALEM

Through Kamtzah and Bar Kamtzah was Jerusalem destroyed; and thus it happened.

A certain man made a feast; he was a friend of Kamtzah, but Bar Kamtzah he hated. He sent a messenger to Kamtzah with an invitation to his banquet, but this messenger making a mistake, delivered the invitation to his master's enemy, Bar Kamtzah.

Bar Kamtzah accepted the invitation, and was on hand at the appointed time, but when the host saw his enemy enter his house, he ordered him to leave at once.

"Nay," said Bar Kamtzah, "now that I am here, do not so insult me as to send me forth. I will pay thee for all that I may eat and drink."

"I want not thy money," returned the other, "neither do I desire thy presence; get thee gone at once."

But Bar Kamtzah persisted.

"I will pay the entire expense of thy feast," he said; "do not let me be degraded in the eyes of thy guests."

The host was determined, and Bar Kamtzah withdrew from the banquet-room in anger.

"Many Rabbis were present," said he in his heart, "and not one of them interfered in my behalf, therefore this insult which they saw put upon me must have pleased them."

So Bar Kamtzah spoke treacherously of the Jews unto the king, saying, "The Jews have rebelled against thee."

"How can I know this?" inquired the king.

"Send a sacrifice to their Temple and it will be rejected," replied Bar Kamtzah.

The ruler then sent a well-conditioned calf to be sacrificed for him in the Temple, but through the machinations of Bar Kamtzah the messenger inflicted a blemish upon it, and, of course, not being fit for the sacrifice (Lev. 22:21) it was not accepted.

Through this cause was Cæsar sent to capture Jerusalem, and for two years he besieged the city. Four wealthy citizens of Jerusalem had stored up enough food to last the inhabitants a much longer time than this, but the people being anxious to fight with the Romans, destroyed the storehouses and brought dire famine upon the city.

A certain noble lady, Miriam, the daughter of Baythus, sent her servant to purchase some flour for household use. The servant found that all the flour had been sold, but there was still some meal which he might have purchased. Hurrying home, however, to learn his mistress's wishes in regard to this, he discovered on his return that this too had been sold, and he could obtain nothing save some coarse barley meal. Not wishing to purchase this without orders he returned home again, but when he returned to the storehouse to secure the barley meal, that was gone also. Then his mistress started out herself to purchase food, but she could find nothing. Suffering from the pangs of hunger she picked from the street the skin of a fig and ate it; this sickened her and she died. But previous to her death she cast all her gold and silver into the street, saying, "What use is this wealth to me when I can obtain no food for it?' Thus were the words of Ezekiel fulfilled:

"Their silver shall they cast into the streets."

After the destruction of the storehouses, Rabbi Jochanan in walking through the city saw the populace boiling straw in water and drinking of the same for sustenance. "Ah, woe is me for this calamity!" he exclaimed; "how can such a people strive against a mighty host?" He applied to Ben Batiach, his nephew, one of the chiefs of the city, for permission to leave Jerusalem. But Ben Batiach replied, "It may not be; no living body may leave the city." "Take me out then as a corpse," entreated Jochanan. Ben Batiach assented to this, and Jochanan was placed in a coffin and carried through the gates of the city; Rabbi Eleazer, Rabbi Joshua, and Ben Batiach acting as pall-bearers. The coffin was placed in a cave, and after they had all returned to their homes Jochanan arose from the coffin and made his way to the enemy's camp. He obtained from the commander permission to establish an academy in Jabna with Rabbon Gamliel as the principal.

Titus soon captured the city, killed many of the people, and sent the others into exile. He entered the Temple, even in the Most Holy, and cut down the veil which separated it from the less sacred precincts. He seized the holy vessels, and sent them to Rome.

From this history of Kamtzah and Bar Kamtzah we should learn to be careful of offending our neighbours, when in so slight a cause such great results may originate. Our Rabbis have said that he who causes his neighbour to blush through an insult, should be compared to the one who sheds blood.

Hannah And Her Seven Sons

During the terrible times which followed the fall of the Holy City, Hannah and her seven sons were cast into prison.

According to their ages they were brought before the tyrant conqueror, and commanded to pay homage to him and his gods.

"God forbid," exclaimed the eldest lad, "that I should bow to thy image. Our commandments say to us, 'I am the Lord thy God;' to no other will I bow."

He was immediately led out to execution, and the same demand made of his brother, the second son.

"My brother bowed not," he answered, "and no more will I."

"Wherefore not?" asked the tyrant.

"Because," replied the lad, "the second commandment of the Decalogue tells us, 'Thou shalt have no other God but me.'"

His death followed immediately his brave words.

"My religion teaches me, 'Thou shalt worship no other God'" (Ex. 34: 14), said the third son, "and I welcome the fate accorded to my brothers rather than bow to thee or thy images."

The same homage was demanded of the fourth son, but brave and faithful as his brethren, he replied, "'He that sacrificeth unto any God save unto the Lord only'" (Ex. 22: 19), and was slain pitilessly.

"'Hear, O Israel! the Lord our God, the Lord is One,'" exclaimed the fifth lad, yielding up his young life with the watchword of Israel's hosts.

"Why art thou so obstinate?" was asked of the sixth brother, when he, too, was brought before the tyrant and scorned the propositions made him.

"'The Lord thy God is in the midst of thee, a mighty and terrible God'" (Deut. 7: 21), he said; and died for the principles he proclaimed.

Then the seventh and youngest boy was brought before the murderer of his relatives, who addressed him kindly, saying:

"My son, come bow before my gods."

And the child answered:

"God forbid! Our holy religion teaches us 'Know therefore this day, and reflect in thy heart that the Lord he is God, in the heavens above and on the earth beneath there is none else' (Deut. 4: 39). Never will we exchange our God for any other, neither will He exchange us for any other nation, for as it is written, 'Thou hast this day acknowledged the Lord' (Deut. 26: 17), so is it also written, 'And the Lord hath acknowledged thee this day, that thou art unto him a peculiar people!'"

Still the tyrant spoke smoothly, and with kind words.

"Thou art young," he said; "thou hast seen but little of the pleasures and joys of life, not as much as has fallen to the portion of thy brethren. Do as I wish thee and thy future shall be bright and happy."

"The Lord will reign for ever and ever," said the lad; "thy nation and thy kingdom will be destroyed; thou art here to-day, to-morrow in the grave; to day elevated, to-morrow lowly; but the most Holy One endures for ever."

"See," continued the other, "thy brothers lie slain before thee; their fate will be thine if thou refusest to do as I desire. See, I will cast my ring to the ground, stoop thou and pick it up; that I will consider allegiance to my gods."

"Thinkest thou that I fear thy threats?" returned the unterrified lad; "why should I fear a human being more than the great God, the King of kings?"

"Where and what is thy God?" asked the oppressor. "Is there a God in the world?"

"Can there be a world without a Creator?" replied the youth. "Of thy gods 'tis said, 'mouths they have, but speak not.' Of our God the Psalmist says, 'By the word of the Lord were the heavens made.' Thy gods have 'eyes but see not,' but 'the eyes of the Lord run to and fro in the whole earth!' Thy gods have 'ears but hear not,' but of our God 'tis written, The Lord hearkened and heard.' Of thy gods 'tis said, 'a nose they have but smell not,' while our God 'smelled the sweet savour.' 'Hands have thy gods but they touch not,' while our God says, 'My hand hath also founded the earth.' Of thy gods 'tis written, 'feet they have but walk not,' while Zachariah tells us of our God, 'His feet will stand that day upon the mount of Olives.'"

Then said the cruel one:

"If thy God hath all these attributes, why does He not deliver thee from my power?"

The lad replied:

"He delivered Chananyah and his companions from the power of Nebuchadnezzar, but they were righteous men, and Nebuchadnezzar was a king deserving of seeing a miracle performed, but for me, alas, I am not worthy of redemption, neither art thou worthy of a demonstration of God's power."

"Let the lad be slain as were his brothers," commanded the tyrant.

Then spoke Hannah, the mother of the boys:

"Give me my child," she cried, "oh, cruel king, let me fold him in my arms ere thou destroyest his innocent young life."

She threw her arms around the lad, clasping him tightly to her bosom, and pressing her lips to his. "Take my life," she cried; "kill me first before my child."

"Nay," he answered, scoffingly, "I cannot do it, for thy own laws forbid; 'Whether it be ox or sheep ye shall not kill it and its young in one day'" (Lev. 28).

"Oh, woe to thee," replied the mother, "thou who art so particular to regard the laws." Then pressing her boy to her heart, "Go, my dear one," she said, "say to Abraham that my sacrifice hath exceeded his. He built one altar whereon to sacrifice Isaac; thy mother hath built seven altars and sacrificed seven Isaacs in one day. He was but tempted; thy mother hath performed."

After the execution of her last son, Hannah became insane, and threw herself from her house-top. Where she fell, she expired.

Happy are ye, ye seven sons of Hannah; your portion in the future world was waiting for you. In faithfulness ye served your God, and with her children shall your mother rejoice for ever in the eternal world.

PART FIFTH. CIVIL AND CRIMINAL LAW--THE HOLY DAYS

Sketch Of Civil And Criminal Codes

"WHEN do justice and goodwill meet? When the contending parties can be made to peaceably agree."

To accomplish this end was the great aim of the ancient Jewish laws, but a marked distinction was made between the civil and criminal branches. In the former cases, arguments could be made before, and decisions rendered by, either the general magistracy or special judges chosen by the contending parties, and many were the fences erected about the judges to keep them within the lines of strict equity, such as the following:

"He who unjustly transfers one man's goods to another shall answer to God for it with his own soul."

"When the judge sits in judgment on his fellow-man he should feel as though a sword was pointed at his heart."

"Woe to the judge who, knowing the unrighteousness of a decision, endeavours to make the witnesses responsible for the same. From *him* will God require an account;"

"When the parties stand before thee look upon both as guilty; but when they are dismissed let them both be innocent, for the fiat has gone forth."

The judge was not allowed to hear anything of a case, save in the presence of all the parties concerned; and he was particularly enjoined to be without bias caused by a difference in the standing or wealth of the parties,; either in favour of the poor against the rich, or of the rich against the poor.

The witnesses in a case were almost as closely scrutinised as the case itself; and they were at once incompetent if they had any personal interest in the suit. If a plaintiff asked for more than he was legally entitled to in the hope of more readily obtaining his due he lost his suit.

While three judges could form a tribunal for the settling of civil cases, that for the judgment of criminal suits was composed of twenty-three judges, and while in the former case a majority of one in the jury, either acquitted or condemned, in the latter a majority of one acquitted, but a majority of two was required to condemn.

The witnesses in criminal suits were thus admonished on being brought into court:

"Perchance you intend to speak from rumour, being the witness of another witness, to tell that which you have heard from a trustworthy man, or perchance you may not be aware that we shall try you with close questions and searching words. Know then, that trials wherein the life of man hangs in the scale, are not like trials concerning worldly goods. With money may money be redeemed, but in trials like this not only the blood of the one unjustly condemned, but that of his seed and his seed's seed, until the end of time, will lay heavy on the soul of the false witness. Adam was created alone one man, and he who destroys a single life will be held as accountable as if he had destroyed a world. Therefore search well thy words. But say not, on the other hand, 'What have I to do with all this?' Remember the words of Holy Writ, 'If a witness hath seen or known, if he do not utter, he shall bear his iniquity;' and remember further, 'In the destruction of the wicked there is joy.'"

The punishments were inflicted in the most humane manner, and the entire code is the perfection of justice tempered by mercy in its truest and highest sense.

No matter how numerous the crimes of an offender might be, one punishment covered them all. A fine could not accompany any other punishment, and in cases of flagellation, the number of strokes was limited in the most extreme cases to thirty-nine.

The judges in capital cases were required to fast all day on the days when they pronounced judgments, and even after the sentence the case was again considered by the highest court before it was carried into effect.

The place of execution was located a considerable distance from the court, and on his progress thereto the prisoner was stopped several times, and asked whether he could think of anything not said which might influence the judges in his favour. He had the privilege of returning to the court as often as he pleased with new pleas, and a herald preceded him, crying aloud, "This man is being led to execution, this is his crime . . . these are the witnesses against him . . . if any one knows aught in his favour let them come forth now and speak the words."

Before his execution he was urged to confess. "Confess thy sins," said the officers; "every one who confesses has part in the world to come." If he offered no confession he was requested to repeat the words, "May my death be a redemption for all my sins."

Capital punishment, however, was of such rare occurrence as to be practically abrogated. In fact, many of the judges declared openly for its abolition, and a court which had pronounced one sentence of death in seven years was called "the court of murderers."

PASSOVER

The feast of unleavened bread, or "Passover," begins upon the evening of the 14th day of *Nissan* (April), and was instituted in commemoration of our ancestors' redemption from Egypt, a memorial for ever. During its continuance we are strictly forbidden the use of any leavened thing.

Moses said to the Israelites in the name of the Lord:

"Draw out and take for yourselves a lamb," &c.

By the observance of this precept they would deserve well of God and He would redeem them, for when He spoke they were "naked and bare" of good deeds and meritorious acts.

"Draw out and take for yourselves a lamb."

Draw yourselves away from the idols which ye are worshipping with the Egyptians, the calves and lambs of stone and metal, and with one of the same animals through which ye sin, prepare to fulfil the commandments of your God.

The planet sign of the month *Nissan* is a lamb therefore, that the Egyptians might not think that through the powers of the lamb they had thrown off the yoke of slavery, God commanded His people to take a lamb and eat it.

They were commanded to roast it whole and to break no bone of it, so that the Egyptians might know that it was indeed a lamb which they had consumed.

The Lord said to Moses, "Tell the children of Israel that they shall borrow of the Egyptians gold and silver vessels," in order that it might not be afterwards said, "The words 'they will make them serve, and they will afflict them,' were fulfilled: but the words 'they shall go out with great substance,' did not come to pass."

When Moses told the Israelites that they, should go up out of Egypt with great substance, they answered, "Would that we could go even empty-handed," like to the servant confined in prison.

"To-morrow," said the jailer to him, "I will release thee from prison, and give thee much money."

"Let me go to-day, and give me nothing," replied the prisoner.

On the seventh day of the Passover the children of Israel passed through the Red Sea on dry land.

A man was once travelling along the road and his son preceded him on the way. A robber appeared in the path, and the man put his son behind him. Then lo, a wolf came after the lad, and his father lifted him up and carried him within his arms.

The sea was before the Israelites, the Egyptians were behind them, so God lifted up His child and carried it within His arms.

When Israel suffered from the hot rays of the sun God "spread the cloud for a covering;" when they were hungry He sent them bread from heaven; and when they thirsted "He brought forth floods from a rock."

Pentecost

The Feast of Weeks, or "Pentecost," occurs upon the sixth day of the third month, *Sivan* (June). It is called the Feast of Weeks because forty-nine days, or seven weeks, duly numbered, elapse between the second day of Passover, when (during the existence of the Temple) a sheaf of green barley was offered, and this festival, when two loaves made of the first flour of the wheat harvest were "brought before the Lord." It is also the anniversary of the delivery of the commandment from Mount Sinai.

Why does not the Bible particularise in this as on other occasions, and say directly, "On the sixth day of the third month was the law given?"

Because in ancient times the men called "wise" placed their faith and dependence upon the planets. They divided these into seven, apportioning one to each day of the week. Some nations selected for their greatest god the sun, other nations the moon, and so on, and prayed to them and worshipped them. They knew not that the planets moved and changed according to the course of nature, established by the Most High, a course which He might change according to His will, and into their ignorant ideas many of the Israelites had entered. Therefore, as they considered the planets as seven, God made many other things depending on that number, to show that as He made them, so had He made the planets.

The seventh day of the week He made the Sabbath; the seventh year he made the year of rest; after seven times seven years, or after seven Sabbatical years, He ordained the Jubilee, or year of release. Seven days He gave to the Passover festival, and seven days to the Feast of Tabernacles. Seven days was Jericho surrounded, and seven priests took seven trumpets and marched round its walls seven times upon the seventh day.

Therefore, after numbering seven weeks during the ripening time of the grain, the Israelites were to hold a holy convocation, to praise the One who can prevent all things, but who cannot be prevented; who can change all things, but is unchangeable.

The first day the Israelites were redeemed from slavery and superstition; the fiftieth day a law was given them for their guide through life; therefore they are commanded to number these days and remember them.

The children of Ishmael, says the legend, were asked to accept the law. "What does it contain?" they asked. "Thou shalt not steal," was the answer. "How can we then accept it," they returned, "when thus was our forefather blessed, 'Thy hand shall be against every man?'"

The children of Esau were asked to accept the law, and they also inquired, "What does it contain?" "Thou shalt not kill," was the answer. "We cannot accept it, then," said they, "for thus did our father Isaac bless us, 'By the sword shalt thou live.'"

When Israel was asked to accept the law, the people answered, "We will do and obey."

New Year, Or The Day Of Memorial

On the first day of the seventh month, *Tishri* (October), is the commemoration of the creation of the world. Then the cornet is blown to announce to the people that a new year has begun its course, and to warn them to examine strictly their conduct and make amends therein where amends are needed.

Would not any person of sense, knowing that he must appear before a Court of Judgment, prepare himself therefor? Either in a civil or a criminal case would he not seek for counsel? How much more, then, is it incumbent upon him to prepare for a meeting with the King of kings, before whom all things are revealed. No counsel can help him in his case; repentance, devotion, charity, these are the arguments which must plead in his favour. Therefore, a person should search his actions and repent his transgressions previous to the day of judgment. In the month of *Elul* (September) he should arouse himself to a consciousness of the dread justice awaiting all mankind.

This is the season when the Lord pardoned the Israelites who had worshipped the molten calf. He commanded Moses to reascend the mount for a second tablet, after he had destroyed the first. Thus say the sages, "The Lord said unto Moses in the month Elul, 'Go up unto me on the mountain,' and Moses went up and received the second tablet at the end of forty days. Before he ascended he caused the trumpet to be sounded through the camp." Since that time it is customary to sound the *Shophar* (cornet) in the synagogues, to give warning to the people that the day of judgment, New Year, is rapidly approaching, and with it the Day of Atonement. Therefore, propitiatory prayers are said twice every day, morning and evening, from the second day of Elul until the eve of the Day of Atonement, which period comprises the last forty days which Moses passed on Sinai, when God was reconciled to Israel and pardoned their transgressions with the molten calf.

Rabbi Eleazer said, "Abraham and Jacob were born in *Tishri*, and in *Tishri* they died. On the first of *Tishri* the universe was created, and during the Passover was Isaac born. On the first of *Tishri* (New Year), Sarah, Rachel, and Hannah, three barren women, were visited. On the first day of *Tishri* our ancestors discontinued their rigorous labour in Egypt. On the first of *Tishri* Adam was created; from his existence we count our years, that is the sixth day of the creation. On that day, too, did he eat of the forbidden fruit, therefore is the season appointed for one of penitence, for the Lord said to Adam, 'This shall be for a sign in future generations; thy descendants shall be judged upon these days, and they shall be appointed as days of pardon and forgiveness.'"

Four times in the year the Lord pronounces His decrees.

First, New Year, the first of *Tishri*. Then the judgments of all human beings for the coming year are ordained.

Second, The first day of Passover. Then the scarcity or fulness of the crops is determined.

Third, Pentecost. Then the Lord blesses the fruit of the trees, or bids them bear not in plenty.

Fourth, The Feast of Tabernacles. Then the Lord determines whether the rain shall bless the earth in its due season or not.

Man is judged on New Year's, and the decree is made final on the Day of Atonement.

Rabbi Nathan has said that man is judged at all times.

Thus taught Rabbi Akiba. "Why does the law command the bringing of a sheaf of barley on the Passover? Because the Passover is the season of the harvest of the grain. The Lord says, 'Offer for me a sheaf of barley on Passover, that I may bless the grain which is in the field.'

"Why does the Bible say, 'Bring two loaves of the new wheat on Pentecost?' Because at Pentecost time the fruit ripens, and God says, 'Offer for me two loaves of the new wheat, in order that I may bless the fruit which is on the trees.'

"Why were we commanded to bring a drink-offering of water into the Temple on the Feast of Tabernacles? Because then is the season of rain, and the Lord says, 'Bring the drink-offering of water to me, in order that I may bless the rain of the year.'

"Why do they make the comet which they blow of a ram's horn? In order that the Lord may remember the ram which was sacrificed instead of Isaac, and allow the merits of the patriarchs to weigh in favour of their descendants, as it is written in the Decalogue, 'Showing mercy to thousands of those who love me and keep my commandments" (Ex. 20: 6).

On New Year's day they recite in the synagogues the record of the binding of Isaac for the same purpose. While God has mercy upon His creatures He gives them a season for repentance, that they may not perish in their wickedness, therefore as it is written in Lamentations 3: 40, we should "search through and investigate our ways and return unto the Lord."

During the year man is apt to grow callous as to his transgressions, therefore the cornet is sounded to arouse him to the consciousness of the time which is passing so rapidly away. "Rouse thee from thy sleep," it says to him; "the hour of thy visitation approaches." The Eternal wishes not to destroy His children, merely to arouse them to repentance and good resolves.

Three classes of people are arraigned for judgment: the righteous, the wicked, and the indifferent. To the righteous the Lord awards a happy life; the wicked He condemns, and to the indifferent ones He grants a respite. From New Year's day until the Day of Atonement His judgment He holds in abeyance; if they repent truly they are classed with the righteous for a happy life, and if they remain un-touched, they are counted with the wicked.

Three sounds for the cornet are commanded in the Bible. A pure sound (*T'kiah*), a sound of alarm or trembling (*T'ruah*), and, thirdly, a pure sound again (*T'kiah*).

The first sound typifies man's first awakening to penitence; he must search well his heart, desert his evil ways, and purify his thoughts, as it is written, "Let the wicked forsake his ways and the man of unrighteousness his thoughts, and let him return unto the Lord."

The alarm sound typifies the sorrow which a repentant man feels for his misconduct and his earnest determination to reform.

The last sound is the pure sound again, which typifies a sincere resolve to keep the repentant heart incorrupt.

The Bible says to us:

"The word is very nigh unto thee, in thy mouth and in thy heart, that thou mayest do it" (Deut. 30: 14). This verse teaches us that repentance is nearer to those who believe in God and His book than fanatics would make it. Difficult penances are ordained for the sinner among them. He must fast many days, or travel barefoot through rugged ways, or sleep in the open air. But we are not required to travel to the nether end of the ocean or to climb to mountain tops, for our Holy Word says to us, "It is not in heaven, neither is it beyond the sea, but the Word is very nigh."

In three ways may we repent:

First, By words of mouth, finding birth in an honest heart.

Secondly, With our feelings, sorrow for sins committed.

Thirdly, By good deeds in the future.

Rabbi Saadiah declared that God commanded us to sound the cornet on New Year's day for ten reasons.

First, Because this day is the beginning of the creation, when God began to reign over the world, and as it is customary to sound the trumpets at the coronation of a king, we should in like manner proclaim by the sound of the cornet that the Creator is our king,--as David said, "With trumpets and the sound of the cornet, shout ye before the Lord."

Secondly, As the New Year day is the first of the ten penitential days, we sound the cornet as a proclamation to admonish all to return to God and repent. If they do not so, they at least have been informed, and cannot plead ignorance. Thus we find that earthly kings publish then decrees with such concomitant, that none may say, "We heard not this."

Thirdly, To remind us of the law given on Mount Sinai, where it is said (Exod. 19:16), "The voice of the cornet was exceeding loud." To remind us also that we should bind ourselves anew to the performance of its precepts, as did our ancestors, when they said, "All that the Lord hath said will we do and obey."

Fourthly, To remind us of the prophets, who were compared to watchmen blowing the trumpet of alarm, as we find in Ezekiel (33: 4), "Whosoever heareth the sound of the cornet and taketh not warning, and the sound cometh and taketh him away, his blood shall be upon his own head; but he that taketh warning shall save his life."

Fifthly, To remind us of the destruction of the Temple and the fearsome sound of the battle-cry of our enemies. "Because thou hast heard, oh my soul, the sound of the trumpet, the alarm of war" (Jerem. 4: 19). Therefore when we hear the sound of the cornet we should implore God to rebuild the Temple.

Sixthly, To remind us of the binding of Isaac, who willingly offered himself for immolation, in order to sanctify the Holy Name.

Seventhly, That when we hear the terrifying sound, we may, through dread, humble ourselves before the Supreme Being, for it is the nature of these martial instruments to produce a sensation of terror, as the prophet Amos observes, "Shall a trumpet be blown in a city, and the people not to be terrified?"

Eighthly, To remind us of the great and terrible Day of Judgment, on which the trumpet is to be sounded, as we find in Zeph. (1: 14-16), "The great day of the Lord is near, and hasteneth much, a day of the trumpet and of shouting."

Ninthly, To remind us to pray for the time when the outcasts of Israel are to be gathered together, as promised in Isaiah (28: 13), "And it shall come to pass in that day, the great trumpet shall be sounded, and those shall come who were perishing in the land of Assyria."

Tenthly, To remind us of the resurrection of the dead, and our firm belief therein. "Yea, all ye that inhabit the world, and that dwell on the earth, when the standard is lifted upon the mountain, behold, and when the trumpet is sounded, hear!" says the prophet Isaiah.

Therefore should we set our hearts to these seasons, and fulfil the precept that the Bible commands us, as it is written:

"And the Lord commanded us to do all the statutes........that it might be well with us at all times" (Deut. 11: 24).

THE DAY OF ATONEMENT

The hearts of all who fear God should tremble with the reflection that all the deeds of the creature are known to the Creator, and will be by Him accounted to them for good or evil. God is ready at all times to acknowledge true penitence; and of repentance there are seven degrees:

First, The righteous man, who repents his misconduct as soon as he becomes aware of his sin. This is the best and most complete.

Secondly, Of the man who has for some time led a life of sin, yet who, in the vigour of his days, gives over his evil ways and conquers his wrong inclinations. As Solomon has said, "Remember thy Creator in the days of thy youthful vigour" (Eccl. 12), While in the prime of life abandon thy evil ways.

Thirdly, Of the one who was prevented by some cause from the commission of a contemplated sin, and who truly repents his evil intention. "Happy is the man who fears the Lord," said the Psalmist. The man, not the woman? Aye, all mankind. The word is used to denote strength; those who repent while still in their youth.

Fourthly, Of the one who repents when his sin is pointed out to him, and he is rebuked for the same, as in the instance of the inhabitants of Nineveh. They repented not until Jonah proclaimed to them, "Yet forty days more, and Nineveh shall be overthrown" (Jonah 3: 4). The men of Nineveh believed in God's mercy, and though the decree had been pronounced against them, yet they repented. "And God saw their work, that they had returned from their evil ways, and God bethought Himself of the evil which He had spoken that He would do to them, and He did it not." Therefore say the Rabbis, "Our brethren, neither sackcloth nor fasting will gain forgiveness for sins; but repentance of the heart and good deeds; for it is not said of the men of Nineveh, "God saw their fasting and sackcloth," but "God saw their *work*, that they had turned from their evil ways."

Fifthly, Of those who repent when trouble befalls them. How much nobler is this than human nature! Instance Jephtah: "Did ye not hate me .... and why are ye come unto me now when you are in distress?" (Judges 11: 8). But the infinite mercy of our God accepts even such repentance; as it is written, "When thou art in tribulation, and all these things have overtaken thee .... then wilt thou return unto the Lord thy God." Founded upon this is the proverb of the fathers, "Repentance and good deed, form a shield against punishment."

Sixthly, The repentance of age. Even when man grows old and feeble, if he repents truly, his atonement will be received. As the Psalmist says, "Thou turnest man to contrition, and sayest, 'Return, ye children of men.'" Meaning, man can return at any time or any age, "Return, ye children of men."

Say the Rabbis, "Although a man has been righteous in his youth and vigour, yet if he rebels against the will of God in his old age, the merit of his former goodness shall be lost to him, as it is written, 'When a righteous man turns away from his righteousness and doeth wrong, and dieth therefor; through his wrong which he hath done must he die' (Ezekiel 18: 26). But a man who has been wicked in his early days, and feels true sorrow and penitence in his old age, shalt not be called 'wicked' any more. This, however, is not gracious penitence when it is so long delayed."

Seventhly, Is the last degree of penitence. Of the one who is rebellious against his Creator during all the days of his life; turns to Him only when the hand of death is laid upon him.

Say the Rabbis, if a person is sick, and the hour of his decease approaches, they who are by his deathbed should say to him, "Confess thy sins to thy Creator."

They who are near the point of death should confess their shortcomings. The sick man is as the man who is before a court of justice. The latter may have advocates to defend him or laud his case, but the only advocates of the former must be penitence and good deeds. As is written in the Book of Job (33: 23), "If there be now about him one single angel as defender, one out of a thousand, to tell for man his uprightness; then is he gracious unto him, and saith, 'Release him from going down to the pit; I have found an atonement.'"

Thus we have seven different degrees of penitence, and he who neglects them all must suffer in the world to come. Therefore fulfil the duties laid upon you; repent as long as you are able to amend. As the Rabbis say, "Repent in the antechamber, that thou mayest enter the room of state."

"Turn ye, turn ye from your evil ways; wherefore will ye die, O house of Israel!" exclaimed the prophet Ezekiel; and what does this warning mean? without repentance ye shall die.

Penitence is thus illustrated by a parable:

There was once a great ship which had been sailing for many days upon the ocean. Before it reached its destination, a high wind arose, which drove it from its course; until, finally, becalmed close to a pleasant-appearing island, the anchor was dropped. There grew upon this island beautiful flowers and luscious fruits in "great profusion;" tall trees lent a pleasing, cooling shade to the place, which appeared to the ship's passengers most desirable and inviting. They divided themselves into five parties; the first party determined not to leave the ship, for said they, "A fair wind may arise, the anchor may be raised, and the ship sail on, leaving us behind; we will not risk the chance of missing our destination for the temporary pleasure which this island offers." The second party went on shore for a short time, enjoyed the perfume of the flowers, tasted of the fruit, and returned to the ship happy and refreshed, finding their places as they had left them; losing nothing, but rather gaining in health and good spirits by the recreation of their visit on shore. The third party also visited the island, but they stayed so long that the fair wind did arise, and hurrying back they just reached the ship as the sailors were lifting the anchor, and in the haste and confusion many lost their places, and were not as comfortable during the balance of their voyage as at the outset. They were wiser, however, than the fourth party; these latter stayed so long upon the island and tasted so deeply of its pleasures, that they allowed the ship's bell of warning to sound unheeded. Said they, "The sails are still to be set; we may enjoy ourselves a few minutes more." Again the bell sounded, and still they lingered, thinking, "The captain will not sail without us." So they remained on shore until they saw the ship moving; then in wild haste they swam after it and scrambled up the sides, but the bruises and injuries which they encountered in so doing were not healed during the remainder of the voyage. But, alas, for the fifth party. They ate and drank so deeply that they did not even hear the bell, and when the ship started they were left behind. Then the wild beasts hid in the thickets made of them a prey, and they who escaped this evil, perished from the poison of surfeit.

The "ship" is our good deeds, which bear us to our destination, heaven. The "island" typifies the pleasures of the world, which the first set of passengers refused to taste or look upon, but which when enjoyed temperately, as by the second party, make our lives pleasant, without causing us to neglect our duties. These pleasures must not be allowed, however, to gain too strong a hold upon our senses. True, we may return, as the third party, while there is yet time and but little bad effect, or even as the fourth party at the eleventh hour, saved, but with bruises and injuries which cannot be entirely healed; but we are in danger of becoming as the last party, spending a lifetime in the pursuit of vanity, forgetting the future, and perishing even of the poison concealed in the sweets which attracted us.

Who hath sorrow? Who hath woe?

He who leaves much wealth to his heirs, and takes with him to the grave a burden of sins. He who gathers wealth without justice. "He that gathereth riches and not by right (Jer. 8: 11), in the midst of his days shall he leave them." To the portals of eternity his gold and his silver cannot accompany the soul of man; good deeds and trust in God must be his directing spirits.

Although God is merciful and pardons the sins of man against Himself; he who has wronged his neighbour must gain that neighbour's forgiveness before he can claim the mercy of the Lord. "This must ye do," said Rabbi Eleazer, "that ye may be clean from all your sins before the Lord (Lev. 16: 30). The Day of Atonement may gain pardon for the sins of man against his Maker, but not for those against his fellow-man, till every wrong done is satisfied."

If a man is called upon to pardon his fellow, freely he must do it; else how can he dare, on the Day of Atonement, to ask pardon for his sins against the Eternal? It is customary on this day for a man to thoroughly cleanse himself bodily and spiritually, and to array himself in white fresh clothing, to typify the words of Isaiah, "Though your sins should be as scarlet, they shall become white as snow."

It happened that the mayor of a city once sent his servant to the market to purchase some fish. When he reached the place of sale he found that all the fish save one had been sold, and this one a Jewish tailor was about purchasing. Said the mayor's servant, "I will give one gold piece for it;" said the tailor, "I will give two." The mayor's messenger then expressed his willingness to pay three gold pieces for it, but the tailor claimed the fish, and said he would not lose it though he should be obliged to pay ten gold pieces for it. The mayor's servant then returned home, and in anger related the circumstance to his master. The mayor sent for his subject, and when the latter appeared before him asked:

"What is thy occupation?"

"A tailor, sir," replied the man.

"Then how canst thou afford to pay so great a price for a fish, and how dare degrade my dignity by offering for it a larger sum than that offered by my servant?"

"I fast to-morrow," replied the tailor, "and I wished the fish to eat to-day, that I might have strength to do so. I would not have lost it even for ten pieces of gold."

"What is to-morrow more than any other day?" asked the mayor.

"Why art thou more than any other man?" returned the other.

"Because the king hath appointed me to this office."

"Well," replied the tailor, "the King of kings hath appointed this day to be holier than all other days, for on this day we hope that God will pardon our transgressions."

"If this be the case thou wert right," answered the mayor, and the Israelite departed in peace.

Thus if a person's intention is to obey God, nothing can hinder its accomplishment. On this day God commanded His children to fast, but they must strengthen their bodies to obey him by eating on the day before. It is a person's duty to sanctify himself; bodily and spiritually, for the approach of this great day. He should be ready to enter at any moment into the Fearful Presence with repentance and good deeds as his companions.

A certain man had three friends. One of these he loved dearly; the second he loved also, but not as intensely as the first; but towards the third one he was quite indifferently disposed.

Now the king of the country sent an officer to this man, commanding his immediate appearance before the throne. Greatly terrified was the man at this summons. He thought that somebody had been speaking evil of him, or probably accusing him falsely before his sovereign, and being afraid to appear unaccompanied before the royal presence, he resolved to ask one of his friends to go with him. First he naturally applied to his dearest friend, but he at once declined to go, giving no reason and no excuse for his lack of friendliness. So the man applied to his second friend, who said to him:

"I will go with thee as far as the palace gates, but I will not enter with thee before the king."

In desperation the man applied to his third friend, the one whom he had neglected, but who replied to him at once:

"Fear not; I will go with thee, and I will speak in thy defence. I will not leave thee until thou art delivered from thy trouble."

The "first friend" is a man's wealth, which he must leave behind him when he dies. The "second friend" is typified by the relatives who follow him to the grave and leave him when the earth has covered his remains. The "third friend," he who entered with him into the presence of the king, is as the good deeds of a man's life, which never desert, but accompany him to plead his cause before the King of kings, who regardeth not person nor taketh bribery.

Thus taught Rabbi Eleazer:

"On this great and tearful day the angel Samal finds no blots, no sins on Israel." Thus he addresses the Most High:

"'O Sovereign Lord, upon the earth this day one nation pure and innocent exists. Even as the angels is Israel on this Atonement Day. As peace exists in heaven, so rests it now upon this people, praying to Thy Holy Name.'

"God hears this testimony of His angel, and pardons all His people's sins."

But though the Almighty thus forgives our sins, we may not repeat them with impunity, for "to such a one as saith, 'I will commit a sin and repent,' there can be no forgiveness, no repentance."

FEAST OF TABERNACLES

The Feast of Tabernacles begins on the fifteenth day of the seventh month, *Tishri* (October), and during its continuance, seven days, the Israelites are commanded to dwell in tabernacles or booths. This is designed to keep fresh in their memory the tents which formed their homes during their forty years' sojourn in the wilderness. The symbols of the festival are branches of the palm, bound with sprigs of myrtle and willow, and a citron.

On this feast we are commanded to rejoice and be glad, for it is not the desire of God that we should always afflict ourselves as upon His precious holy day, the Day of Atonement. No; after humbling our hearts and returning to our Creator, we are enjoined to rejoice with our families and neighbours; therefore, we call this holy day the season of our rejoicing.

The Lord said, "This is not to be to you a fast as the Day of Atonement; eat, drink, be merry, and sacrifice peace-offerings thereon." The Bible says, "Seven days unto the Lord;" therefore we should in all our merriment devote a few serious thoughts to Him.

The Omnipotent King has commanded us to remove from our permanent dwellings and live for seven days in booths. This precept teaches us that man should put no trust in the magnificent structures he may have raised and adorned with ornaments of value, nor to place his confidence entirely upon human beings, even though rulers in his land; but to rely solely upon the Almighty, the One who said, "Let the universe come into being;" to Him alone is the power and the dominion. He alone will never change, or be other than He has proclaimed Himself, as it is written, "God is not a man that He should lie" (Num. 23: 19), and He alone can prove our sure protection.

The Feast of Tabernacles is held in the autumn, after the fruits of the field have been garnered in the storehouses, according to the words of the Bible, "The Feast of Tabernacles shalt thou hold for thyself seven days when thou hast gathered in the produce of thy threshing-floor and thy wine-press" (Deut. 16: 14).

At this time, when a man sees plenty around him, his heart perhaps may grow haughty, he may feel like enriching his house and furnishing it with elegance; for this reason he is commanded to leave it for a season, and dwell in booths, where his thoughts may be directed to God. That in the dwelling rudely put together, and unprotected from the rain, he may remember that through the rain sent by the Most High in its due season did the profusion of his crops result, and with this reflection appreciate the fact that all he possesses he owes to the goodness of God, and not to his own intelligence or strength.

This dwelling in booths is also to bring to mind the manner in which the Israelites lived for forty years after they left Egypt. With merely temporary walls to protect them from summer's heat and winter's cold, from wind and storm. God was with them through all their generations, and they were protected from all evil.

According to the opinion of some of the Rabbis, the Israelites did not really dwell in booths in the wilderness, but were surrounded by clouds--by seven clouds. Four clouds, one at each of the four sides; a fifth, a shadow, to protect them from the hot rays of the sun; the sixth, a pillar of fire, to give them light by night (they being able to see as clearly by night as by day); and the seventh, to precede their journeying and direct their way.

The children of Israel departed from Egypt in *Nissan* (April), and obtained immediately these booths, which they made use of for forty years. Thus they were in booths during the entire cycle of the year, and we could as easily commemorate this fact in the spring as in the fall, in the summer as in the winter. Why, then, has God made autumn, and neither spring nor summer, the season of observance? Because if we dwelt in booths in the summer, it would be a question whether we did so in obedience to God's behest or for our own gratification; for many people seek airy retreats during this season; but in the fall, when the trees lose their leaves, and the air grows cold and chilling, and it is the time to fix our houses for the winter, then by inhabiting these temporary residences, we display our desire to do as our Creator has bidden us.

The Feast of Tabernacles is also the Feast of Ingathering, when we should thank God for the kindness shown us, and the treasure with which He has blessed us. When the Eternal has provided man with his sustenance, in the long evenings which follow he should meditate and study his Bible, and make this indeed a "feast to the Lord," and not entirely for personal gratification.

The four species belonging to the vegetable kingdom, which we use on this festival, are designed to remind us of the four elements of nature, which work under the direction and approval of the Most High, and without which all things would cease to exist. Therefore the Bible commands us on this "feast of the Lord" to give thanks, and bring before Him these four species, each typifying one of the elements.

"Ye shall take for yourselves (Lev. 23: 40) the fruit of the tree *hadar*" (the citron). Its colour is high yellow and resembles fire. The second species is the palm branch (Heb. *Lulab*), The palm is a high tree, growing up straight in the air, and its fruit is sweet and delicious to the taste; this then represents the second element, air. The third is the bough of the myrtle, one of the lowliest of trees, growing close to the ground; its nature, cold and dry as earth, fits it to represent that element. The fourth is "the willow of the brook," which grows in perfection close beside the water, dropping its branches into the stream, and symbolising thus the last element, water.

The Bible teaches us that for each of these four elements we owe especial thanks to God.

The citron we hold in the left hand, and the other three we grasp together in the right. This we do because the citron contains in itself all that the others represent. The outside skin is yellow, fire; the inside skin is white and damp, air; the pulp is watery, water; and the seeds are dry, earth. It is taken into the left hand, because the right hand is strongest, and the citron is but one, while the other emblems are three.

These four emblems represent likewise the four principal members of the human body. The citron is shaped somewhat like a heart, without which we could not live, and with, which man should serve his fellows; the palm branch represents the spine, which is the foundation of the human frame, in front of which the heart lies; this signifies that we should serve God with our entire body. The branches of the myrtle resemble a human eye, with which man recognises the deeds of his fellows, and with which he may obtain a knowledge of the law. The leaves of the willow represent the lips, with which man may serve the Eternal and thank Him. The myrtle is mentioned in the Bible before the willow, because we arc able to see and know a thing before we can call its name with our lips; man is able to look into the Bible before he can study the same. Therefore, with these four principal parts of the human frame should we praise the Creator, as David said, "All my bones shall say, O Lord, who is like unto thee?"

The great Maimonides, in his work called "*Moreh Nebuchim*" (The Guide of the Perplexed), explains that God commanded the Israelites to take these four emblems during this festival to remind them that they were brought out from the wilderness, where no fruit grew, and no people lived, into a land of brooklets, waters, a land flowing with milk and honey. For this reason did God command us to hold in our hands the precious fruit of this land while singing praises to Him, the One who wrought miracles in our behalf, who feeds and supports us from the productiveness of the earth.

The four emblems are different in taste, appearance, and odour, even as the sons of men are different in conduct and habits.

The citron is a valuable fruit; it is good for food and has a most pleasant odour. It is compared to the intelligent man, who is righteous in his conduct towards God and his fellow-man. The odour of the fruit is his good deeds; its substance is his learning, on which others may feed. This is perfect among the emblems, and is, therefore, always mentioned first, and taken by itself in one hand.

The palm branch brings forth fruit, but is without odour. It is compared to those people who are learned, but who are wanting in good deeds; they who know the law, but transgress its mandates.

The myrtle is compared to those people who are naturally good, who act correctly towards God and man, but who are uneducated.

The willow of the brook has neither fruit nor odour; it is, therefore, compared to the people who have no knowledge and who perform no good deeds.

If all unite together, however, and offer supplication to the Most High, He will surely hearken to their words, and for this reason Moses said to the Israelites, "And ye shall take unto yourselves," &c.; meaning, to your own benefit, to praise the Lord during the seven days of the festival with these emblems, and to exclaim with the same "*Hoshaánah*" (O, save us now), and "Oh, give thanks to the Lord, for His mercy endureth for ever."

The Rabbis have said that he who has failed to participate in the keeping of the Tabernacle Festival in Jerusalem has failed to taste real enjoyment in his life. The first day of the feast was kept with great solemnity, and the middle days with joy and gladness in various methods of public amusement.

The Temple in Jerusalem was provided with a gallery or the women, which was called the apartment of the women, and the men sat below, as is still the custom of the synagogue. Thither all repaired. The young priests filled the lamps of the large chandeliers with oil, and lighted them all, even that the place was so bright that its reflection lighted the streets of the city. Hymns and praises were chanted by the pious ones, and the Levites praised the Lord with harps, cornets, trumpets, flutes, and other instruments of harmony. They stood upon fifteen broad steps, reaching from the lower floor to the gallery, the court of the women. And they sang fifteen psalms as they ascended, beginning with "A song of Degrees," and the large choir joined voices with them. The ancient Hillel was accustomed to address the assemblages on these occasions.

"If God's presence dwells here," he was used to say, "then are ye here, each one of you, the souls of each; but if God should be removed from your midst through disobedience then which of you could be here?" For the Lord has said, "If thou wilt come to My house, then will I come to thy house, but if thou refusest to visit My dwelling, I will also neglect to enter yours;" as it is written, "In every place where I shall permit My name to be mentioned I will come unto thee and I will bless thee" (Exod. xx. 21).

Then some of the people answered:

"Happy were the days of our youth, for they have not set to blush the days of our old age." These were men of piety.

Others answered:

"Happy is our old age, for therein have we atoned tot the sins of our youth." These were repentants.

Then joining together, both parties said:

"Happy is the one who is free from sin; but ye who have sinned, repent, return to God, and ye will be forgiven."

The festival was continued during the entire night; for when the religious exercises concluded the people gave themselves up to innocent but thorough enjoyment.

This festival was also called the "Festival of Drawing Water."

Because, during the existence of the Temple, wine was offered during the year for a burnt-offering, but on the Feast of Tabernacles they offered two drink-offerings, one of wine and one of water. Of the other they made a special festival on the second day of the Tabernacle assemblage, calling it the Feast of Drawing the Water. It was founded upon the words of the prophet:

"And ye shall draw water with joy from the fountains of salvation."

"HANNUCKAH," THE FEAST OF DEDICATION

This festival is observed for eight days during the ninth month *Kislev* (December), and commemorates the dedication of the Temple after it had been defiled by Antiochus Epiphanes, whose armies were overthrown by the valiant Maccabees, Hashmoneans.

The Most Holy One has frequently wrought wonders in behalf of his children in their hour of need, and thereby displayed His supreme power to the nations of the world. These should prevent man from growing infidel and ascribing all happiness to the course of nature. The God who created the world from naught, may change at His will the nature which He established. When the Hashmoneans gained, with the aid of God, their great victory, and restored peace and harmony to their land, their first act was to cleanse and rededicate the Temple, which had been defiled, and on the twenty-fifth day of Kislev, in obedience to the teachings of the Rabbis, we inaugurate the "Dedication Feast" by lighting the lamps or candles prepared expressly for this occasion. The first night we light one, and then an additional one each succeeding night of its continuance. We also celebrate it by hymns of thanksgiving and hallelujahs.

This feast is foreshadowed in the Book of Numbers. When Aaron observed the offerings of the princes of each of the tribes and their great liberality, he was conscious of a feeling of regret, because he and his tribe were unable to join with them. But these words were spoken to comfort him, "Aaron, thy merit is greater than theirs, for thou lightest and fixest the holy lamps."

When were these words spoken?

When he was charged with the blessing to be found in Numbers 6: 23, as will be found in the Book of Maccabees in the Apocrypha.

The Lord said unto Moses, "Thus say unto Aaron. In the generations to come, there will be another dedication and lighting of the lamps, and through thy descendants shall the service be performed. Miracles and wonders will accompany this dedication. Fear not for the greatness of the princes of thy tribe; during the existence of the Temple thou shalt sacrifice, but the lighting of the lamps shall be for ever, and the blessing with which I have charged thee to bless the people shall also exist for ever. Through the destruction of the Temple the sacrifices will be abolished, but the lighting of the dedication of the Hashmoneans will never cease."

The Rabbis have ordained this celebration by lighting of lamps, to make God's miracle known to all coining generations, and it is our duty to light the same in the synagogues and in our homes.

Although the Lord afflicted Israel on account of iniquities, He still showed mercy, and allowed not a complete destruction, and to this festival do the Rabbis again apply the verse in Leviticus 26: 44:

"And yet for all that, though they be in the land of their enemies, will I not cast them away, neither will I loathe them to destroy them utterly, to break my covenant with them, for I am the Lord their God."

And thus do the Rabbis explain the same

"Will I not cast them away." In the time of the Chaldeans I appointed Daniel and his companions to deliver them.

"Neither will I loathe them." In the time of the Assyrians I gave them Matthias, his sons and their comrades, to serve them.

"To destroy them." In the time of Haman I sent Mordecai and Esther to rescue them.

"To break my covenant with them." In the time of the Romans I appointed Rabbi Judah and his associates to work their salvation.

"For I am the Eternal, your God." In the future no nation shall rule over Israel, and the descendants of Abraham shall be restored to their independent state.

The dedication commemorated by Hannuckah occurred in the year 3632-129 B.C.E.

Purim

This festival, occurring on the fourteenth day of the twelfth month, Adar (March), is to commemorate the deliverance of the Hebrews from the wiles of Haman, through the God-aided means of Mordecai and Esther.

Although the Holy One threatens the Israelites, in order that they may repent of their sins, He has also tempted them, in order to increase their reward.

For instance, a father who loves his son, and desires him to improve his conduct, must punish him for his misdeeds; but it is a punishment induced by affection which he bestows.

A certain apostate once said to Rabbi Saphra:

"It is written, 'Because I know you more than all the nations of the earth, therefore I visit upon you your iniquities;' how is this? If a person has a wild horse, is it likely that he would put his dearest friend upon it, that he might be thrown and hurt?"

Rabbi Saphra answered:

"Suppose a man lends money to two persons; one of these is his friend, the other his enemy. He will allow his friend to repay him in instalments, that the discharge of the debt may not prove onerous; but from his enemy he will require the amount in full. The verse you quote will apply in the same manner, 'I love you, therefore will I visit upon you your iniquities;' meaning, 'I will punish you for them as they occur, little by little, by which means you may have quittance and happiness in the world to come.'

The action of the king in delivering his signet ring to Haman had more effect upon the Jews than the precepts and warnings of forty-eight prophets who lectured to them early and late. They clothed themselves in sackcloth, and repented truly with tears and fasting, and God had compassion upon them and destroyed Haman.

Although the reading of the Book of Esther (*Megilah*) on Purim is not a precept of the Pentateuch, 'tis nevertheless binding upon us and our descendants. Therefore the day is appointed as one of feasting and gladness, and interchange of presents, and also of gifts to the poor, that they too may rejoice. As in the decree of Haman, no distinction was made between rich and poor, as all alike were doomed to destruction, it is proper that all should have equal cause to feel joyful, and therefore in all generations the poor should be liberally remembered on this day.

THE END

Made in United States
Orlando, FL
31 May 2024

47408990R00176